THE NEW
GOOD LIFE

BALLANTINE BOOKS

NEW YORK

THE NEW GOOD LIFE

LIVING BETTER THAN EVER
IN AN AGE OF LESS

John Robbins

Published in the United States by Ballantine Books, an imprint of The Random House Publishing Group, a division of Random House, Inc., New York.

BALLANTINE and colophon are registered trademarks of Random House, Inc.

Grateful acknowledgment is made to the following for permission to reprint previously published material:

ECONOMIC POLICY INSTITUTE: "Household Debt as Percentage of Annual After-Tax Income," data excerpted from *The Economic Policy Institute: The State of Working America*. Reprinted by permission of The Economic Policy Institute.

HARPERCOLLINS PUBLISHERS, INC.: Excerpt from *Lit from Within* by Victoria Moran, copyright © 2001 by Victoria Moran. Reprinted by permission of HarperCollins Publishers, Inc.

MARY RITA SCHILKE KORZAN: "When You Thought I Wasn't Looking," by Mary Rita Schilke Korzan, copyright © 1980 by Mary Rita Schilke Korzan. Reprinted by permission of Mary Rita Schilke Korzan.

LIBRARY OF CONGRESS CATALOGING-IN-PUBLICATION DATA
Robbins, John.
The new good life: living better than ever in an age of less / John Robbins.
p. cm.
Includes bibliographical references and index.
ISBN 978-0-345-51984-9
eBook ISBN 978-0-345-52023-4
1. Thriftiness. 2. Finance, Personal. 3. Money—Psychological aspects.
I. Title.
HG179.R5442 2010   332.024—dc22   2010010552

Printed in the United States of America on acid-free paper

www.ballantinebooks.com

2 4 6 8 9 7 5 3 1

FIRST EDITION

Book design by Casey Hampton

Contents

Who's the wealthiest person you've ever known?

Most of us, when asked that question, think of the people we've known who were richest in monetary wealth.

But what if you asked the question differently?

In terms of what really makes life worth living, who's the wealthiest person you've ever known? Have you known anyone who has truly made the world a better place? Have you known anyone whose life is so filled with joy, who cares so deeply, who loves so richly that—whether or not they are financially abundant—their lives are a blessing to the rest of us?

When we say someone is a "success," what do we mean? Do we mean that she or he is an emotionally balanced, loving human being? Do we mean that this person is creative and artistic and adds beauty to the world?

Not usually. Instead, most of us reserve the word "success" for people who have made a lot of money.

This is how we impoverish ourselves.

This is why we need a new vision of the good life.

Introduction

We have now entered an entirely new phase in our nation's and our world's economic existence. We have come to the end of the financial world as we have known it.

The assumptions of the past are no longer reliable or credible. Not that long ago, General Motors represented 10 percent of the U.S. economy and was the world's largest employer. But in 2008, the company lost nearly 90 percent of its value. The following year, the company that had long been considered the backbone of the U.S. economy went bankrupt.

Is it possible that an entire nation could go bankrupt? It's not only possible, it's already happened. Iceland was a model of strong economic growth in the 1990s and beyond, and one of the world's most highly functioning economies. In 2007, Iceland ranked number one among all the world's nations in terms of the Human Development Index. But in 2008, Iceland literally went bankrupt. Unable to pay its external debts, the Icelandic currency, the krona, became essentially valueless in the rest of the world.

What will happen in the U.S. economy in the years to come is deeply uncertain. Although some economists and public officials have declared the worst behind us, most of them have a vested interest in a positive outlook. A sober look at the facts can be unsettling. The year 2010 began with nearly one in three U.S. homeowners owing more on their mortgages than their homes were worth, and that figure was expected to soon reach one in two. Today, foreclosures are filed in the United States every seven and a half seconds.

Facing daunting deficits, cities, counties, and states have been making staggering and unprecedented budget cuts. Fearing bankruptcy, governments at every level have seen no alternative but to dramatically decrease services across the board, including some considered essential for public safety. The cuts have been so severe, they haven't been made with scalpels. They've been made with meat axes.

The level of affluence many Americans had come to take for granted is becoming out of reach for rapidly growing numbers of people. Today, more Americans are going bankrupt than are graduating from college. In many states, unemployment is at a seventy-year high, and the unemployed are confronting a job market that is increasingly bleak. The ranks of the poor are swelling with failed business owners, office workers, salespeople, and longtime homeowners. In major cities, requests for emergency shelter are doubling annually. People who have never before needed food aid are applying for food stamps in record numbers. Millions of people are losing their health insurance along with their jobs.

Ominous comparisons have been made to the 1930s, but there are fundamental differences, some of which may actually make it harder for the economy to recover from the current crisis. Then, we had no national debt. Today, we have become the greatest debtor nation in human history. Then, saving was seen as a virtue. Now, the average American owes 25 percent of his or her annual income to credit card debt alone. Then, the environment was relatively pristine, natural resources were abundant, and the United States produced more oil than it used. Today, perils such as global warming and dependence on imported oil threaten to undermine economic progress. And in the 1930s, U.S. military spending amounted to 5 percent of the world's total. Now, it's 45 percent.

Meanwhile, for the past few years, something extraordinary has been happening at the North Pole. For an increasing number of weeks each summer, the Arctic ice pack has melted sufficiently that it has become briefly possible for a ship to travel from the Atlantic to the Pacific without going through the Panama Canal or around the Cape of Good Hope. This has never happened before, in all of recorded human history.

Atmospheric carbon dioxide levels are now the highest in three million years. These trends foretell a future of melting glaciers, acidifying oceans, rising sea levels, disappearing species, and an unstable climate—all of which will put additional stress on an already beleaguered world economy.

Can a world that has plunged into harsh and uncertain financial times find a way to switch from fossil to renewable fuels? Can a society that is standing on unstable fiscal footing manage to halt the deterioration of the environment? If not, will we come to liquidate the planet's ecological assets? And what will be the economic consequences?

Just about everyone at every level of monetary existence is impacted. In 2007, *Forbes* named Adolf Merckle as one of the fifty richest billionaires in the world, with a fortune of nearly $13 billion "and growing." He and his family owned many businesses, including Germany's largest pharmaceutical wholesaler (Phoenix Pharmahandel), one of the country's major generic drug manufacturers (Ratiopharm), and large parts of a cement company (HeidelbergCement) and a vehicle manufacturer (Kässbohrer). You would think that a man of that immense wealth could withstand the current crisis. But in January 2009, Adolf Merckle threw himself in front of a train, committing suicide, utterly despondent over the extent of his financial losses.

The anguish is palpable. The uncertainties in our financial system have produced a crisis of confidence at every level. Is there any way that this fiscal predicament, as disorienting and devastating as it is, could also serve a positive and benign purpose? Is there any path by which we could experience what has become a cascade of grievous economic events not as victims, but with clear intentions, wise actions, and fulfilling outcomes? Has there ever been a moment with a greater need to become more intelligent and more conscious in our relationship to money?

Some of us experience economic hard times as frightening and malevolent. But I think there is a genuine alternative. The challenges we face truly do have another potential. We can experience them, with all their very real hardships, in a way that brings out the best in us, but in order for that to happen, we must transform our entire relationship to money. And that is the point and purpose of this book. I want to help you achieve financial freedom, even within a profoundly unstable economy and a world too often succumbing to fear.

We all know the colossal importance we have come to attach to our economic status. Regardless of whether we are rich or poor, it's hard to exaggerate the role that money plays in our lives. Is there any area of life it doesn't touch? The foods we eat, the clothes we wear, the places we live, the kinds of work we do, the futures we dream of, whether we marry or not, whether we have children or not, even who we love— these are all affected by how we relate to the money in our lives.

I have a dear friend with whom I've become very close in recent years. He and I talk about almost everything. We confide in each other to such an extent that we even know details of each other's sexual history and experiences. But I've noticed something. Even with all that we have shared, even with all the comfort we've created together, he isn't able to talk freely and openly about money.

Recently, when I asked him why, he said it's because talking about money makes him feel uncomfortable and vulnerable. In this, I don't think my friend is at all unique. Money issues seem uniquely capable of triggering our attachments, hopes, and aversions, and of bringing up feelings we are uncomfortable with, such as fear, envy, and shame. When it comes to money, otherwise kind and sensible people sometimes become fearful and crazy.

Here's what I hope to convey in this book:

However much money you have or don't have, your relationship to the money in your life can be transformational. It can be a doorway into greater consciousness, into greater integrity, and into greater freedom.

And one more thing. I do not say this glibly. I say this in all humility and in all seriousness. It's obvious that there are limitations and restrictions that come with having financial challenges. What is not so obvious, and what is crucial to realize, is that there are also opportunities, openings, and possibilities.

This book is about your relationship to money. It's about finding a new freedom, a new truth, and a new joy in your relationship to it. It is a guide to developing a relationship to money that is fulfilling, that is sane and wise, that enables you to thrive, and that connects you to your powers of renewal and creativity.

As I've realized how hard it is for most of us to talk openly and freely about money, I've come to understand that there is profound human treasure hidden in the darkness. By shedding light on an area of our lives that has so much importance and yet can be so delicate and sensitive, we can find new possibilities for healing. We can become more able to make conscious and fulfilling choices around money. We can become better able to align our money decisions with our deepest core values and our highest commitments.

The goal, and it's a far more reachable one than most of us realize, is financial freedom. We tend to think that only if we have vast sums of money can we be financially free. But becoming financially free, as we shall see, is not determined by the amount of money you make. Part of accomplishing financial freedom is what I call "the new frugality." This isn't your grandmother's frugality. This isn't about deprivation. It's about choice and self-determination. Have you noticed that when you feel deprived, you don't stay on track? That's true about budgets, diets, and anywhere else we want to make changes. This book isn't about self-denial. You don't have to move into an apartment the size of a prison cell, clip coupons, and eat nothing but canned beans for every meal. Quite to the contrary, the new frugality can be an adventure and a great deal of fun.

It's a game, really. The object of the game is to see how much you can lower your spending while raising your quality of life.

I will show you how radical and energizing it can be to play this game, instead of playing the game most people play. Our consumer society wants you to play the "you are what you buy" game. Our consumer society tells you it is your patriotic duty to go to the mall even if you have to go into credit card debt. Remarkably, this was President George W. Bush's advice to the country after the devastating terrorist attacks on the United States on September 11, 2001: "Go shopping." Deep down, we all knew that this advice was wrong and would ultimately not address our needs for healing or for community.

We've all seen bumper stickers that say "He who dies with the most toys wins." That's the old game; that's the old way of defining success; that's the old "good life." In the new good life, the point is not to have the most toys, but the most joys.

The new way of defining success is liberating. Now you're playing a game that lowers your cost of living and protects you from being exploited. Now you're playing a game that is good for your spirit, that is healthy for your relationships, that is in service to the wider earth community—and that is crucial for your financial sanity.

This game isn't about denying your pleasures. It's about plugging the money leaks that you may have been only dimly aware of, but which have been draining you. Some of us buy rich and expensive foods and then pay for costly health care to deal with the problems that come from overeating. Some of us buy things we don't need and then pay for larger residences or storage space to house the things we have accumulated. This book will help you to identify where your spending patterns are inconsistent with your life's greater fulfillment. It's about the joy of living with a purpose larger than consumption. It's about living less from image and more from the creative spark of your own spirit. It's about expanding the love and laughter in your home rather than increasing the square footage of your home.

The point of this game is to achieve an overflowing life, a generous life, an exciting life, a joyful life, while spending less. The rationale behind the new frugality is not to become a miser (the word "miser" comes from the same root as the word "miserable"). The goal is to live better for less. The point is to have less stress in your life and more true wealth.

This isn't achieved by depriving yourself. It's accomplished by spending your money with a clarity of purpose. When you eliminate wasteful spending in every area of your financial life, you can focus your spending on what you really care about. Your spending can become more intelligent and more productive. And when you stop scrambling to earn money to pay for stuff that doesn't really make your life better, you have more time for the things that matter most to you.

I believe there is a hidden blessing in the economic crisis, in the necessary return to reality from a make-waste society. Many of us know, at some level, that we have become caught up in something deeply out of balance, that we are going way too fast, that we are speeding past too many of the things and moments that could really matter. Many of us sense that life is too precious and too precarious to live the way we are living. This book will help you to prosper in times of economic distress, and also to appreciate the sometimes bitter medicine that our society needs in order to regain its soul.

PART ONE

HEALING YOUR RELATIONSHIP WITH MONEY

ONE

Rags and Riches

Recently, Lexus spent many millions of dollars on an ad campaign that wasn't exactly subtle. The ads trumpeted: "Whoever said money can't buy happiness isn't spending it right." The message, of course, was that you *can* buy happiness, providing you spend $50,000 or so on one of the company's luxury cars.

This kind of thing happens at all ends of the economic spectrum. Yesterday, I saw a McDonald's ad on a billboard. Several of their coffee beverages were pictured, along with the bold and prominent question "Who says you can't buy happiness?"

Similarly, years ago when I was working for my father and the ice cream company he cofounded and owned (Baskin-Robbins, 31 Flavors), the marketing department came up with what they considered a brilliant idea for a new advertising slogan. The new motto was to become the centerpiece of the company's marketing efforts. It was to be featured in radio, TV, and newspaper ads and displayed prominently in many of the retail stores. The new slogan was "We make people happy."

Both the marketing executives and my father were delighted with the proposed new motto. I, however, was not, and our differences sparked an intense conversation.

"What I like about the slogan," my dad argued, "is that we are communicating fun and happiness. That's what people want."

"Yes, people want to have fun and be happy," I agreed. "But it's not actually accurate. We don't *make* people happy. We sell ice cream."

"Don't get technical," he reprimanded. "You're making things too complicated."

I, of course, loved ice cream, to the point that I sometimes devoured a quart at a sitting. I knew intimately most of the hundreds of flavors the company had brought to market over the years. I thought many of the flavors were wonderful, and I'd had a hand in creating a number of them.

Up until this moment, I'd had no problem with the company's other advertising slogans. In fact, I was delighted that a huge photograph of me as a child, smiling while eating an ice cream cone, was prominently displayed on the wall behind the counter in hundreds of stores. And I happily sang the radio jingle that had been the centerpiece of ad campaigns in previous years: "Look for the sign with the big thirty-one—It's Baskin-Robbins, where ice cream's fun!" But there was something about this new slogan that disturbed me.

"Happiness is something we create by how we live our lives," I reflected. "It's something we bring about by living with respect for ourselves and for others. It's not something that can be bought and sold. We sell a product that is fun and provides temporary pleasure, but that's not the same thing as *making* people happy."

My dad was far from pleased. "What do you think you are, a philosopher?" he scolded. "Stop analyzing everything. We're talking about an advertising slogan, and you're making it into some kind of deep abstract discussion. Cut it out."

"What's the point, then?" I asked.

"The point is to sell ice cream."

"That's what I'm saying. That's what we do. We manufacture and sell ice cream. It takes a lot more than an ice cream cone to make someone happy."

"They can also buy quarts, half gallons, and ice cream cakes."

My heart sank. I knew he was right, in terms of what would effectively sell the product. This was, after all, what advertisements are meant to do. Customers appreciated the experience, the image, the feeling of being happy that Baskin-Robbins ice cream stores represented. I knew the slogan would be effective. But still, something bothered me.

THE FORGING OF A CONSCIENCE

Despite my concerns, the company adopted the motto, and "We make people happy" went on to become one of the most successful marketing slogans in the history of the American food business. Successful, that is, in terms of increased ice cream sales. Baskin-Robbins, founded the year I was born, was rapidly becoming the biggest and most profitable ice cream company in the world.

I, however, remained troubled. I knew how high ice cream is in saturated fat and sugar, and I was coming to see the link with heart disease. An ice cream cone never killed anyone, but the more ice cream people eat the more likely they are to develop health problems, and the company naturally wanted to sell as much ice cream as possible. It was disturbing to consider that people might suffer more heart attacks as a result of the company's meteoric growth.

In 1967, my uncle Burt Baskin, the company's other founder, died of a heart attack. A big man, he was only fifty-four years old. I was overwhelmed with grief for the loss of my beloved uncle and increasingly troubled by the existential dilemma I was facing.

I asked my father if he thought there might be any connection between the amount of ice cream my uncle ate and his fatal heart attack. "Absolutely not," he snapped. "His ticker just got tired and stopped working."

It was not hard to understand why my father wouldn't want to consider that there might be a connection. By that time he had manufactured and sold more ice cream than any other human being who had ever lived on this planet. He didn't want to think that ice cream harmed anyone, much less that it had anything to do with the death of his beloved brother-in-law and business partner. But I could not keep from wondering.

My dad had groomed me since my earliest childhood to one day succeed him at Baskin-Robbins. The company was expanding rapidly, with annual sales in the billions of dollars. But despite the considerable lure of great wealth, I felt called to a different way of life, one whose purpose wasn't focused on making the most money but on making the biggest difference. Every new generation has an instinct to step out on its own, but what was stirred in me felt somehow much deeper than a stereotypical father-son generational split.

As a teenager, I had read the writings of Henry David Thoreau, who challenged the relentless pursuit of money and social status. "I love to see anything," he wrote, "that implies a simpler mode of life and a greater nearness to the earth." Seeing people too often make themselves what he called "slaves to the acquisition of money and things," he suggested that "a man is rich in proportion to the number of things he can do without."

Thoreau's books inspired me to think about topics that were never discussed in the household in which I grew up—issues such as the importance of contact with the natural world, self-reliance, personal conscience, and social responsibility. Meanwhile, I was living in a home with an ice cream cone–shaped swimming pool and a soda fountain that offered guests all thirty-one flavors. My father was proud of his Rolls-Royce and the many expensive classic cars he collected. His yacht was named *The 32nd Flavor*.

If money and ice cream were all that was needed to make a person happy, I would have been jubilant. But I wasn't, and my distress kept growing stronger. I had the distinct impression that even though humanity now had the potential to live upon this earth with more ease and comfort than had ever been possible in human history, we were collectively moving farther and farther away from that possibility.

I thought that Gandhi was right when he said that there is enough for everyone's need, but not for everyone's greed, and so it pained me to see how often money was becoming the goal of our lives, rather than a tool in service to our ultimate goals.

It would be twenty more years before the hit film *Wall Street* would appear, in which the lead character Gordon Gekko, played by Michael Douglas, would fervently declare that "Greed is good." But it was already clear to me that the pursuit of a prosperity driven by voracious consumption was taking root, and that it beckoned the eventual destruction of much that is good in our spirits and our world. If these trends were to continue, I feared, the global economy would become gargantuan in its excesses and grotesque in its inequalities.

I was born at the pinnacle of the old good life with its promise of un-limited consumption, and was poised to champion it into a new genera-tion. I could not have forecast the collapse of major financial institutions that predatory lending and unrestrained greed would precipitate in the economic crisis that began in 2008. But I knew that ideas and ways of treating people and the earth were spreading over the world that were socially unjust, spiritually unfulfilling, environmentally unsustainable, and morally bankrupt. It was dawning on me that I would have to change my life to the core.

I did not find it easy, however, to explain my thoughts and feelings to my father, a conservative businessman who never went a day without reading *The Wall Street Journal.* He had come of age during the Great Depression of the 1930s, while I was becoming an adult in the 1960s. Our lives were shaped by very different times.

"It's a different world now than when you grew up," I told him. "The environment is deteriorating rapidly under the impact of human activities. Every two seconds a child somewhere dies of hunger, while elsewhere there are abundant resources going to waste. The gap be-tween the rich and the poor is widening. We live now under a nuclear shadow, and at any moment the unspeakable could happen. Under these circumstances, can you see that inventing a thirty-second flavor would not be an adequate response for my life?"

A CHOICE FOR INTEGRITY

It was my father's dream that I would eventually take over the business, and he offered me an opportunity that would surely have meant a life of immense wealth. But something deep inside me kept pulling me in a different direction. Money, it seemed to me, was valuable only as a means to other ends, and I rebelled against the mind-set that made peo-ple measure their self-worth by their net worth. I wanted to use my life to help bring about a world of greater respect, understanding, and in-tegrity.

When I was twenty-one, deeply troubled by the damage I saw being done to our world by the forces of materialism and entitlement, I not only told my father that I didn't want to work with him at Baskin-Robbins any longer, but also that I didn't want to depend on his financial achievements. I did not want to have a trust fund or any other access to or dependence on his money. I wanted to discover and live my own values, and I knew that I wasn't strong enough to do that if I remained tethered, even a little, to my father's fortune.

My father was hurt and angry, and felt justifiably that I was rejecting his life's work. He also thought I was making a huge mistake, and he didn't hesitate to tell me so. "You're obviously intelligent," he said, shaking his head. "And you're obviously sincere. But you are also obviously insane."

It was very painful for me when my dad's disappointment turned to bitterness. I never wanted to hurt him, and his disapproval and anger were hard to take. I found it difficult to talk with him about why I needed to make such a radical break, and why I needed to walk away so totally from the business he had worked so hard to build and the money he had worked so hard to earn. I didn't fully understand it myself. It was ice cream he was selling, after all, ice cream that I loved eating as much as anyone. It wasn't a health food, but it certainly wasn't evil. It's not like Baskin-Robbins was manufacturing plutonium triggers for nuclear weapons.

Yet still, something in me was calling me elsewhere, and like a caterpillar called to spin its cocoon and enter a transformational process, I could not deny my destiny. If I were to refuse that call, I might end up rich, but I would surely end up untrue to myself and unhappy. To live against our innermost values can make us sick. It also can lead to disingenuous, counterfeit, or artificial lives.

It would be many years before my dad and I were able to reconcile, but I am glad to say that we eventually did. There came a day, for example, after years of struggle, when he told me that he had come to respect me for the choices I had made. "You marched to a different drummer," he said, and there was even some approval in his voice.

I was grateful for his acceptance and respect, and touched by his recognition that I had never meant to hurt him but had instead been following a call that existed within my own nature. Ironically, it was Thoreau who first coined the phrase "a different drummer," in what has become one of the world's most time-honored quotations: "If a man does not keep pace with his companions, perhaps it is because he hears a different drummer. Let him step to the music which he hears, however measured or far away."

LIFE AFTER ICE CREAM

After walking away from the ice cream fortune, I now had to work my way through my studies at the University of California, Berkeley. I did this by washing dishes twenty hours a week and taking on a variety of other part-time jobs. I must admit, too, that I had another, somewhat less admirable source of income. I won enough money in poker and bridge games that, along with the other money I was earning, I managed to pay for all my expenses in my final two years of school and to save a few thousand dollars as well. This savings then allowed me to take the next step in my journey.

After graduating in 1969, I moved with my wife, Deo, to Salt Spring Island, off the coast of British Columbia, where for less than $2,000 we bought several acres of land in a remote corner of the island. Here, more than a mile from our nearest neighbor, we built a tiny one-room log cabin in which we lived for the next ten years, 1969–1979, growing most of our own food. Our only furniture was a little table, two chairs, and a bed, which I made out of materials left over from the cabin-building project. We had no closets, but that was not a problem, because we each had only a single set of clothes.

It may be cliché to say so, but though we had little money, we never felt poor. In fact, I now look back at those years as among the richest of my life. We had good work to do in a beautiful and pristine environment, with clean air and water, and deep silence in which to meditate. We had by then adopted a regular practice of doing yoga and meditating for several hours a day, which, along with the joy of our relationship, nurtured an inner richness in our lives.

I felt alive in a way I never had before. When I awoke in the morning, I was glad and grateful, and when I closed my eyes at night I was at peace. For the first time in my life, I felt at home in myself. Having made a clean break from my family's expectations for my life, I was now free to be myself, to search for and discover my values, to bring my life into harmony with the real purposes for which I had been born.

Something deep inside me was beginning to awaken. I was a caterpillar no more.

Having grown up in cities, surrounded by the hustle and competition that so often characterize modern life, both Deo and I wanted to know if something else was possible and might even be more fulfilling.

We didn't know all the latest data on population growth or species extinction, but something in our bones told us that humanity was on a collision course with tragedy, and we felt compelled to step out of the rat race so we could more authentically step into our lives.

Committed to simplicity and having little money, we spent only about $500 a year during our first five years on the island, and for the next five years, after our son, Ocean, was born, only about $1,000 a year.

I was keenly aware of how extreme our experience and choices were. I didn't undertake these adventures because I thought anyone else should give everything up and start over on a tiny island, or reduce their spending to such a radical level. I certainly never thought of what we were doing as a model for anyone else to replicate. We made the choices we did simply because at the time they seemed to provide us with the most direct path to living authentic lives and to discovering new perspectives on what really matters.

Of course, even spending as little as we did, the money had to come from somewhere. I was young and inexperienced, and had very little in the way of talents or abilities to offer to others in exchange for money. When we arrived on the island, we had a small amount of savings beyond what was needed to build our little cabin. But that was only enough to see us through a year or so.

Then, one day I was hitchhiking to town to get a new tarp for the woodpile. I didn't go to town often, but on this particular day I got into a conversation with the young man who gave me a ride. When he found out that I did yoga, he said he had always wanted to learn and he knew several others on the island who also would like to learn. Out of the ensuing discussion, I ended up teaching yoga classes for a few local people. The classes were popular, and they grew; within a year we were holding yoga retreats on the island for people from Vancouver, Victoria, and Seattle. We always charged on a sliding scale, depending on people's ability to pay, and we offered free scholarships or work trades to anyone who needed them.

From our yoga classes and retreats, we managed to make about $2,000 a year, but we spent so little that we were actually able to save money during this time. In fact, in most years we were able to save half our income.

Deo and I kept careful track of each dollar we spent and earned, and agreed to thoroughly discuss together any major expenditure, which we defined as anything over five dollars. We bought seeds to plant and a few gardening tools, and we purchased whatever food we couldn't grow. We didn't have enough space or time to grow grains, but we could buy them in bulk quite inexpensively. Once, we bought a twenty-five-pound sack of organically grown red spring wheat for five cents a pound. We used a hand-cranked grain mill to grind the wheat, which lasted us quite a while, as we tended to prefer brown rice, cooked millet, or buckwheat as our staple grains, rather than our homemade wheat breads.

Once a year, in late fall, we would place an order with a food co-op or a health food store on the mainland and arrange to have it delivered to us on the island. This was our major purchase of the year. It typically came to around $300, which was in some years over half our total annual expenditures. The order consisted of sacks of beans (adzuki, garbanzo, and pinto); grains (wheat, brown rice, millet, and buckwheat); seeds for kitchen sprouting (lentils and alfalfa); nuts (walnuts, almonds, and filberts); sunflower seeds; specialty items such as tahini, tamari, and miso; plus a few other odds and ends. Other than that, we ate what we grew or foraged.

One does get tired of rice and beans, so we worked hard to have as much variety in our diet as we could. In late spring, and during summer and fall, our garden was a cornucopia of delights. In fall, we picked and stored boxes of apples from abandoned orchards. In winter, we ate alfalfa and lentil sprouts, along with our stored winter squashes, potatoes, onions, cabbages, rutabagas, carrots, parsnips, beets, and other root vegetables, and, of course, plenty of rice and other grains, and beans. But the mainstay of our winter diet turned out to be kale. We found varieties of this wonderful dark green leafy vegetable (such as Siberian kale) that could tolerate the cold Canadian winter, and we grew great quantities of it. During the winter we would walk out to the garden, brush the snow off the leaves, and pick them fresh for that day's meals.

So enamored did we become with the marvelous dark green leaves of this vegetable, and so dependent on it for our winter nourishment, that when Deo became pregnant, four years into our time on the island, we briefly considered naming our son-to-be "Kale."

For much of the year, we spent many hours a day working in the garden, and in the winter we would go on long walks to collect wheelbarrows full of leaves and other organic materials from the forest that we could use to make compost. We made a lot of compost.

It was hard work, and it was good work. We became intimate with the seasons, able to notice subtle changes in the weather patterns, and in awe of the power of the natural world. It was deeply enriching, and it was also quite humbling.

In the beginning we were novices and made a lot of silly mistakes. The one I remember with perhaps the most embarrassment happened during our first year. We had decided to grow cabbages and had obtained packages of cabbage and other vegetable seeds through the mail. Once a week, the post office delivered our mail to a box that was about a mile's walk through the woods from our cabin.

We had prepared the soil for planting, carefully following the instructions in our organic gardening books. Now what? Neither of us had ever planted a vegetable seed before. In fact, neither of us had ever grown anything up until that moment. Yet, naïve and idealistic, we were now intending to grow most of our food.

It said on the seed package to plant the cabbage seeds every three inches, in rows three feet apart, and then to thin the seedlings so that the plants would be eighteen inches apart in the rows. It's probably only necessary to plant in straight rows, I thought, when farmers are using tractors and other mechanical means of cultivation. But we were doing everything by hand. So, I reasoned, thinking myself to be quite clever, it shouldn't be necessary to plant in rows at all.

Guided by such thoughts, I proceeded to scatter the seeds in a small section of the garden, without any particular order. I intended to thin them when they came up so that they had enough room to grow, but there was no need, I believed, for linear rows. That isn't how nature does things, I thought. I had had enough of cities, with their straight lines and right angles everywhere.

Things, however, did not work out quite the way I had planned. Within a few days, many little green sprouts appeared in the area where I had spread the cabbage seeds. This seemed like a step in the right direction, but there was a problem. Never having grown cabbage before, neither of us had any idea what a cabbage seedling, a baby cabbage plant, would look like. How were we to know which of the sprouts that were emerging from the soil were cabbages and which were weeds? Anyone who had ever seen a cabbage seedling would know, of course, but we hadn't ever had that experience and so were left to our own, as it turned out rather pathetic, devices.

There was, you see, a particular type of little sprouted seedling that began almost immediately to appear in large quantities in the area where I had planted cabbage seeds. Naturally, I assumed those must be the baby cabbage plants. Accordingly, I pulled out any other kinds of sprouts that appeared in the days and weeks to come, thinking they must be weeds. Meanwhile, we carefully watered and cared for the ones I had determined were the cabbages, so that they might grow optimally.

Within a few weeks it gradually became clear that the "cabbage plants" we were so ardently tending looked a great deal like certain plants that were growing wild outside the garden. Could it be, I wondered, that those wild plants were somehow related to the cabbages we were growing? Could it be that we had fortuitously stumbled upon a garden site next to where some kind of wild cabbages were growing? Could these wild plants be the original plants from which our food cabbages have been bred?

Unaware of the extent of my ignorance, I continued to cultivate and care for the young plants I had deemed to be cabbages, and sure enough they grew magnificently. They grew so fast and strong, it was as though they were native to the area. And indeed, it turned out that they were. For as time went by and spiky purple blossoms appeared on the plants, I came slowly to grasp that I had thinned out all the actual cabbage plants and had instead been cultivating a very fine collection of wild thistles.

This was only one of many humbling experiences I had that showed me again and again how ignorant and unprepared for this kind of life I was. We persevered, however, and somehow got through that first year, and in time we became quite proficient at growing vegetables. We also learned that the roots of thistles are edible, if you cut off the tough outer bark and cook them properly. I never did grow fond of thistles, though through the years we did eat many wild plants, including dandelions, lamb's-quarters, stinging nettles, wild mushrooms, thimbleberries, black-berries, and the unopened fronds of wild ferns called fiddleheads. A word of warning, though: Don't eat any wild plants unless you are certain they are edible. There were a few times that we ate plants we mistakenly thought were edible, and I can tell you that you don't really want to have those kinds of experiences. I am grateful for it all, though, and eating plants we shouldn't have provided another major opportunity to learn a deeper humility, and to become more aware of how we human beings, magnificent ants that we are, must live with a deep respect for the powers of this beautiful planet.

THE NEW GOOD LIFE

We were learning to thrive on less money than we had ever dreamed possible. Of course, some people might interpret this to mean buying many things as cheaply as possible. Even though I, too, love bargains, this was not our goal. In fact, our relentless effort as a culture to obtain as much as we can as cheaply as we can has cheapened our lives and made Wal-Mart the largest and most profitable business in the world.

Wal-Mart and similar companies sell a lot of stuff at low prices, but the new good life isn't about getting a lot of stuff at low prices. It's about consuming less and consuming far more intelligently. It's about making a most critical distinction between wants and needs. It's about not letting things that are only wants take on the importance of true needs.

A basic tenet of some schools of Buddhist philosophy is that suffering in the human experience is caused by attachment to excessive and unnecessary desires. And yet, isn't that exactly what's been at the core of the *old* good life? Aren't excessive and unnecessary desires exactly what modern advertising is designed to promote?

If everything we look at is generating dissatisfaction, how does that affect us as people? If we're constantly being lured to buy a new cell phone, a bigger house, an upgraded computer system, or a new car, how does that affect our prospects for self-contentment and inner peace? Do we start looking at people and saying that if they don't make our lives more pleasant, they are disposable? Do we become less capable of being faithful to ourselves and one another?

The new good life requires a different set of tools and a different way of looking at things. It doesn't require abstinence or austerity, but it does ask each of us for a new thoughtfulness about the way we live and a sober skepticism toward the corporate agenda. It does entail a refusal to be entranced by the messages bombarding us day and night from a culture that sometimes seems to be trapped in a hypnotic trance.

Americans now spend nearly seven times as much time shopping as they do playing with their kids. Thirty-four percent of Americans polled ranked shopping as their favorite activity, double the number who preferred being in nature.

Is there something infantile about a world that so excessively values immediate gratification? Is there something impoverishing about a culture that encourages us to understand and express our identities through the brands and products we consume? Is there something sad about a society that believes spending money is the route to feeling good about ourselves?

On the other hand, I don't think that how thrifty you are is any indication of your level of moral or spiritual attainment. I don't think the person who spends less is somehow superior to the person who spends more. That would just be the old good life in reverse. That would just be the mirror image of the idea that the person with the biggest house or most prestigious car or biggest bank account is the more successful human being and has more value than others. I have no desire to replace conspicuous consumption with conspicuous frugality.

The new good life is neither one of self-denial nor self-indulgence. It's a path of self-awareness and self-knowledge. It's a way of living with respect for yourself, respect for others, and respect for the life of this beautiful planet we share.

You don't have to deprive yourself of anything that gives your life meaning and substance. You don't need to turn your back on all material things, and you certainly don't have to become a Puritan. To the Puritans, of course, life was grim, and temptations to sin were always lurking everywhere. They actually passed laws against laughing on Sunday.

That's not my approach. Rather, I speak to these issues from a practical perspective. I look out at the world today and I see a time of great economic uncertainty, a time when so many safety nets are being shredded, a time when the planet is groaning under the weight of our out-of-control consumption. In such circumstances, anything we can do to both create financial freedom and lessen our global footprint is more than a good thing.

It is a survival imperative.

LIFESTYLES OF THE RICH IN SPIRIT

Like just about everybody I know, I have struggled with money. My use of money has been personal, eccentric, inconsistent, and sometimes confusing. I could make a long list of things I have purchased over the course of my life that turned out to be wasteful and unnecessary. My hope and my goal is that the amount I am adding to that list is decreasing, and that I am able, as time goes by, to bring my life into greater alignment.

After fifteen years in Canada, Deo and I moved back to the United States in 1984. Our son, Ocean, was then ten years old, and we were looking for the best school for him. We found it near the small town of Santa Cruz, California, so this is where we relocated. I had by that time developed a thriving bodywork practice, offering a form of deep therapeutic massage, and by keeping our expenses low we had been able to save more than a year's worth of living expenses.

It was then that I began writing my first book, *Diet for a New America*. It took me two and a half years, working between fifty and seventy hours a week. During that interval, we managed on the money we had saved from my bodywork practice and on the money Deo brought in by cleaning houses and doing bookkeeping. It was, I suppose, an act of faith to take so much time to write a book—time during which I was making no money. I was an unknown and unpublished author, and there certainly was no reason to believe the book would sell well, or that I would even find a publisher. But I never doubted that this was what I was called to do, and neither did Deo. Somehow we both just knew that this was our path.

To my astonishment, in the years that followed, *Diet for a New America* became a bestseller, with sales eventually passing well beyond the one million mark. I was on the cover of many national magazines, and my life story got a lot of publicity. Still, we continued to live simply.

Four years after the book was published, I got a phone call. There was an upbeat female voice on the line. She said she was with a television show, and they wanted to do a program on me and my work.

"What's the name of your show?" I asked.

"*Lifestyles.*"

"Never heard of it," I said.

"We're in every major market in the country."

A national show, I thought, that's interesting. But I needed more information, and so I asked, "What time are you on in my area?"

After she told me the particulars, I put the phone down and fetched a newspaper to check if the show was in my local listings. This seemed like a straightforward thing to do, but when I found the spot, I was shocked, for it said *Lifestyles of the Rich and Famous*. This was a wildly popular television show in the eighties and nineties that exalted the extravagant lifestyles of the world's wealthiest people. Many shows were filmed on private islands and aboard personal jets, looking in awe at lifestyle choices that might have made medieval kings appear frugal. The show's host, Robin Leach, ended each episode with his signature phrase, "Champagne wishes and caviar dreams."

Hardly believing what was happening, I returned to the phone and told her what it said in my paper.

"Well, yes, that's the full name of our show."

I probably should have been diplomatic and tactful. My efforts in that direction, however, were not very effective. "I hate your show," I told her. "You glorify the shallowest parts of people. Your motto should be 'Shop Till the Planet Drops.' "

"I'm sorry you feel that way," she replied, seemingly unfazed, "but on our behalf, let me say that we don't put people down. We try to be positive."

I wasn't impressed and took the occasion to tell her so. When every religion and spiritual lineage known to humankind has taught that happiness cannot be attained through material acquisition, what kind of television show is it that preaches just the opposite? With the world ecology teetering on the edge, what kind of show glorifies an orgy of unsustainable consumption?

"I can't believe you're calling me," I said, finally. "I'm the total opposite of everything you're about."

"Let me explain," she persisted. "Once a year we're allowed to do a different kind of show. Once a year we do a show on philanthropists who donate to humanitarian causes. We feature people who use their wealth for the good of their fellow human beings."

"That's very nice," I replied. "I wish you did that show every week, and once a year you did your stupid show."

She laughed, which confused me all the more. I was totally serious. Twenty years earlier, I had walked away from the kind of lifestyle her show made such a fuss about, to live a far more simple and earth-friendly life. As far as I was concerned, her show had no place in a world deteriorating rapidly from the very lifestyle choices the show extolled.

Then it occurred to me what must be happening. She must be assuming I was still connected to Baskin-Robbins, and that I was rich. I tried to be patient as I told her that I had walked away from all that years before, had been totally on my own ever since, and had no connection to any of the Baskin-Robbins money. But, if anything, she now seemed to intensify her efforts to talk me into being featured on the show.

I decided to make one more stab at straightening things out. "Could you just tell me one thing? Why in the world would you want to do a show on me? I'm not rich, and, quite frankly, I find your show disgusting."

She sighed, but persevered. "Well, yes, I understand, but you see, some of us on the staff here have read your book, and we think your message and your life are extraordinarily important, and we want to use the program to get your message out to a large audience of people who otherwise might never be exposed to it."

Now it made a bit more sense, and I must admit I was flattered. But still, even though she meant well, I couldn't see how it could work. I tried to explain to her how we lived. Our home was small—so tiny, in fact, that the room my wife and I slept in was also our living room and kitchen, and our son's room was a converted closet. Our only car was a fifteen-year-old Datsun station wagon that had been driven more than two hundred thousand miles, and looked it. It ran and we were happy, but our lifestyle was quite a far cry from anything I thought they would ever be interested in filming.

"That doesn't matter," she assured me. "We'll find a way to make it work. We'll think of something."

I'm not sure what came over me, but I said okay, and we made a date for them to come. When the time arrived, we cleaned the place up. Not that it took long. You could vacuum our whole home in about ten minutes.

And then a gigantic van arrived. On its side were written the words, "Lifestyles of the Rich and Famous." I knew because I was peeking through the blinds.

The van door opened, and a rather heavyset fellow, who I later learned was one of the cameramen, approached the door. He knocked, and I answered. "Excuse me," he said. "Sorry to bother you. But we're looking for the home of a John Robbins, and we seem to have gotten lost. Your house number is the same as his."

At this point I figured I had better make the best of it. "That's me," I said, smiling. "Come in and make yourself at home."

He looked perplexed. "This," he said doubtfully, "is where you live?"

"Yes," I said. "Please come in."

He turned toward the van and the others. "This is the right place," he shouted. Then he laughed. "Doesn't look like the places we go to, usually."

As they entered, I attempted to be a good host. "Have a seat," I said to the cameraman, gesturing toward our only chairs. These were chairs that had been purchased several decades before as a Sears dinette set. Over the years, one of our cats had decided that these chairs were his personal scratching posts. At first I had tried to stop him, but it was to no avail, and I had eventually given up the effort. He had enjoyed himself shredding the chairs, so that by this time there was mostly stuffing showing. I had come, over the years, to look upon the chairs as a kind of art form, the artist in this case being a cat.

That did not seem, however, to be the way the cameraman saw things. "No, thank you," he said stiffly. "I'll stand."

Then I met the woman who had made the original call, a delightful woman, actually, and before long we were under way.

They interviewed me quite a few times over the ensuing days and filmed me speaking at a fund-raiser for EarthSave, a nonprofit organization I had founded.

After the first morning of shooting, Deo made us all a fabulous lunch, with fresh organic vegetables from our garden and from the local farmers market. The cameraman told me that he'd been with the show for years, filming palatial mansions and estates, and yet had never before been invited to have lunch with the people they were filming. I told him I thought that was sad, but I was glad, at least, that he was having a different experience now.

As time went along, I talked a good deal on camera about the environmental situation, and how our patterns of consumption were damaging the world and the future of all life. I spoke about the urgent need for all of us to create lifestyles and public policies that helped us to walk more lightly on the earth, that did not create so much waste or use so much energy. I pointed with dismay to the ever-widening gap between the rich and the poor.

When the time came to say good-bye, I realized how much fun it had been. The entire crew had been more than respectful toward me. As they left, the cameraman and other crewmembers told me they had enjoyed themselves very much, learned a great deal, and were going to be far more mindful of their own consumption in the future. The woman who had made the original call told me I had no idea how much this had all meant to her. She hugged me, and while she was at it, she told me that doing this show was one of the highlights of her life. "I'm so happy and proud," she said.

I was moved, and the feeling lingered for a while after they all left, until it dawned on me that I had no idea what would appear on television in the end. They had, after all, taken many hours of film. Someone would create the show by cutting and splicing in the editing room. I didn't know what to expect.

It was therefore with some trepidation that I pulled our small television out of the closet the day they first aired the show. But actually, they did a marvelous job, and the program, which turned out to be one of their most popular ever, was eventually aired thousands of times on stations all over the world.

The show's host, Robin Leach, called me "the prophet of nonprofit." I rather liked that, especially considering some of the other things I've been called. There was one thing that I was sure they would cut, but they left it in—my saying that I admired Thoreau, and quoting him: "I make myself rich by making my wants few."

At one point in the show, the camera was sweeping across the room, and there were the chairs, at which point Robin Leach announced (and I have no idea where he got this) that "every stick of furniture in their house is recycled."

But what was most amazing of all to me was that at the end, they brought up on the screen for everyone to see a beautiful picture of the earth from space. I'm sure you can picture the photo—our precious blue-green planet, suspended among the stars like an exquisite jewel. They left this photo up there for a long time, instead of jumping from one image to the next every microsecond, as is so often done on TV, and they played beautiful music to accompany the image.

And then Robin Leach said something I could hardly believe I was hearing on this, of all shows: "This man's life goes to prove that whoever believes, 'He who dies with the most toys wins,' doesn't see the whole picture." And there was the picture of the whole earth from space.

I don't want to make too much of this, because I know it was just a television show. But I was moved by what transpired, because if a show as incorrigibly shallow as *Lifestyles of the Rich and Famous* could, even for a few minutes, broadcast this kind of message, then maybe there are beneficent forces at work that may yet see us through.

Maybe we won't have to wait until the last river has been poisoned, the last acre of fertile ground has been paved over, and the last forest has been converted into a shopping mall, to learn that we can't eat money.

Maybe the day is not that far off when we will honor those who excel at giving, not those who excel at getting. Perhaps it won't be long before we recognize and appreciate the many courageous people who work day in and day out, not just to make the biggest buck, but to make the world a better place.

Maybe the work so many people are doing to create a thriving and sustainable way of life for all might actually be taking root—even in some of the most unlikely places.

AND THEN . . .

In the years after *Diet for a New America* was published, I began touring North America, speaking to larger and larger crowds, and in the process making more and more money. Still, we lived simply, so we were able to save substantial amounts and help support causes and people we loved and cared about. I found it a joyful privilege to be making a good income while doing work I loved. I felt immensely fortunate and grateful.

Born into wealth, I had chosen to leave that behind and had lived for many years with few financial resources. But now I was making significant money doing work that made a difference, and quite frankly I was delighted. While the amount we had did not compare to what would have been mine if I had stayed at Baskin-Robbins, it came from work I believed in with all my heart. Subsequently, I wrote a number of other books that also sold well, so as the years went by our net financial worth grew considerably.

Then, in January 2001, something happened that changed the course of our lives. At the time, Deo and I were living with our son, Ocean, and his wife, Michele. Michele had moved in with us in 1994, and now, six and a half years later, she was pregnant with identical twins. They were due in mid-March, but on January 7, 2001, Michele gave birth to two extremely premature identical twin boys, River and Bodhi. The little fellows were so tiny and so unready for life that they could not possibly have survived without massive medical intervention, and even with it they barely made it. They spent their first six weeks of life in the intensive care unit of a hospital, where, despite the best efforts of the hospital staff, they turned blue from lack of oxygen many times a day. It took an enormous effort by all of us, but they are now dear sweet loving boys whom we love with all our hearts. And yet the beginning of their lives was marked by repeated and substantial oxygen deprivation to their brains. They have had and very likely will always have many special needs.

There were, of course, major financial implications to all of this, and I felt grateful that Deo and I had sufficient savings and income that we could provide many forms of financial support. At the same time, I realized this could well be a lifelong situation. At the very least, we would need to provide for our special-needs grandchildren for decades to come.

A friend of mine, Richard Glantz, offered to help. A lawyer and a valued member of the board of EarthSave, Richard was very wealthy, and his financial and legal counsel had often been profoundly important to EarthSave's development and growth. I trusted him greatly.

Richard offered me the opportunity to place our money in a fund that he controlled, and in which his great wealth was invested. Our money would be pooled with his own, with the money from a number of his family members and other friends, and with the endowments of a number of progressive nonprofits and charities on whose boards he served. He believed the investment could be counted on to provide a steady and favorable annual return. The return he promised was less than the stock market had produced during the 1990s, so it didn't seem suspicious to me. I liked the steadiness and the fact that I wouldn't have to manage the money myself. Richard, who by all appearances was an expert and highly sophisticated financial adviser, would be handling it. Given the twins' ongoing special needs, it seemed like a godsend that we could get a good return on our money reliably and safely.

For the next seven years our investment did indeed earn a respectable rate of annual return, and it was very steady, just as Richard had promised. I withdrew only enough to pay the taxes on the income, as I wanted to increase our savings as much as I could in order to prepare for the twins' long-term needs, and for Deo's and my retirement. In time, I invested our entire life savings with Richard. Most years, the investment was earning 2 or 3 percent higher than the interest rate on our small mortgage, so eventually, to take advantage of that difference, I mortgaged our home to the maximum in order to increase the amount of money we had in the fund. I knew that Richard was doing the same with his homes, and it seemed perfectly safe. Richard told me—correctly—that the SEC had investigated the fund in 1992 and had given it a clean bill of health, and that it was run by the former chairman of NASDAQ. NASDAQ is the largest electronic screen-based equity securities trading market in the United States, and has more trading volume per hour than any other stock exchange in the world. It seemed totally legitimate. The returns we were getting were good but not sky-high, so I thought I was being prudent in investing our money this way.

But on December 11, 2008, Richard called with excruciating news. He had invested the money, it turned out, with a man who had just been arrested for perpetrating the most massive financial fraud in world history, the former NASDAQ chairman Bernard Madoff. The epic swindler, you may know, was responsible for the disappearance of somewhere on the order of $65 billion. He stole more money, over a longer period of time, from more people all over the world than any thief in history.

On that phone call, we learned that more than 95 percent of our net worth had been stolen. Every cent we had put into the fund was gone. Because we weren't direct investors (I didn't even know who Madoff was prior to his arrest), there was no hope of ever recovering a penny from any kind of insurance, public or private, or from the money that would eventually ensue from the liquidation of Madoff's remaining assets.

Like us, Richard was ruined financially, only he had the added guilt of having brought people he loved into what proved to be a total disaster. He wanted to help people and thought he could, but it turned out to be a financial catastrophe for all of us.

At first, I felt such enormous shock that I genuinely wondered if it might kill me. The anguish was so intense I could hardly sleep, and when I did, my sleep was roiled with nightmares. Fear became my constant companion. When I heard someone say that money doesn't buy happiness, I wanted to tell them they were full of crap. When you don't have enough to meet your basic needs, money is massively important. At that moment, without any question I would have been far happier, far less frightened, and far more able to take care of my family if I had more money. I was in despair and I was terrified.

Earlier in my life, I had walked away from an immense amount of money by choice, and I had lived without much for many years after that. I was young when I had made that decision, and the money I walked away from hadn't felt like mine, anyway. It was my father's company and fortune. I had made a choice to live by my own values. It was a choice for freedom and integrity. But now I was in my sixties, as was my wife. We were living with and helping to raise our special-needs grandchildren. And the money that had been stolen from us was our life savings, the material fruits of forty years of dedicated work. Yes, we knew how to live simply, but still, the loss felt devastating. The worst part was that I didn't see any way that I could ever get out of the financial abyss.

Through my life choices, I had tried to distance myself from the forces of greed and entitlement that have hurt so many people, and yet I had unwittingly made myself vulnerable to the crimes perpetrated by a man, Bernard Madoff, who was named by *Newsweek* in 2009 as the greediest human being to have ever walked the earth. I would have liked to talk to my parents about all this—perhaps for advice, or emotional support, or maybe even, under such extreme circumstances, to ask for a short-term loan—but my father had died nearly a year previously, and my mother was suffering from advanced Alzheimer's disease, so that was not possible.

I felt waves of shame. I had let my family down. I had put all our eggs in one basket. I had made a lot of money over the years, saved it diligently, had created financial security for my family, and now it was suddenly all gone. It seemed impossible for us to keep our home. Would we end up on the street? What would happen to the twins?

Reeling with shock and pain, I realized that I had to mobilize and to act, and do it quickly. I had to cope, not mope. I had to find a way to experience my grief as a strength, rather than as a vulnerability or a weakness. Bernard Madoff stole our money, but I wasn't about to let him steal the rest of our lives.

With the support of many friends, we began as soon as possible to dig ourselves out of the very deep financial hole into which we found ourselves so suddenly and unexpectedly plunged. We stayed purposeful, coordinating our team effort, taking one step at a time. Within three weeks we had rented out rooms in our house and had been generously lent a motor home that we rented out as well. We sold much of our furniture, electronics, and other possessions. Deo took a job as a personal assistant. I began feverishly working on a new book, took a position consulting for Whole Foods Market, and began charging for my lectures, something I had stopped doing many years before. Michele took on a part-time job (as though being the mother of twins with special needs wasn't already plenty of work), Ocean greatly increased his workload, and all of us cut our expenses to the absolute minimum. Painfully, I had to stop financially supporting causes and people I loved, although I hoped and prayed this would somehow prove to be only temporary. Many dear friends (most notably Glenn and Amy Bacheller, and Judith Morgan) stood by our sides through it all, as we grieved, made some tough choices, and tried to envision a possible future for our family. A close friend and fellow activist, Patti Breitman, circulated a letter in the vegetarian, sustainability, and social justice communities, telling of our plight. This letter was later signed and further distributed by many other friends and colleagues. I will never forget the many people who reached out to us with loving-kindness in our time of desperate need.

So many people were so compassionate and so caring to us then that even now, just remembering it, brings tears to my eyes. We barely made it, but with the loving support from many friends (which took a variety of forms, including gifts and low-interest loans), and a tremendous amount of continual work and sacrifice from each adult family member, we were able, as if by a miracle, to keep our home and thus to keep our family intact, and I was able to continue to do the work I am called to do.

With humility and gratitude, I vowed to try to be worthy of the trust that had been placed in me. The generosity of others gave me a renewed appreciation for the words of the Dalai Lama:

> If you think only of yourself, if you forget the rights and well-being of others, or, worse still, if you exploit others, ultimately you will lose. You will have no friends who will show concern for your well-being. Moreover, if a tragedy befalls you, instead of feeling concerned, others might even secretly rejoice. By contrast, if an individual is compassionate and altruistic, and has the interests of others in mind, then irrespective of whether that person knows a lot of people, wherever that person moves, he or she will immediately

make friends. And when that person faces a tragedy, there will be plenty of people who will come to help.

Born into riches, I've gone from there to chosen rags, to self-made riches, to unchosen rags, to now recovering and once again creating sufficiency. Through it all, I've come to realize that the journey I've been on has given me something precious, something actually more valuable than the fortune I walked away from, and worth more than the millions of dollars I earned and saved before they were stolen.

It's often been said that there are no luggage racks on hearses. No matter what worldly possessions any of us have acquired, we leave it all behind in the end.

What, then, do we take with us?

There is a story about a teacher who asked his students, "If I have five hundred dollars, and in the course of my life I give away four hundred dollars, how much do I have at the end of my life?"

The students eagerly answered, "One hundred dollars."

"That's what you might think," the teacher said. "But the deeper truth is that if I have five hundred dollars here on Earth, and I give away four hundred dollars, then at my death what I will have is four hundred dollars. Because in the end, all you have is what you have given."

TWO

Getting to Know Your Money Type

Each of us has our own money story. You now know something of mine, of how my life has evolved financially. You, of course, have your own story. Whether we are rich or poor, each one of us has had a journey in regards to money, a journey with many twists and turns, with challenges and wounds, with times of darkness and times of light. Through it all, each of us has developed our unique ways of thinking about and handling money.

How well do you know your money personality? Do you know, when it comes to your attitudes, feelings, and beliefs about money, how you compare to the average person? Do you know your strengths and weaknesses? Do you know the gifts and the pitfalls that come with your particular money style? Do you know what tendencies you revert to under money stress?

The money styles we have developed are a result of the experiences we have each had during the course of our lives, and they are also a result of certain indwelling patterns we each carry. In order to become financially free and self-aware, we need to understand the life experiences we have had with money, and we need to recognize the deep organizing patterns within our psyches that influence our experience. We need to understand the money archetypes that play out with tremendous power in our financial lives.*

It was Carl Jung who first discovered that humans have "preconscious psychic dispositions" around which our life experiences constellate. These archetypes have extraordinary impact on the way each of us experiences our wounds and our healings, our losses and our victories, our choices and our fortunes.

Knowing the archetypes that play out in your money life is a step in the journey to having a happier and more life-supporting relationship with money. Having insight into your money type gives you new understanding of yourself, your choices, and your behaviors. And it helps you to appreciate others' styles, so you can recognize your differences and use them constructively.

In this chapter I will share with you six basic money archetypes that I believe are alive in our collective money journey at this moment in history, and which make up the dominant forces in each of our money personalities. These are:

The Saver
The Innocent
The Performer
The Sensualist
The Vigilant
The Giver

Does each person express one type and one type alone? No. These are universal archetypes that live to some degree in all of us, so you will probably find something of yourself in each of the six types. But not equally.

* Recognizing that people have widely different relationships with money and respond very differently to financial stress, many authors, psychologists, and financial advisers have sought to identify these archetypes in order to help people see themselves and others more clearly. My understanding of the inner inclinations and patterns that people carry around financial matters has drawn particularly on the work of Brent Kessel, and on the work of Olivia Mellan, Deborah L. Price, Laura Rowley, David Keirsey, Carol Pearson, the psycho-spiritual typology known as the Enneagram, and the Jungian-based Myers-Briggs typology.

As a result of early life experiences, family histories, genetics, ancestral memories, and prenatal factors, most of us emerge from childhood with one or two of the six archetypes playing dominant roles in our money lives, and with a few others playing lesser but still significant parts. These predominant archetypes, in conjunction with the other types that play supporting roles, essentially define your money personality.

Are some types inherently better or worse than others? No. There is absolutely no hierarchy among the money archetypes. Our society tends to esteem and reward certain types more than others, but that represents a cultural phase, a temporary artifact of social conditions. The deeper truth is that each archetype has its own shadows and its own gifts. Each has its distinctive liabilities and assets. Each entails certain dangers and carries certain powers. Each type has its own internal structure, and each involves certain characteristic behaviors, attitudes, defenses, and motivations. Each archetype brings its own burdens and its own blessings.

Sometimes you experience the unhealthy tendencies and traits that are characteristic of your types, and other times you express the healthier and more life-affirming qualities. No matter how evolved you are, in the course of your life there will inevitably be times that you experience the lower aspects of your types, the compulsions and pathologies. And no matter how wounded or broken you feel, there will be other times that you will know and embody the brighter possibilities of your types.

As you proceed along the path your money archetypes present, you will learn something that is of utmost importance to your financial freedom, to your physical health, and to your spiritual well-being. You will learn that you have everything you need to turn compulsion into choice, adversity into prosperity, and darkness into light.

THE SIX MONEY ARCHETYPES

The Saver

Savers tend to plan their financial affairs and are typically careful in their budgeting, cautious in their spending, and conservative in their investing. They like having a steady paycheck, living within their means, and saving on a regular basis.

People in whom the Saver archetype is strong tend to have remarkably little interest in keeping up with the Joneses. They equate money, and particularly savings, with security for themselves and for their families. For them, having money is more exciting than almost anything they could buy with it. As children, Savers were the ones who counted the money in their piggy banks rather than spending it.

Their friends may think Savers are prone to be cheapskates, but they don't mind. They don't look at their frugality as being stingy; they see it as being safe. And safety, to a Saver, is of paramount importance.

Savers don't particularly like spending money on anything they believe are frills or luxuries. If their savings diminish, even if the numbers are still substantial, they may feel uneasy or anxious. They need to feel that they have a strong safety net in place.

When Savers do purchase things, they get more pleasure if the items were a bargain. Always aware of how much things cost, they are on the constant lookout for sales and are genuinely excited when they see an opportunity to get things that they buy regularly for less.

Savers tend to remember where they bought many of the things they have purchased, and they have a pretty good idea of what they spent. They notice the price of gas at local gas stations and make it a point to fill up where gas is least expensive.

Generally quite responsible around money issues, Savers rarely go into debt and would prefer to do without rather than to run up a credit card balance. If they ever took a financial risk and it didn't work out well, or ever wasted a significant amount of money, they may have a hard time forgiving themselves and getting over it.

Savers are apt to carefully monitor their bank statements, and they may give a lot of thought to the amount of money they will need to retire. When buying appliances, they look for energy-efficient models. When shopping for a car, gas mileage and anticipated maintenance costs play a major role in their choice. They pride themselves on getting good deals and are likely to do thorough research before making a major purchase. They get annoyed when they see people wasting money.

The messages about money that Savers give to their children are the ones they live. Saving comes first. When a small child has a birthday, they might give him or her a piggy bank. As their children grow up, they might give them an allowance, but it won't be excessive and they will encourage them to put part of it each week in the piggy bank. When their children are old enough, they will take them to a bank and open up a savings account for them. For a high school graduation gift, they probably won't buy their children a car or an iPod. If they can afford it, they might buy them a life insurance policy.

Savers don't like wasting anything. They eat everything on their plates. Their old shirts become rags; their plastic bags get rinsed and reused; and they wear extra sweaters rather than turn on the heat. They may be workaholics who hang on to a job out of a sense of financial duty even when it's killing them.

Savers are vividly aware of the uncertainty of our current financial era. For them, frugality isn't just common sense; it's a necessity. When they are distressed, it calms them down to think about how much money they have saved. Deep down, they feel that their survival and that of their family depends most of all on the amount of their savings.

No one likes losing their life savings. But for those in whom the Saver archetype is strong, the loss of savings can be traumatic. If the loss is major and sudden, they may experience such overwhelming pain that they lose the ability to cope.

I speak from personal experience here. The Saver archetype is large in my psyche. When our life savings were abruptly lost in the Madoff fraud, I felt for a time as though the very ground of my being was sucked out of me. It would have been disastrous to linger in these feelings, though, because my family's financial survival was at stake. I had to work hard to get over the trauma so that I could begin to think and act with clarity.

When major financial misfortune occurs, it helps greatly to know where your real wealth lies. Savers tend to be prudent and responsible people, but if you make your life all about money, then if you lose it you feel like you've lost everything. I know of four different Madoff victims who committed suicide.

The Shadow Side of the Saver

Today, when the economic downturn is causing so much stress, many of us need to be reminded that saving money is a central part of any sound financial plan. But as with any archetype, there is a dark side to the Saver. Savers love to delay gratification. Sometimes they delay it so completely that it never comes. If by some miracle they were ever to get a massage, they might spend the whole time thinking about whether they were getting their money's worth. If a close friend were to suffer a devastating financial blow, they might be more quick to judge their friend's actions that left them vulnerable than to offer them support. They can be afraid to spend money or to give it to others. They may not know the pleasure of generously giving to those in need.

In the extreme, Savers can become so obsessed with saving money that their lives are drained of joy. They can become so worried that their money might someday run out that they descend into hoarding, counting and recounting their savings, hardly noticing that their life spirit has contracted into density and fearfulness.

At its lowest levels, the experience of the Saver archetype is fraught with tension and rigidity. However much money they save, however much money they have, they still feel pain, loneliness, and isolation. They become living statements of the Greek proverb: "A miser is ever in want." At the most unhealthy extreme, their attachment to material things leaves little space in their heart for living connections with other people or with the natural world.

One of the most infamous examples of the Saver archetype at its lowest level was a businesswoman named Hetty Green, who lived in Vermont and New York. When she died in 1916, her estate was valued at nearly $200 million, which is equivalent to more than $3 billion today. The richest woman in the world, she never turned on the heat or used hot water. She wore the same black dress every day, and she changed her undergarments only after they had worn out. She ate only cold oatmeal, and she once spent an entire night looking for a lost stamp worth two cents. When her son, Ned, broke his leg as a child, Hetty tried to get him admitted to a hospital charity ward. She was recognized, though, and as a result her son was refused entry, at which point she stormed away in anger, vowing to treat his wounds herself. Left without medical attention, Ned's leg ended up having to be amputated.

Perhaps the most famous example in English literature of the extreme dark side of the Saver archetype is Ebenezer Scrooge, the main character in *A Christmas Carol* by Charles Dickens. A coldhearted, tightfisted, selfish man who despises Christmas and all things happy and generous, he is finally transformed in the course of the novel by the three ghosts of Christmas. He comes eventually see that money is not an end in itself, and that hoarding money for its own sake is not a path to anything but emptiness. Money, he comes to understand, is a resource and a tool, and is valuable in proportion to the ends to which it is used.

The Evolving Saver

Today, we are just emerging from decades when personal savings have been at an all-time low, when maxing out on credit card debt and buying a home with no money down have been seen as viable financial strategies, when the Saver archetype was viewed as a party pooper. As a result, many of us today desperately need the higher and healthier levels of the Saver archetype to be activated in our psyches. We need to learn how to plan joyfully for retirement, how to live within our means, how to systematically pay down our debts, and how to save happily for a rainy day. Frugality is, at long last, coming back into style. The wisdom of the Saver in its higher aspects will stand many of us in good stead in the days to come.

The Saver archetype, like all money archetypes, is a path. At one end, at its negative pole, lies miserliness and hoarding. In the middle, there are many people who derive more pleasure from saving money than from spending it, whose lives, while not ruled entirely by fear, are still beset by low background levels of anxiety and agitation. At the higher end lies the mature form of the Saver archetype. Here are people whose lives are graced by prudence, thoughtfulness, and the responsible wisdom born of self-sufficiency. This is not the self-sufficiency of building a fortress or acquiring an immense savings account so they'll never need anyone else. It's the joyful self-sufficiency the poet Walt Whitman expressed when he wrote "Henceforth, I ask not good fortune. I myself am good fortune."

Along the path of the Saver archetype, the very sense of time changes. At its lowest level, the Saver hoards desperately in fear of the future. In its more common form, people go about their lives saving money whenever they can, their brows knit with concern about the future. In its highest form, the Saver archetype takes joy in planning and building a future that can bring out the best in the human spirit. At its highest level, the Saver lives with great respect for the future, embodying the Iroquois Confederacy maxim: "In our every deliberation, we must consider the impact of our decisions on the next seven generations."

The Evolved Saver

The mature form of the Saver archetype carries a deep sense of reverence for the passage of time and understands the intimate interweaving

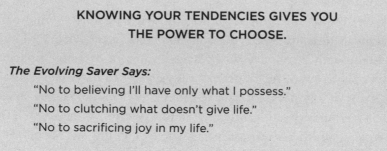

**KNOWING YOUR TENDENCIES GIVES YOU
THE POWER TO CHOOSE.**

The Evolving Saver Says:

"No to believing I'll have only what I possess."

"No to clutching what doesn't give life."

"No to sacrificing joy in my life."

The Evolving Saver Says:

"Yes to giving and receiving."

"Yes to feeling safe in the world."

"Yes to true wealth and true self."

of the past, the present, and the future. If we were, as individuals and as a culture, to embody the highest levels of the Saver archetype, we would not fear the future but would find joy in doing what we can to make it as beautiful and as happy as possible. We would be grateful for every opportunity we might have to leave our children a better future. We would find our pleasures and our fulfillment while being responsible in our use of resources and in conserving the natural world. Rather than saving money for its own sake, we would also save our world from pollution, we would save our minds from the toxicity of fear, and we would save our fellow human beings from poverty and loneliness. We would experience the new good life to be immensely satisfying, for we would know that when our time comes to leave this world, it would be a better place for our having been here.

We would live with infinite gratitude to all things past, infinite service to all things present, and infinite responsibility to all things future.

The Innocent

All of us begin our lives innocently. As little children, we have no ability to survive on our own and certainly no skill or understanding of the laws of money. We are completely dependent on our parents and/or other adults to take care of our survival needs.

It is a sadness of modern life that as we grow up and learn to take responsibility for ourselves, so many of us lose touch with the freedom, the playfulness, and the openheartedness of our childhood. Many of us become so embroiled in meeting the serious demands of adulthood that something in our psyches turns rigid and we lose a sense of wonder before the mysteries of life.

This may be a greater loss than most of us realize. Rachel Carson, the biologist and writer who is often considered the founder of the modern environmental movement, attributed her keen sensitivity to the interconnectedness of ecological systems to never having lost her sense of innocence. "If I had influence with the good fairy who is supposed to preside over the christening of all children," she wrote, "I should ask that her gift to each child in the world be a sense of wonder so indestructible that it would last throughout life."

The dictionary defines innocence as "freedom from guilt or sin through being unacquainted with evil." As a financial archetype, Innocents have little desire to become acquainted with money. They never place a high priority on learning how to earn, save, or manage their financial lives.

As children, Innocents aren't the kids who play store, they aren't the ones who put up lemonade stands in order to sell lemonade, and they aren't the ones who constantly pester their parents to buy them things or to give them bigger allowances. They have extraordinarily rich imaginations and they have vivid and powerful dreams, but they don't dream of being the next Donald Trump. They live in more mythological realms.

As adults, Innocents often have great gifts and talents. Their openhearted natures can make them warm and even delightful friends. Sometimes they are artistic, creative, or adventurous. But when it comes to money, many of them feel hopelessly confused.

Some Innocents are the children of wealthy patriarchs who controlled everything to do with the family's finances and were far from transparent about how they handled money. Others are the children of people who struggled financially for their entire lives and believed that "people like us will never have money." But whatever their backgrounds, their characteristic feeling around money is bewilderment. As a result, even the routine tasks of money life can be difficult.

They may have a hard time paying bills on time. They may not fully understand their phone bills, their credit card bills, or the statements they get from the bank. The financial records they keep may be disorganized and incomplete. They are more apt than most other financial archetypes to incur bank charges and overdraft fees, and to be in credit card debt without realizing how much interest they're being charged. Many years, they wait until the last minute to do their taxes. If their checkbooks happen to balance, they regard it as a minor miracle.

Often, Innocents possess talents that aren't rewarded financially in our society. They may be caregivers, musicians, or artists. They may be poets, teachers, or nurses.

Because Innocents tend to be such trusting people, they may be the most likely of all financial archetypes to be taken advantage of by friends, family members, and others. They might buy things because they're worried about hurting the feelings of salespeople.

The Innocent is the most likely archetype to buy lottery tickets, to gamble compulsively, or to become involved in pyramid schemes. They may believe that only good luck or grace can rescue them, that only some kind of financial windfall can provide them with security.

The spending patterns of Innocents tend to be haphazard at best. They may drive five miles out of their way to purchase gas that is ten cents a gallon cheaper, without thinking of the gas and time they use up in the process. They may agonize for a half hour at a garage sale over whether to buy a $5 toaster, and then the next day impulsively buy a $100 handbag.

Innocents are the most likely of all archetypes to be confused about where their money is going.

The Shadow Side of the Innocent

At the lower levels of the archetype, Innocents become depressed by their lack of financial skill. And at the lowest levels, when Innocents are depressed, they don't exercise or do other things to kick their games back into high gear. Instead, their thoughts are filled with "If onlys." "If only I came from a wealthier family," "If only the people I depended on had taken care of me," "If only my boss wasn't such a jerk," "If only my relatives hadn't betrayed me," "If only the bank would make an error in my favor, and I'd suddenly find a million dollars in my account."

In the darkest manifestation of the archetype, Innocents see themselves as victims and blame their financial woes on others. They have a long list of reasons for why their lives don't work and the injustices that have been perpetrated upon them. Some of these abuses may indeed have occurred, and they may, in fact, have experienced more than their share of financial and emotional misfortunes. But what marks the most toxic form of the Innocent archetype is self-pity and an overarching sense of entitlement. They hold others responsible for their misfortunes, want others to rescue them, and seek to become dependent on others financially. Their avoidance patterns can become so entrenched that they develop addictions—to alcohol, drugs, gambling—in the effort to distract from their pain.

The Evolving Innocent

Of course, the vast majority of Innocents never descend to such an extreme level of darkness. The world is full of Innocents who muddle along, not harming anyone but not particularly happy with themselves or their lives, wishing and hoping things would get better for them financially, but not believing they can ever initiate and sustain a thriving relationship with money.

I have a friend named Margie who carries a lot of the Innocent archetype. The only daughter in a family with four kids, she grew up in a home in which boys were raised to earn and manage money, and girls were raised to care for the home and the children. It was the 1950s, a time when many American families were supported by a single wage earner. Throughout her childhood she loved babysitting, and when she was paid for her services she would simply give the money to her father, for he took care of all the family's finances and financial decisions. When her friends and family members had birthdays, she never thought to buy them presents; instead she would draw them pictures. She has always been gregarious and openhearted. And she never learned how to manage finances.

As Margie got older, the world changed, and it wasn't what her parents and education had prepared her for. She never married, and while she worked hard in multiple jobs, she never seemed to have a stable footing in the financial world. Feeling overwhelmed by anything to do with money management, she tended to avoid it altogether. "It just works out," she would say, "or it doesn't. But either way, it's over my head!"

Like many Innocents, Margie spent erratically. Once I visited her home in January and it was fifty degrees inside. She had no heat on, she said, because she was trying to save on heating costs. The very next week

I came over again, only this time I found her home to be toasty warm. The thermostat on the wall was set at seventy-five degrees. "I just got paid," she explained when I inquired about the difference.

I've always known Margie to be a generous friend. She would think nothing of staying up all night to help a loved one recovering from surgery, or of taking care of a friend's kids for the day in a time of crisis. She never shunned taking responsibility, except when it came to money. There, she would fear it like the plague.

Every so often, Margie would make an effort to get her financial house in order but rarely met with any success. Always a believer in the power of the mind, she would write affirmations such as, "I am rich and prosperous and have all the money I want." Unfortunately, this didn't work quite the way she hoped, typically leading only to spending binges and ever larger credit card bills.

A few years ago, Margie lost one of her jobs, and she got into so much credit card debt that she was finally forced to face her financial demons. It was either that, she realized, or they would completely destroy her life.

With some coaching from a friend, Margie took stock of her income and her fixed expenses, decided to track what she spent and what she earned, and made a tentative budget for the next three months. She still tended to become easily confused about money matters, but she was now resolute in her feeling that she needed to attain some measure of control and pay down her credit card debts. It wasn't easy for her, and she had to trim her costs of living in a lot of areas. She also had to give up her fantasies of being somehow rescued by a knight in shining armor, or of prosperity somehow magically appearing if only she thought the right thoughts. Margie still believed in the power of affirmations, but now she wrote things such as, "I take responsibility for my spending. I am learning to be careful, wise, and responsible with money." Step by step, Margie learned to manage the small stream of money that flowed through her life. As she did so, her life became more stable, and she began to feel better about herself.

Margie has worked hard and applied herself to an area of weakness, and in the process, she has turned it into something of a strength. She has always loved to give to others generously of her time and energies. Now she mentors girls from low-income backgrounds in basic budgeting and financial management. "I know what it's like to not have those skills," she says, "and I want to help others to learn."

Margie has begun to claim control over an area of her life—her money life—that had been utterly bewildering. Her story is an example of an Innocent working her way through the continuum of possibilities, gradually growing toward the higher possibilities of the archetype.

Mature Innocents won't usually become financial wizards, because their natural talents and gifts typically lie in other areas. But as they gain confidence and competence in their money lives, their other interests cease to be incapacitated by their financial issues and instead begin to be supported. Where before their financial confusion had sabotaged the rest of their lives, now their money world becomes a source of sustenance for the many other things they love to do. Their natural openness and sense of wonder becomes grounded in a foundation that can sustain a healthy and responsible life.

The work of those in whom the Innocent archetype is strong is to grow up without forsaking their ideals. It's to claim their own powers and to trust their own capabilities. At lower levels of the archetype they see their mistakes and failures as proof of their incompetence. At higher levels they see them as opportunities to learn.

Although Innocents tend to have an aversion to keeping careful track of their finances, they gain an enormous amount from doing so. As they start to develop genuine financial expertise, every area of their lives is touched and transformed. Where before there had been the need to hide and obfuscate, now there is the capacity to be visible, present, and engaged. Where before there had been shame, now there is growing self-respect. Where before there had been victimhood, now there is the development of competence.

As parents, evolving Innocents are careful to transmit positive and healthy messages to their children about their relationships with money. Both through their words and their actions, they tell them, "You will be successful at whatever you choose to undertake in your life. You will be great at anything you really want to do. You are a talented and wonderful human being, and you have the ability to make money and handle it with grace and respect."

The Evolved Innocent

The self-realized Innocent, like the fully evolved embodiment of every other archetype, has been through an arduous healing journey and has a great deal to offer others. Mature Innocents have known the experience

---

KNOWING YOUR TENDENCIES GIVES YOU
THE POWER TO CHOOSE.

The Evolving Innocent Says:

"No to blaming others for my financial problems."

"No to remaining incompetent and helpless around money."

"No to feeling sorry for myself."

The Evolving Innocent Says:

"Yes to my ability to learn how to handle my finances."

"Yes to my creativity and my competence."

"Yes to enjoying the freedom that comes with taking full responsibility in all areas of my life."

---

of clinging to outdated beliefs and traveling on self-defeating paths. At the same time, they know how toxic pity can be, and so they never pity another person. They understand the difference between pity and compassion. They reach out to help those who are needing or hurting with a profound respect for the capability, intelligence, and strength at the core of every person. Having come to know and trust their own powers, they can transmit to others a belief in their own resilience, their ability to overcome obstacles, and their capacity to mend from whatever addictions or pain might for now be holding them hostage.

If the highest possibilities of the Innocent archetype were more present in our lives, we would honor the many kinds of intelligence by which human beings can know the world. We would deepen in our respect for intuition and empathy, for musical and emotional wisdom, as well as for analysis and logic. Most of all, we would know that the innocence of childhood can be more than a beautiful but passing life stage. The sense of wonder and awe before the mysteries of life that are part of a healthy childhood would sustain us as adults and would be fertile sources for the artistic and spiritual dimensions of our lives.

Albert Einstein was such an Innocent. Widely recognized as one of the most brilliant scientists in human history, he actually struggled in his early years with money and, remarkably, even with academics. A late talker who almost flunked out of high school, he possessed a deeply inquisitive nature that made him often appear dreamy. As he learned to focus his remarkable brilliance, he never forgot how deeply important it is to stay in touch with our sense of wonder. "The most beautiful thing we can experience," he wrote, "is the mysterious. It is the source of all true art and all science." Einstein felt sad for those "to whom this emotion is a stranger, who can no longer pause to wonder and stand rapt in awe."

The Performer

We all need attention. Children can die from a lack of it, and prisoners who are deprived of others' attention by being placed in isolation often develop serious mental disorders. The human psyche seems to require a certain amount of attention from others to thrive.

Performers are more aware than any other archetype of the significance and power of others' attention. They're always alert to who is being noticed. Their idea of a great time is to have a room full of enthusiastic listeners or to be on stage in front of a captivated audience. They relish being admired and enthralling others, bringing them joy and making them laugh. For Performers, nothing is as irresistible as other people's attention, because for them, attention is equivalent to love.

For those in whom this archetype is dominant, money is a tool to enhance their ability to get the kind of attention they want. As Marilyn Monroe, a famous Performer, put it, "I don't want to make money. I just want to be wonderful."

We all want to be recognized and appreciated, and we all enjoy looking good in others' eyes. People whose basic financial archetype is the Performer, however, are so keenly aware of the image that they project that this determines many of their major life decisions. It often governs what they spend their money on and may even influence who they love.

Compared to other money styles, a higher percentage of a Performer's total spending goes to clothing, hair care, jewelry, beauty products, cosmetics, and other ways to enhance their appearance and body image. They dress to impress.

Performers focus on external signs of wealth and beauty because they believe that this is the surest way to gain recognition, acceptance, and love. Having the latest smart phone, seeing a new movie on opening night, getting the latest cosmetic surgery, and even going on a fancy vacation can feel like an imperative if it will enable them to get the kind of attention they want. More than other archetypes, they'll be drawn to driving prestigious cars and displaying other signs of status.

When overweight Performers take steps to lose weight, their primary motivation is less likely to be concern for their health and more likely to be concern for how others see them.

It's nearly impossible for a female Performer to meet another woman and not notice how she is dressed, how her hair is done, and whether she's got a stylish handbag. She may be a feminist, but you can't convince her that being liberated means wearing sensible shoes.

Although men tend not to be fond of clothes shopping, the male Performer enjoys it more than most. Regardless of his economic status, he always makes it a point to be sharply dressed.

There is a great strength in this archetype, for it is Performers who most deeply grasp the implications of how they appear to others. In many situations and professions, how people look and the impression others have of them is of central importance. Performers recognize that generating the right image will raise their sales figures, help them get well-paying jobs, or lead to other forms of financial success. They know that people in our society tend to trust and follow others who radiate a sense of accomplishment.

Studies have shown that men who are seen as attractive are more likely to be leaders and to make more money than those who are seen as less attractive. The same is largely true for women. Many studies have shown that women who are seen as beautiful are noticed far more and make considerably more money than those who are seen as less so. If they're waitresses, they get bigger tips. If they're attorneys, they win more cases in front of juries. If they're in the corporate world, they get more promotions. If they marry, it's often to wealthier partners.

Performers, more than any other financial archetype, use money to generate and project whatever self-image they believe will bring them the good things in life. As Carrie Bradshaw, the lead character in the TV series *Sex and the City,* puts it: "I like my money right where I can see it, hanging in my closet."

The Shadow Side of the Performer

As with all archetypes, there is a shadow side to the Performer. They can become so caught up in appearances that they neglect their feelings and their relationships with others. They are vulnerable to marketing and advertising efforts to convince them that in order to keep up their image they just have to have the latest technology.

In the extreme, they buy things they can't afford just to make others think more highly of them. Mistakenly believing that anyone who projects a more affluent image than they are able to must be happier than they are, they are uniquely susceptible to ad campaigns like the one for the Mercedes E350 that promised, none-too-subtly, "More horses, Bigger engine, Increased envy."

An example of the money mismanagement that can plague the Performer archetype in its lower levels is the rise and fall of the rap artist and dancer MC Hammer. In the early 1990s, Hammer was at the peak of a hugely successful performing career. His albums had sold more than fifty million copies, and he had a net worth of nearly $40 million. He built a mansion in Fremont, California, which included a recording studio, a thirty-three-seat theater, two swimming pools, tennis courts, a baseball diamond, a bowling alley, and a totally mirrored bathroom. The mirrors he installed throughout the house cost more than $100,000. He had gold-plated gates placed at the entrance to the property, with his name prominently inscribed.

The great Indian sage Mahatma Gandhi, known for truly walking his talk, once said, "My life is my statement." Hammer, known for his flashy wardrobes, shiny suits, and baggy pants, once said that his lifestyle was his fashion statement. Unfortunately, looking good proved to be costly for him. In 1996, he filed for bankruptcy, telling the court that his debts exceeded his assets by more than $4 million.

Today, MC Hammer is still a Performer, but he has risen from the depths of the archetype to a far more functional place. He works as a television show host, performs occasionally at concerts and other functions, and tries to live within his means.

The Evolving Performer

In the lower levels of the archetype, Performers seek others' admiration for their own self-aggrandizement. But as they evolve, Performers use their abilities to attract others' attention in order to fulfill higher purposes. They use their sensitivities less self-consciously and more on behalf of the well-being of others and of the greater Earth community.

At every level, Performers know that how they look and how others perceive them really does matter. The question is whether their intention to use their appearance is motivated by egotistic desires or by desires to serve and contribute to others.

As Performers work their way upward along the continuum of possibilities inherent in their type, they can often help others understand how they are being seen. If someone suffers from feeling invisible, the evolving Performer may be just the person to help, to take that person under their wing and help them to come out of their shell, to help them learn how to express themselves so that their gifts will be recognized and appreciated. Keenly sensitive to how people are received by others, they can help their friends and family members develop a personal style that is creative, authentic, and effective.

Performers always love others' attention and always thrive in the spotlight, but as they evolve, the craving to be seen as special gives way to more contentment and self-acceptance. As their need to be seen in a particular way by other people recedes, their focus on their inner lives and feelings becomes sharpened. Their sense of self-worth and self-respect are increasingly self-generated, and they begin to embody the truth in the saying that "character is who you are when no one is looking."

As teachers, Performers in the brighter dimensions of the archetype have a unique ability to present information and material that inspires others. Some of the most powerful ministers have been Performers manifesting their more evolved potentials. Their sense of humor, eloquence, and charisma enable them to uplift and motivate their congregations. Similarly, many recording artists and musicians are Performers who use their musical gifts to bring energy, excitement, harmony, and new possibilities to their listeners. At the higher levels of the archetype, Performers bring consciousness and healing to their friends, families, and audiences, bathing others in an atmosphere of hope and goodwill.

The Evolved Performer

Since its founding in the 1930s, the Gallup Organization has polled people in the United States every year to determine the most widely admired people. In December 1999, they compiled the results from nearly seventy years of polling and produced a list of the most admired people from the twentieth century. Mother Teresa and Martin Luther King, Jr., were first and second on the list. John F. Kennedy was third.

Kennedy was president for only two and a half years, and most commentators agree that his policies and decisions weren't sufficiently remarkable to account for the great esteem in which he is still held by so many. It was the image he presented, most agree, that made him so memorable.

Kennedy was a masterful Performer, who almost certainly would never have become president if it weren't for his finely honed sensitivity to how he was seen. In September and October 1960, Kennedy debated then-vice-president Richard Nixon in the first televised U.S. presidential debates. Radio listeners generally thought Nixon won the debates, but television viewers overwhelmingly thought Kennedy won. On November 8, Kennedy defeated Nixon for the presidency in an extraordinarily close election. In the national popular vote, Kennedy surpassed Nixon by only two-tenths of 1 percent (49.7 percent to 49.5 percent).

Throughout his presidency, Kennedy projected an image of vitality and virility. It wasn't until 2002, when the Kennedy library allowed historians access to the medical archives, that the truth became known. Ironically, the president most Americans saw as the embodiment of youthful vigor and health was, in fact, a very ill man with a bad back, digestive problems, and Addison's disease. Just to get through the day he took twelve different medications, including phenobarbital, Librium, meprobamate, Nembutal, Demerol, methadone, codeine, oral and injected cortisone, and testosterone. Six times a day White House physicians injected Novocain, procaine, and other painkilling medications into his back. When he wasn't in the public eye, he often walked on crutches. Yet, ever the Performer, Kennedy successfully presented an image to the world of being fit, dynamic, and energetic.

At the peak levels of the Performer archetype are people who elevate themselves in the glow of the attention they relish, in order to serve the highest aspirations of the human spirit. According to some of the people who were closest to him, Martin Luther King, Jr., was always extremely aware of his appearance. As a young man, he spent much of his pocket money on clothes and other things to enhance the way he was seen. Today, it is almost universally recognized that this remarkable man used the immense recognition and even glory he received as a world leader to advance the cause of human rights and the dignity of all people. It may seem trivializing to call a man of his stature a Performer, but in the very finest and highest possible sense of the archetype, this is what he was.

KNOWING YOUR TENDENCIES GIVES YOU THE POWER TO CHOOSE.

The Evolving Performer Says:

"No to being defined only by the image I project."

"No to evaluating myself only through others' eyes."

"No to obsessively seeking the approval of others."

The Evolving Performer Says:

"Yes to cultivating the beauty that comes from within."

"Yes to living by my inner wisdom."

"Yes to living with joy, self-confidence, and power."

The Sensualist

It is inherent in human nature to live in our senses and seek pleasure. All of us appreciate immediate gratification. For Sensualists, though, more than any other financial archetype, the desire for pleasure and instant gratification is felt so keenly that it plays a dominant role in their financial lives.

Once their basic needs are met, and sometimes even before they are, Sensualists view money as a means to buy goods and services that bring pleasure. For this archetype, saving for a rainy day seems a little silly. It's far more important to enjoy the sunshine right now.

If they experience good financial fortune, Sensualists are overjoyed with thoughts of what they can buy. For them, "be here now" means not worrying about the future. Focused on the present, they tend to be impulsive and spontaneous in their spending. To deny themselves the pleasures that money can buy feels like self-betrayal.

The archetype cuts across class lines and is found at every level of income. Sensualists who have little money are sometimes intensely drawn to thrift stores, close-out sales, and garage sales.

Sensualists have a heightened receptivity for sensory experience and pleasure. Their spontaneity and fun-loving nature can be charming and make them attractive to romantic partners. They seem to overflow with abundance and to know how to enjoy life. Some Sensualists have a series of relationships, but if they marry and try to settle down things may not go so well. They have a tendency to be distractible and scattered, they do not want limits put on themselves, and they may have difficulties with commitment.

Sensualists assume others get pleasure from immediate gratification just as much as they do, and they are happy if they are able to provide it to others. They often eagerly look forward to holidays and birthdays and will sometimes spend lavishly on presents.

Compared to other financial archetypes, Sensualists make less distinction between items that are necessary and those that are luxuries. They may relish fine dining, good wine, fancy organic face creams, and maybe even spa weekends. When buying sheets, they'll be drawn to the most luxurious options with the highest thread counts. Their homes are often filled with toys.

Sensualists are inclined to deals that promise "no money down" or "buy now, pay later." Their sense of the present is so strong and their sense of the future so amorphous that it's almost as though this means these items are free.

When Sensualists feel depressed, bored, or lonely, they sometimes use credit cards to self-medicate. At the end of the month, they may not have a clue where their money has gone. The very word "budget" can make them feel claustrophobic. Their motto could almost be "Ready, aim, spend."

Those people in whom the Sensualist archetype is strong derive much pleasure from spending money. They don't want their children to feel deprived, so they'll give them as big an allowance as they can afford, and maybe bigger. They aren't concerned about spoiling them; they want to give them the best things money can buy. When their kids are young, they might take them to a toy store and happily ask, "What do you want to get?" Later, when the children graduate from high school, Sensualists might take them to dinner at a fine restaurant. They might give them a luxury vacation, whether they can afford it or not.

Sensualists are happy when spending money to provide themselves or others with pleasure. If they won the lottery, they'd probably buy a new car and a new house, and throw quite the party. Most likely, the money would all be gone within a few years.

The Shadow Side of the Sensualist

As with every financial archetype, there is a shadow side to Sensualists. They have a harder time than most other archetypes tightening their belts when money is short, and they are the most likely of all types to go into debt to maintain the lifestyles to which they are accustomed.

Some Sensualists judge themselves harshly for not being in control of their spending. But in the descending spiral that marks the dark side of the archetype, this does not lead to a change in direction. Instead, Sensualists may try to drown out the feelings of guilt by seeking even more immediate pleasure. Seeking solace from a growing inner emptiness by spending more money, they derive less and less pleasure from their purchases and from their life. At its most toxic extreme, the dark side of the Sensualist's journey leads ever deeper into debt, and ever deeper into despair.

At its lowest levels, Sensualists' spending becomes compulsive. They lose the ability to ask whether their spending is actually enhancing their life, and they increasingly put themselves and their loved ones in financial peril. As both their debt and their hopelessness increase, they resort to the remedy with which they are most familiar—spending their money in an effort to distract themselves from the harm their spending is causing. Their addiction to immediate gratification overpowers even their most basic common sense.

Sometimes our entertainers and sports stars play out before us the workings of our own psyches and lives. Jack Clark was one of the great Major League Baseball players in recent years and a painful example of what can happen when the Sensualist archetype goes awry.

In 1992, the slugger was in the middle of a three-year contract with the Boston Red Sox, paying him nearly $9 million. However, that year the baseball player filed for bankruptcy, with his debts exceeding his assets by $7 million. The problem? "He had some expensive hobbies," Clark's lawyer told the Associated Press, "and I think they got ahead of him." I'd say. Once, on the way to the ballpark, he passed a car lot and liked the look of some fancy cars he saw there. He dropped in and quickly bought two for $90,000 each before continuing on to the game. His bankruptcy filing revealed that Clark owned eighteen cars, including several Ferraris, one of them a 1990 model that cost $717,000. At the time of his bankruptcy, Clark still owed money on seventeen of his eighteen cars.

The Evolving Sensualist

What Jack Clark did with his money represents a stunning degree of irresponsibility, so it's easy to condemn such spending. But staying balanced and sane around money in this culture is not easy for people whose natures include a strong dose of the Sensualist.

The particular vulnerabilities of the Sensualist are systematically exploited by an advertising industry that employs creative geniuses and spends hundreds of billions of dollars to get people to buy products whether or not they need them, and whether or not they can afford them. Sensualists, because they are so inclined to immediate gratification, have a heightened susceptibility to advertising's predations.

It's tempting to pass judgment on Sensualists who spend themselves into irresolvable debt, and criticize them for their lack of concern for the future. But for at least the last half century, much of our economy has been based on getting people to spend money as if there were no tomorrow.

The corporations that profit from your purchases do not want you to be in control of your spending. They want you to be obsessed with spending, addicted to spending, anything that will keep you waiting in line at the store or clicking away at your computer to buy ever more of the products and services they sell.

People in civilized nations used to be called "citizens." Now we are identified as "consumers" (a term that means, according to the dictionary definition of "consume," people who "use up, waste, destroy, and squander").

How did this happen? Consumerism, it turns out, was invented in the twentieth century, when it was believed that the economy would flourish only if people were encouraged to buy more goods. In 1955, an influential U.S. retail analyst, Victor Lebow, explained this new way of thinking: "Our enormously productive economy . . . demands that we make consumption our way of life, that we convert the buying and use of goods into rituals, that we seek our spiritual satisfaction, our ego satisfaction, in consumption. . . . We need things consumed, burned up, worn out, replaced, and discarded at an ever increasing rate."

Our very language has shifted to reflect this preoccupation with consumption and spending. We now call that portion of our income that is not required to cover our basic needs by the phrase "disposable income," as though there was something intrinsic to this part of our income requiring us to dispose of it. What if we called it "conservable income"?

And we speak of consumer "goods," as though items for sale possessed some intrinsic goodness. Wouldn't it be more accurate to call them consumer "products"?

If we continue in this direction, to keep up with the times maybe we will need to change the phrase in the Declaration of Independence about our inalienable rights to read: "Life, liberty, and the pursuit of material possessions."

The financial mayhem that unfortunately exists in the lives of many Sensualists today attests not to an inherent defect in this archetype, but to the massive and overwhelming forces that have been exerted to get us to find our satisfactions, our pleasures, and even our identities through what we purchase. We have literally been encouraged to love things and use people, rather than the other way around.

The Sensualist archetype, like all financial archetypes, is a path. At its worst, it leads to compulsive shopping, spending addiction, and a fixation on immediate gratification that can destroy people and families. In the middle, there are a great number of people who enjoy the things they buy and make their minimum credit card payments every month but feel stuck on a financial treadmill.

At the higher end lies the mature form of the Sensualist archetype. Here are people whose pleasures are healthy for themselves and for others. Here are people who take great joy in life, but now take no pleasure in anything that causes harm to themselves or others, in the present or in the future.

The Evolved Sensualist

Mature sensualists are able to appreciate high-quality items without losing their sensitivity to the consequences or costs of these products. Mature Sensualists love the smell and taste of good coffee, and care whether it's the product of fair trade; they are fond of fine chocolate but deplore the use of slavery in cocoa production; they appreciate fine jewelry but detest the horrors of conflict diamonds. They may still take pleasure in cell phones and digital cameras, but they don't want the need for minerals for use in our electronics products to fuel wars in Africa and elsewhere.

Evolved Sensualists relish how much pleasure, joy, and richness they can derive from nonmaterial things. They treasure moonlit walks, beautiful sunsets, time in nature, playing with children, good company, and other joys that lighten the heart without lightening the wallet.

A friend of mine has a great deal of the Sensualist archetype in his money personality. A generous man who was for many years fairly wealthy, he would eagerly look forward to Christmas, for then he would lavish expensive presents on his children and other members of his family. But then money became much tighter for him, and he was forced to make many changes in his lifestyle.

A few years ago, as Christmas was approaching, he was speaking to me of these changes and bemoaning the fact that he didn't have enough money to buy his children much in the way of presents. He began complaining about how expensive children were. But he caught himself and said, "Expensive, did I say? I meant priceless."

We both laughed. And then it was as if he possessed a magic wand and waved it across his heart. And this is the change he made, with the help of his wonderful wife. That year and all the years since, his family has celebrated a buy-nothing Christmas. Instead of purchasing gifts, they find creative ways to express their appreciation for one another. Sometimes they make things for one another, such as art or pottery or carved walking sticks. Other times they write letters or poems, or make collages with images cut out from magazines that represent the joys they wish for one another in the coming year. Then, on Christmas morning, after they have shared these homemade gifts, they each take a turn to speak of what they appreciate in themselves and what they wish for themselves in the year to come. His kids have told others at their school of this new way of celebrating Christmas, and the practice has begun to spread from family to family.

It's a sweet and personal thing, this man and his family having a noncommercial Christmas. But it's also more. For them, and I think in a way for all of us, it is a step into the new good life.

If we were, as individuals and as a culture, to embody the highest levels of the Sensualist archetype, we would take delight in our relationships and in the beautiful innocence of our children. We would protect especially the most impressionable among us, our children, from the ravages of commercialism. Recognizing the harm that is being done to the average American child, who sees more than a quarter million advertisements between the ages of two to eleven, we would put a stop to

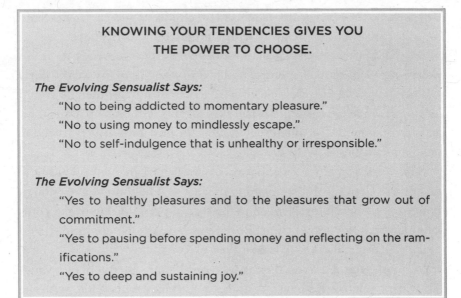

**KNOWING YOUR TENDENCIES GIVES YOU
THE POWER TO CHOOSE.**

The Evolving Sensualist Says:
"No to being addicted to momentary pleasure."
"No to using money to mindlessly escape."
"No to self-indulgence that is unhealthy or irresponsible."

The Evolving Sensualist Says:
"Yes to healthy pleasures and to the pleasures that grow out of commitment."
"Yes to pausing before spending money and reflecting on the ramifications."
"Yes to deep and sustaining joy."

the unrelenting exploitation of our youth. We would fulfill Plato's definition of education as teaching children to find pleasure in the right things.

The Sensualists do not have it easy in a culture where consumption and debt have been mistaken for the good life. Of all financial archetypes, they have been the most vulnerable to—and the most harmed by—the American "dream" of unlimited consumption.

Maybe it is they who will lead us to a new vision of the good life, one in which we know the joys of learning to live elegantly with less, and one in which we take tremendous pleasure in the beauty, the love, and the kindness we can create together, now and for our future.

The Vigilant

Of all the financial archetypes, Vigilants are the most resolute about fulfilling their duties and responsibilities. Practical and down-to-earth, they are the bedrocks of society. If there's a job to be done, you can count on them to apply themselves fully and to see it through.

Dependable, helpful, and hardworking, Vigilants play by the rules.

They don't mind working long hours and may end up being the ones who do the thankless tasks that others avoid. They enjoy spending money for things that bring them pleasure or make them more attractive, but they rarely go overboard. They know the value of a dollar, and they don't like to see money misused.

As shoppers, Vigilants are annoyed by how shoddy modern merchandise can be. "If you have to replace it in five years," they exclaim, "then it's no bargain." They don't mind spending more for something if they're convinced that in doing so they'll spend less in the long run. When shopping, they aren't often impulsive or frivolous. If you were to describe their shopping personality in a single word, it would be "sensible."

Though not nearly as focused on saving as Savers, Vigilants believe in having emergency funds, money they have set aside to be used in case of an unforeseen need. When advising their children about money management, they'll warn them always to be careful.

Vigilants gain a feeling of security from historical continuity. They feel unsettled when large companies that have been around for a long time cease operations. They aren't happy in situations where the rules seem always to be changing, or where long-established ways of doing things are not respected. They trust that in the long run, discipline and teamwork will pay off. They like people who are reliable.

The Vigilant puts a high value on tradition, both at home and in the larger world. If they're wealthy, they might collect antiques. If they go on a vacation, it will likely be to a place they've been before or to a place that carries some kind of historical meaning.

Before making any clothing purchase, the female Vigilant thinks about what she already owns and what she would wear with any new items she might buy. She also considers how much use she might get from an item of clothing, and may have a policy against buying anything if it's only for a single event. She's aware of the latest trends but prefers clothes that will remain stylish over the years.

In school, vigilants are hardworking and industrious and are usually respectful to their teachers. They follow directions dutifully, do homework meticulously, and turn their assignments in on time. As adults, they keep meticulous track of their financial records, do their taxes carefully, and are never late in filing their returns. If they ask for an extension, it's usually because others have not gotten information or forms to them that they need in order to do the job thoroughly.

When it comes to major purchases such as cars and appliances, Vigilants tend to be loyal to companies and brands whose products they have owned in the past, as long as they have had good experiences. They'll keep a car that they like for many years. The fact that it has a lot of mileage on it doesn't bother them. In fact, it gives them a feeling of security. They tend to like old things.

As mates, Vigilants are loyal. As parents, they are responsible. In organizational dynamics, they are a stabilizing influence. They like to see things run smoothly.

The Shadow Side of the Vigilant

Vigilants take their financial responsibilities seriously, and in most cases they are trustworthy providers, supervisors, and protectors. As with every archetype, though, there is a shadow side to the Vigilant.

In the darker levels of the Vigilant archetype, they may spend an excessive amount of time analyzing their financial data. Even if their family economics are in decent condition, they may be hypercritical of their spouses and their children for spending too much. They may become so preoccupied with their fears of loss that they become exhausted, lose their capacity for joy, and go emotionally numb.

At the lowest and unhealthiest levels of the archetype, Vigilants feel so profoundly frightened of any kind of change that they can become nearly frozen with anxiety. Terrified of new situations, they feel inadequate and afraid of being exploited. The future becomes fraught with uncertainty and danger. The only assurance is that things will get worse and there will be increasing pain. Vigilants at this level of toxicity can become so enraged at those they see as troublemakers that they can become violent and willing to follow demagogues who promise to make things right again. Their anger can lead them to take the law into their own hands—hence the term "vigilantes."

At the darkest level of the archetype, their attention increasingly fixates on potential threats, hazards, and difficulties. They may ruminate obsessively about past financial decisions, brooding about times they felt taken advantage of or mistakes they've made. In the extreme, Vigilants feel that they must always remain on guard. Their focus is always on what's wrong. Their thoughts of the future are filled with catastrophic expectations.

The Evolving Vigilant

Of course, most Vigilants never descend to such severe states of darkness. They may have some hard moments, but by and large they are a stable and diligent group.

Because they aren't showy, Vigilants can be taken for granted and may not get the gratitude they deserve. But we would be a far less stable society without the blessings that Vigilants bring us. In their higher levels of manifestation, they are constant and conscientious, and they provide many kinds of tireless service to others.

At the brighter levels of the archetype's continuum, Vigilants are wonderful friends. Loyal and stable, they provide a calm and comforting presence in times of disturbance or stress. They make excellent neighbors, there to help when help is needed. As teachers, they are patient and respectful. Expecting their students to apply themselves and do their best, they transmit their belief in their students' ability to do well.

Inspired Vigilants bestow on their children a sense of confidence and safety in the world. Because of their steadfast nature, they imbue their children with a sense of inner confidence that will sustain them throughout their lives. They pass on the belief that for every problem there is a solution if we take the time and give it the attention it needs.

In their more evolved manifestations, Vigilants make excellent leaders who have a deep sense of fair play and who aren't overly dramatic or self-aggrandizing. Their attunement to fairness and issues of justice can make them a kind of moral compass for our culture. Mature Vigilants make outstanding public officials, because they have a natural instinct to protect the many from the greed and corruption of the few.

The Evolved Vigilant

One of the founding fathers of the United States, Thomas Jefferson, was an extraordinary Vigilant. The third president and the principal author of the Declaration of Independence, he is today widely recognized as one of the greatest presidents, and one of the most brilliant geniuses, in U.S. history. When President John F. Kennedy welcomed forty-nine Nobel Prize winners to the White House in 1962, he said, "I think this is the most extraordinary collection of talent and of human knowledge that has ever been gathered together at the White House—with the possible exception of when Thomas Jefferson dined alone."

Though he lived more than two hundred years ago, Jefferson's insights and call to vigilance continue to inspire the world's first mass experiment in democracy. It was Jefferson who declared that "the price of liberty is eternal vigilance."

As an illumined Vigilant, Thomas Jefferson combined a deep sense of morality, a respect for the power of our economic institutions, and a very real concern that money and the power it brings not become overly concentrated in the hands of the few. It's remarkable how relevant the wisdom of this inspired Vigilant remains today.

Jefferson warned us against accruing debt, both as individuals and as a nation. "Never spend your money before you have it," he said. "It is incumbent on every generation to pay its own debts—a principle which if acted on would save one-half the wars of the world." He warned us, also, against too large a gap between the rich and the poor, saying, "Man is the only animal which devours his own kind, for I can apply no milder term to the general prey of the rich on the poor."

As to the path to happiness and the good life, Jefferson reminded us that, "It is neither wealth nor splendor, but tranquility and occupation which give happiness."

In the modern era, many of us tend to view the wisdom of the past with suspicion, as if it couldn't possibly be relevant to our times. If something is new we may assume it's better; if it's old we may assume it's outdated or obsolete. Fortunately we have Vigilants, with their deep regard for lineage and history, to remind us how important it is to respect our elders and to use the wisdom of the ages to better understand ourselves and our times.

In a time of increasingly rapid change, the wisdom of our enlightened Vigilants can help connect us to our roots. In a world in which so many people are seeking instant gratification, they can help us all to remember what really matters. In an era when corruption and greed have grown powerful, they can help restore us to decency, balance, and justice.

> ## KNOWING YOUR TENDENCIES GIVES YOU THE POWER TO CHOOSE.
>
> *The Evolving Vigilant Says:*
>   "No to fearing it can only get worse."
>   "No to trying to control everything."
>   "No to seeing change as a threat."
>
> *The Evolving Vigilant Says:*
>   "Yes to the power of working together for the common good."
>   "Yes to taking responsibility for what is mine to do and letting the rest go."
>   "Yes to both treasuring tradition and embracing change."

The Giver

For the Giver, the purpose of money is to help others, to provide support, to make a difference through love.

Givers are the providers, the nurturers, the caretakers. They are the ones who are delighted to cook for others, who think nothing of spending hours in the kitchen making a fabulous meal for their family or friends, and yet if eating alone might just as soon throw something in the microwave.

Givers are the ones who, if a friend is struggling financially, will be more likely to provide financial aid than to save for their own retirement. If possible, they may try to find a way to assist anonymously, because they don't want the recipient of their gift to feel indebted. If they give money to charities or causes, they don't particularly want to see their names listed publicly as supporters, because they find it beside the point and even embarrassing.

The message that Givers want to impart to their children about money is that among its many functions, money can be used to help others. When their children have birthdays approaching, they might use the occasions to teach them about people who are in need. Rather than purchasing gifts, they might give them a certain amount of money and invite them to choose a cause or charitable organization to which to contribute the money they've been given.

The Giver archetype comes alive in most people to some extent when they become parents, when it comes naturally to be attentive and protective of their children, spending money and time to provide them with the support they need to thrive. But there are those in whom the Giver archetype is activated in many relationships throughout the course of their lives.

They are the ones who tend to care for others before themselves. If Givers have the resources available, they may loan money to a family member or friend who wants to start a business, buy a house, or even just keep up with rent payments—knowing these loans might not be repaid. They enjoy giving their time, attention, and skills to benefit others, particularly if they feel that doing so genuinely makes a difference. When they sees friends or family members in need, they dream of winning a lottery so they could help them.

Givers will often have a cheaper car or live a simpler lifestyle than they could afford, because they won't tend to spend a lot of money for their personal needs if it would cut into their ability to provide for other people. While other archetypes might experience this as a sacrifice, Givers don't. They often get more pleasure from helping others than they do from buying things for themselves. It's looking after others that brings joy, meaning, and richness into their lives.

When shopping for clothes, the female Giver thinks about what her partner or friends or children might enjoy seeing her wear. If she buys something for herself, she's also likely to buy something for someone dear to her. When traveling, she'll buy gifts for friends and family, sometimes rather than buying things for herself.

The Giver may choose to be a stay-at-home mom, even though this role is often underappreciated. She may be willing to accept financial sacrifices, leaving behind a career to become a homemaker, because she sees the benefits of being home for her children and for her marriage. To her, the sacrifices she makes are well worth it, for they create lasting bonds and a stronger family.

Givers are often the financial caretakers for their families. From the point of view of an outsider, it may look like they are giving too much. But Givers take pride in providing for their family financially, so much so that if they aren't able to supply sufficient support to their family, they feel deep pain and regret.

As someone in whom the Giver archetype is strong, I experienced this when we lost our life savings in the Madoff fraud. I could barely tolerate the feeling that I had let down the people I love. I was filled with feelings of shame and horror that those who depended on me would have to suffer for my mistake. I am grateful that, with the help of many wonderful friends and a lot of sacrifice and hard work, we were able to begin regaining our financial footing. Yet I still feel a profound sense of loss that I am not able to give as much money to causes and people I want to support.

The Shadow Side of the Giver

As with all archetypes, there is a dark side to the Giver.

Of all archetypes, Givers are the most likely to sacrifice their dreams for the sake of others. They may have a hard time spending money on themselves and feel guilty if they do because others need it more. If they are wealthy, they may be generous, but if their generosity arises out of a sense of guilt about their relative affluence, rather than out of a sense of compassion and connectedness with others, it will bring them little joy.

At the lower levels, Givers believe they will not be loved or accepted unless they give to others. As a result, they may have a hard time identifying or expressing their own needs, and they can become preoccupied with the needs of others. They may become so identified with being "the giver" that their giving becomes more about the perpetuation of a self-image than about responding to the authentic needs and realities of the person to whom they are "giving."

This is the darker side of the archetype, in which the Giver's sense of value and self-worth become contingent upon always giving. Needing to give in order to feel good about themselves, they may go into debt, both financially and emotionally, in order to continue their "generosity." If someone in their life is addicted to alcohol, drugs, or gambling, their giving may become what the Twelve Step community calls "enabling": doing something for someone else that they could—and should—be doing for themselves. They may feel that their efforts to help are necessary, but in reality they are allowing the addiction to continue by preventing the addict from facing the consequences of their actions.

At the lower levels of the archetype, Givers try to meet their own needs by projecting them onto others. They may not grasp that when people give from such motivations, it often causes the recipients of their efforts to feel objectified, demeaned, disempowered, or patronized. Givers may then feel taken advantage of and may not understand why people don't feel more grateful to them. Increasingly resentful that others aren't more appreciative, they may redouble their efforts to give to others, who still don't feel nurtured or thankful. Instead, they feel smothered.

Givers at this level of confusion may repeatedly feel obligated to give more to others than they can afford. They may find themselves repeatedly needing to rescue a child, a spouse, a friend, or a parent from one dismal circumstance or another. Replaying this pattern may make them feel needed, but it will also almost certainly make them feel exhausted, aggrieved, and impoverished.

At the lowest and most toxic levels of the archetype, Givers may lose themselves so totally in trying to meet the needs of others that they may feel a compulsive obligation to respond to others' needs—whether or not they have been asked for assistance, and whether or not their help is useful or wanted.

The Evolving Giver

Thankfully, the vast majority of people in whom the Giver archetype is strong never descend to such a dark level of compulsion. They may have been taught "It's better to give than to receive" and so have a hard time receiving from others. But most have a genuine desire to help others and are capable of learning from their experiences. They eventually release their attachments to negative patterns that do not really serve anyone.

As parents, healthy Givers understand the beauty of unconditional love and recognize that setting limits is part of that love. They can and do say "No" when it is appropriate to do so. No, you may not play video games all day. No, you may not eat just cookies for breakfast. No, you may not hit your sister. No, we will not spend hundreds of dollars on toys.

The wisdom of the enlightened Giver is evident in the old saying, "Give a man a fish and he can eat for a day; teach him to fish and he can eat for the rest of his life." At higher levels of understanding, Givers know that the purpose of giving is never to foster dependency, but always to help the other to grow strong and capable. If in the role of parent, therapist, teacher, nurse, or mentor, an enlightened Giver takes responsibility for the learning or healing situation in the beginning, always with the goal of helping the child, client, student, patient, or protégé to grow more capable of autonomous functioning. Whatever form their nurturing takes, their intention is to help others to become as self-sufficient as possible.

In the healthier levels of the archetype, Givers share their time and talents as well as their treasure. Grateful for the opportunity to give to others, they derive a tremendous amount of joy from the vital role they play in supporting others' well-being. Their giving conveys their respect for themselves and their respect for those for whom they have the happy privilege of providing care and support.

In today's me-first culture, a certain cynicism has set in regarding Givers. It's as though many of us assume such people must necessarily be coming from the lower levels of the archetype. We suspect that those who are giving something are doing so only because they expect and want something in return. But the truth is that there lives in almost all of us an instinct to care for others, a need, in fact, to express our caring and love for others in ways that matter. For those of us in whom the Giver archetype is strong, that need can be so compelling that if it isn't expressed, the result will be not only frustration, but illness. On the other hand, if it is expressed, the results will not only be joyful but potentially world changing.

The Evolved Giver

In the early 1950s, polio was the most frightening public health problem in the modern world. Annual epidemics were getting worse, and the victims were usually children. In 1952, there were three hundred thousand cases and sixty thousand deaths. Enormous numbers of people had been paralyzed by this dreaded disease. And each year was worse than the year before. People were terrified.

Meanwhile, the scientist Jonas Salk had been working sixteen hours a day, seven days a week, year after year, trying to discover a vaccine to prevent the disease. Finally, on April 12, 1955, exactly ten years to the day after the death of President Franklin D. Roosevelt, the world's most famous polio victim, it was announced that the Salk vaccine had been proven to be both safe and effective. Within minutes of the announcement, church bells were ringing across the country, factories were observing moments of silence, synagogues and churches were holding prayer meetings, and parents and teachers were weeping with joy.

Within hours, politicians around the country were eagerly rushing to congratulate Dr. Jonas Salk. The Eisenhower White House presented Salk with a special presidential medal declaring him a "benefactor of all mankind." Overnight, Salk became one of the most famous and celebrated people in the world. He was the recipient of the nation's first Congressional Medal for Distinguished Civilian Service, and a plethora of honorary degrees.

Ten years later, on April 12, 1965, leaders of the Senate and House presented Salk with a joint resolution expressing the nation's gratitude to him, and President Lyndon Johnson called him to the White House to congratulate him personally. There had been barely one hundred cases of polio reported in the previous year. "This represents an historic triumph of preventive medicine," said the surgeon general, "unparalleled in history."

It's almost impossible to exaggerate the financial fortune that could have come to Jonas Salk if he had sought to capitalize on his discovery and fame. But Salk functioned at the highest level of the Giver archetype. When the American journalist Edward R. Murrow asked Salk, "Who owns the patent on this vaccine?" Salk famously replied, "Well, the people, I would say. There is no patent. Could you patent the sun?" Later, he added, "I feel that the greatest reward for doing is the opportunity to do more."

As a result of his refusal to patent the vaccine it was able to be distributed on a massive scale, even in the world's poorest countries.

In his life and his work, in his brilliance, his dedication, and in his desire to give over the fruits of his labor to the public good, Jonas Salk represented the highest levels of the Giver archetype. If anyone deserves to be called a true world hero, it is Jonas Salk and people like him.

Of course, most Givers never achieve the prominence and recognition that came to Dr. Jonas Salk. Most, unfortunately, receive little acknowledgment or reward for their efforts on others' behalf. They are the nurses and teachers, the bus drivers and plumbers, the artists and farmers, the scientists and businesspeople, and many others who work day in and day out to make life a bit more bearable and, if possible, a bit more beautiful for the rest of us. They are the mothers and fathers who

> ### KNOWING YOUR TENDENCIES GIVES YOU
> ### THE POWER TO CHOOSE.
>
> *The Evolving Giver Says:*
>   "No to being a victim of others' needs."
>   "No to having to prove my worth."
>   "No to unending sacrifice."
>
> *The Evolving Giver Says:*
>   "Yes to respecting myself and others."
>   "Yes to thriving in all my relations."
>   "Yes to living with consciousness, compassion, and caring."

sacrifice so that their children will have a better life. They are the people who look after the elderly, the sick, the impoverished, and the disabled.

As a society, we don't reward caregivers very highly, either with status or with financial remuneration. But we owe an incalculable debt to the Givers, for in their generosity and caretaking they represent a counterforce to the unrestrained greed that has become such a plague in our time. To the degree that the archetype of the Giver is active in the higher levels in our psyches and in our culture, we become more generous people, our lives are enriched with abundance, and our world knows more trust and less fear. We understand the truth that, in Anne Frank's words, "No one has ever become poor by giving."

Today, when the growing gap between the haves and the have-nots on our planet has become a worldwide catastrophe, we need the mature forms of the Giver archetype more than ever. If the wisdom of the enlightened Giver were to seep more fully into the larger reality of our times, the living waters of compassion and caring would flow far more freely through our world.

The Spanish poet Federico Lorca did not live to see the worldwide rejoicing that took place on the day it was announced that Dr. Jonas Salk had discovered a vaccine that could safely and effectively prevent polio. He did not know that one day we would have it within our grasp, as we in fact do today, to totally eradicate this ancient scourge from the earth forever.

But he did foresee another day of even greater rejoicing, a day we could possibly yet see in our lifetimes if somehow we were able as a society to manifest fully the highest wisdom of the Giver archetype. "The day that hunger is eradicated from the earth," he wrote, "there will be the greatest spiritual explosion the world has ever known. Humanity cannot imagine the joy that will burst into the world on the day of that great revolution."

WORKING WITH THE ARCHETYPES

Do you recognize yourself in any of the financial archetypes? Do you identify with some more than others? Some of the archetypes may be part of your familiar experience and self-image, while others may seem far more distant or even foreign. But each type represents energies that manifest themselves in all of our psyches to at least some degree.

Whatever combination of archetypes reflects your experience, if you are able to meet each of the archetypes in yourself with kindness and compassion, you will become better able to understand yourself, and better able to appreciate others whose basic types differ from your own.

The more aware you become of the beliefs and patterns inherent in your dominant money types, the freer you will be to realize and express their more evolved aspects. The more conscious you become of your tendencies, the more often and the more steadily you will dwell in the happiest and most lucid dimensions of your nature. The more alert you are to both the hazards and the opportunities implicit in your money journey, the less time you will spend feeling anxious, resistant, reactive, or emotionally volatile—and the more time you will spend feeling capable, free, clear, and emotionally available.

Are there advantages for couples? Yes, and they can be of vital importance. Becoming aware of the differing money archetypes that prevail in your own and your partner's money life can make the difference between a relationship that thrives and one that dies.

More divorces occur as a result of money problems than any other cause. At the same time, the costs of divorce, both financially and emotionally, are immense. Instead of arguing over who is right, knowing your different money types can allow for the creation of a climate of respect. It can enable you to see the weak areas and blind spots that each of you carries in your money life, and help you appreciate the positive strengths that each of you brings to the economic partnership. With this understanding, empathy has a chance to take the place of criticism, and both members of the couple can recognize the real and separate responsibilities each is carrying in the work of making the partnership successful.

Each money archetype represents not just a different money personality, but also a different style of seeking happiness and ensuring survival. As you become more aware of how your dominant archetypes differ from that of your partner, you will see how often money issues are not just about money, but represent deeper issues involving love, power, security, and self-esteem. When faced with money crises or critical money decisions, many people tend to revert to the lower level of their financial archetypes, which is often an ineffective approach governed by the reptilian brain. At that point, a two-year-old has essentially taken over your psyche and is running your financial life. With a language to discuss what is happening in respectful ways, you can support each other in accepting your feelings and shifting to the higher and more mature level of your prevailing archetypes. Then you can become more genuinely grateful for the gifts each provides to enhance the financial and emotional relationship.

Whether you are part of a couple or not, knowing your money archetype gives you a vehicle for self-discovery and renewal, and a way to discover previously untapped sources of power. Identifying which archetypes are active in you can give you a clearer perception of your strengths and weaknesses. It can allow you to have direct insight into the specific steps you need to take to balance your financial life with your spiritual life and to achieve success in both.

Whatever archetypes are dominant for you, your destiny is to fulfill their highest potential. There is nothing to be gained in envying other archetypes or imitating their strengths. Your calling is to be entirely yourself and to be true to who you are. Your task is to become the fullest realization of the beauty that resides in your nature. Your job is to find the real treasure at the heart of your life.

Whatever your basic types, your life is an experience of the human condition. You have good days and you have bad ones. You have times of grace and times of hardship. If you are someone who's known more than your share of darkness and suffering, if you have found yourself more often at the bottom than the top, perhaps this poem by an anonymous author may speak to you as much as it does to me:

I asked for strength, that I might achieve.
I was made weak, that I might learn humbly to obey . . .

I asked for health, that I might do great things.
I was given infirmity, that I might do better things . . .

I asked for riches, that I might be happy.
I was given poverty, that I might be wise . . .

I asked for power, that I might have the praise of men.
I was given weakness, that I might learn to care . . .

I asked for all things, that I might enjoy life.
I was given life, that I might enjoy all things . . .

I got nothing I asked for—but everything I had hoped for.
Almost despite myself, my unspoken prayers were answered.

I am, among men, most richly blessed.

There are those who believe that having more money is a sign that God has blessed your life, but I tend to look at it a little differently. I believe that money is a resource, just as faith, laughter, friends, health, creativity, and the capacity for joy are resources. In the end, financial freedom is less about how much money you have and more about remembering—and fulfilling—your true purpose for being alive.

The old good life has been about climbing the ladder of socioeconomic status. The goal has been to get and have more. The new good life is about ascending through the possibilities inherent in your basic archetypes so you can fulfill the highest callings of your spirit. Whatever your basic type, may you move along its continuum to become increasingly awake to your greatest gifts and your deepest peace.

THREE

Four Steps to Financial Freedom

How exactly does one evolve? How can you spend more time in the higher manifestations of whatever archetypes are large in your money life and less time in the lower ones?

In this chapter, I will present you with four practical steps to help you move into the higher realms of your dominant archetypes. These exercises will give you a better picture of what is actually going on in your financial life. Distilled from work presented by Joe Dominguez and Vicki Robin in their classic bestseller, *Your Money or Your Life* as part of a nine-step program to support financial liberation, these four steps are simple—and life changing.

Once you take these steps, instead of guessing, you'll know. Instead of wishing and hoping that things will get better, you'll be better able to manifest the full power of your intentions. Instead of stumbling in the dark, you'll be grounded in reality.

In order to become more conscious and successful in your financial dealings, you need practical and specific information. These steps will give you that information. Your awareness around the money that enters and leaves your life will deepen in connection to reality, and this will give you the traction you need to become more powerful and more effective in every aspect of your life that involves money.

You don't necessarily even have to do these exercises in order to benefit from them. You can gain value from simply reading them. But you will likely get *far* more value if you actually do them.

The good life is inspired by love and guided by knowledge. When it comes to money, ignorance isn't bliss; it's foolishness.

STEP NUMBER ONE:
KNOWING YOUR FINANCIAL NET WORTH

The first step in taking stock of your financial situation is to calculate your financial net worth. We're not talking here about your self-worth. We're not talking about all the wonderful skills and talents you have, the marvelous gifts that are yours to give, or your capacity to bring beauty and love into the lives of others. We're not talking about your education, your knowledge, or your sense of humor. Those things are important, absolutely, but now we're going to be eminently practical. We're going to talk specifically about money, and to be more precise, about *your* money.

We're talking dollars here, naked and simple. We're talking the language of bankers and the IRS and accountants. If you want to give direction and clarity to your financial life, if you are going to take the reins, this is the solid information you need to have.

Money issues can bring up all kinds of emotions and feelings, but keep in mind as you move through these steps that this isn't about pride and ego. It's not about how things could or should have been different, or would have been different if only something or somebody had been different. It's not about regret or guilt.

This is about being clear, realistic, and courageous in confronting your financial reality, as it is today. It's about knowing exactly how much money you have and owe right now. It's about facing the truth of your financial situation directly.

Of course, that's not easy. I shared all this with a friend recently, and she quipped, "I believe in looking reality straight in the eye and denying it."

Many people resist actually calculating their financial net worth. Keep in mind that no one else will see your data, unless you choose to share it with them. Some of us are afraid that the amount might not measure up to our self-image. It might not correlate to how we present ourselves to the world. We might learn something that we would rather not know.

All of this can be challenging. We all have a part of ourselves that would rather stick our heads in the sand, that would rather not know what's going on. If you are frightened that you might find something out that would be hard to accept, you're not alone. I feel that way, too, sometimes. But this isn't about pride or shame. It's about knowledge and empowerment. It's about deciding to see, rather than groping along blindly in the dark.

Okay? Here's how it's done:

1. **First, make a list of your liquid assets.** This list includes any or all of the following:

   Cash on hand
   Savings or checking accounts
   Brokerage accounts
   Bank CDs
   Stocks
   Mutual funds
   Money market funds
   Life insurance (current cash value)
   IRAs, Keoghs, and 401(k)s
   Debts owed to you

   Then, assign an accurate current dollar figure to each of these liquid assets. Add these figures together, and you've got the current monetary value of your liquid assets.

2. **Next, make a list of your fixed assets (your "stuff").** Your list might include any or all of the following:

   House
   Car(s)
   Furniture
   Art

    Clothes and shoes
    Electronics (TV, sound system, computers, printer, camera,
       cell phone, etc.)
    Jewelry
    Sports equipment
    Bicycle or motorcycle
    Household appliances
    Power tools
    Anything else you have that could be sold or that has financial
       value

Then, assign an accurate current dollar figure to each of these fixed assets.

If you have accumulated a lot of stuff, it may take you a while to list and assess everything, but the more thorough and inclusive you are in making the list and in assigning monetary values to each item on the list, the more you will get out of this exercise.

The point is to assign an *accurate* and *realistic* cash value to each item on your list. The value you want to use here is *not* the amount you paid for the items; it is what the items could easily be sold for *today*. If you own a home, you might check with a real estate agent for an up-to-date picture of its value. For a car, use the private party value (a figure midway between the wholesale and retail bluebook value). For smaller things, be realistic about what you could get for them on an online resale site or at a garage sale. Remember, for the purposes of this exercise we aren't talking about the sentimental value of these things. Your scrapbook of photos from your childhood probably has great value to you, but for the purpose of this exercise you need to give it the dollar figure it would fetch at a garage sale, which I'm sorry to say is probably close to zero.

You are creating a balance sheet, in measurable monetary terms, of your assets and liabilities. You are taking stock of your financial situation, as it is, here and now.

It can be a little disheartening to realize that the couch you bought new for $1,200 a couple years ago actually isn't worth anywhere near that much today. If you were to sell it on craigslist, you might get only $200 for it, even if it's in great shape (which it probably isn't). The same is true for clothes or artwork or other things that you may have purchased at retail. They almost certainly aren't worth today anywhere near what you paid for them. If you need a reality check, you can get one rather quickly by checking the asking price of comparable used items on craigslist or eBay, or by actually trying to sell some things to a used item dealer, at a garage sale, a flea market, or on craigslist.

Once you've given each item a realistic value, add these figures together, and you've got the current monetary value of your fixed assets.

3. **Add together the current monetary values of your liquid and fixed assets, and you have the current monetary value of your total assets.**

4. **Now, make a list of your liabilities.** This list might include any or all of the following:

> Credit card debt
> Home mortgage
> Balance due on car loan(s)
> Bank loans
> School loans
> Loans owed to friends
> Unpaid medical or dental bills
> Other unpaid bills (including phone, gas, water, electricity, etc.)
> Taxes you owe for past income
> Any other debts, child support payments, etc.

Assign a dollar figure to each of the liabilities on your list, add them up, and you've got the current monetary value of your liabilities.

5. **Take the total value of your assets and then subtract the total value of your liabilities, and you've successfully calculated your net worth.**

Congratulations. You've now taken a step in financial self-awareness that few people ever actually take.

Now you know where you stand.

You might be surprised by the results. You might find you have more than you had thought, or you might find you have less, but either way you are now working from actual reality, and that is a necessary and essential step on any path to greater financial freedom.

Some people who do this exercise discover they have a negative financial net worth—that their liabilities are greater than their assets. It may be painful to find this out, but if this is the case for you, resist the temptation to criticize or punish yourself and instead recognize and appreciate yourself for doing what may be the hardest thing of all, which is to directly face your situation. If you have the courage to do that, you've won half the battle already.

If encountering your actual financial predicament brings up feelings of shame, please know that you're far from alone. Many people sometimes feel that way, myself included. At different times, I've felt shame for many aspects of my financial life. I've felt shame for needing and at other times I've felt guilty for having. I've felt shame for being poor and I've felt guilty for being wealthy. It's all too easy to feel bad about our financial reality, which is one of the reasons we avoid confronting it directly.

Remember, you aren't doing this exercise to feel bad about yourself. You're doing it to know the truth. You're doing this to restore hope, faith, and trust.

Once you've done this step, you'll know what you really have or owe. Now let's turn to step two, and find out what you really make.

STEP NUMBER TWO:
KNOWING YOUR *REAL* HOURLY WAGE

You have a limited number of hours and days on this earth. Each moment is unique and will never come again. Yet most of us have absolutely no idea how much of our precious time and life energy we are exchanging for the salary or wages or other income we make. Oh, we think we know. Some of us might say, "I earn eight hundred dollars a week, I work forty hours a week, so I trade one hour of my life energy for twenty dollars." The trouble is, it's not nearly that simple—not by a long shot, as you'll soon discover in this exercise.

The idea here, as Vicki Robin puts it, is to "establish the actual costs in time and money required to maintain your job." This, in turn, enables you to compute your real hourly wage.

Vicki and her late partner Joe Dominguez have done a marvelous job in developing this idea, and I recommend *Your Money or Your Life* highly to anyone wishing to explore this concept in greater depth. "Think of all the ways," they write, "you use your life energy that are directly related to your money-earning employment. Think of all the monetary expenses that are directly associated with the job. In other words, if you didn't need that money-earning job, what time expenditures and money expenditures would disappear from your life?"

Most people spend a great deal of time and money on things that are employment related without realizing it. Some of us enjoy our work, but many of us find our work environments unfulfilling. And when we finally get away from work—work that we may have done only because we were paid to do it—we very well may want to spend money to feel better.

Some of us spend money going out to eat because we work so many hours that we don't have time to cook, or we spend money on child care because we don't have time to care for our own kids, or we pay people to clean our homes because we don't have the time or energy to do it ourselves.

Americans now work an average of nine full weeks more each year than do our counterparts in western Europe—eleven and a half weeks more than the Germans. Our workdays are longer, our workweeks are longer, and our vacations are disappearing. In fact, one-quarter of American workers got no vacation at all last year. Even medieval peasants worked less than we do.

There are forms of employment that are so draining of our time and energy that we have little left for our families. This can result in costs that are literally incalculable. How can you measure the costs of kids drifting into drug addiction or of emotionally devastating divorces?

Most of us are grateful to have paid work, but if we do, we need to know what we are actually making per hour. The point of the following exercise is for you to determine for yourself the real trade-offs in time and energy associated with your employment and other means of obtaining income. You can understand how much you really make only if you uncover the hidden costs of the things you do to earn income. This is important whether you work a stable forty-hour week, are self-employed, or if your work life takes another form.

Okay, here we go.

Commuting

An increasing number of people now work from home. But for the vast majority, whether you drive a car, walk, ride a bicycle, or take cabs, buses, or subways, it takes time to get to and from work. And unless you walk, it costs money. For a hypothetical example, let's say you commute by car five days per week. And let's say your commute is 30 miles each way, and it takes you 45 minutes to drive each way. Using those numbers, your weekly commute would total 7.5 hours and 300 miles.

The American Automobile Association (AAA) calculates the per-mile costs of driving. These costs vary depending on the type of car you drive, the number of miles you drive annually, and the price you pay for gas. But on average, according to the AAA, it costs about 60 cents per mile to drive a car in the United States. (This includes gas, depreciation, maintenance, repairs, insurance, and registration.)

If the hypothetical numbers we are using here were accurate representations of your commuting experience, and if we use the AAA figure of 60 cents per mile, your commute costs you 7.5 hours and $180 a week, plus any parking fees, bridge tolls, and so forth.

If you walk, ride a bicycle, or take public transportation to work, your dollar costs will be lower, but your time costs could be just as great or even higher. If you work from home, of course, then your work-related travel costs will be far less, perhaps limited to errands and business trips.

> **Take a few minutes now to estimate your actual weekly costs of commuting, in time and money. You should arrive at a dollar figure and an hourly figure. Write these numbers down, because you're going to use them later.**

Clothes

Getting dressed for work is another time- and money-consuming task that most of us take for granted. But we usually wear different clothes for work than the ones we wear on our days off. This is obviously true for nurses and others who wear uniforms, and for construction workers who wear hard hats and steel-toed boots. But it's also true for people in many less obvious lines of work. Office workers, for example, are often expected to wear tailored suits, high heels, pantyhose, or neckties.

How much time do you spend on personal grooming, including shopping for clothes, shaving products, and cosmetics; time at the hair salon; time spent shaving, putting on your clothes in the morning, and taking them off when you get home; dry-cleaning and laundering; and putting on makeup? Maybe 2.5 hours a week? And how much money do you spend? If the amount you spend annually on clothes and cosmetics for work is, say, $1,200, that comes to $23 a week.

Take a few minutes now to estimate your actual weekly costs of dressing, personal grooming, and cosmetics for your work life. Once again, you should arrive at both a dollar figure and an hourly figure. Write them down, because you will need them for later use.

Meals

Many people would like to prepare their lunches at home, knowing they would save significant money and get better nutrition, but they aren't able to do so because their lives are so time-stressed by their work life. And then, for dinner, they buy expensive packaged and processed convenience foods because they are too tired to cook. Some people spend time waiting in line at a deli to buy food, and others spend time waiting in line at the employees' cafeteria. And some spend time and money on weight-reduction programs to try to get rid of the extra weight from eating unhealthily and not having time to exercise. Plus, maybe there's morning coffee and doughnuts.

People who buy their lunches from a local deli spend about $30 more per week than if they made lunch at home. Many people find that they purchase and eat particular kinds of food to reward themselves for hanging in there in an unpleasant work environment, and these usually aren't the healthiest kinds of food. This, too, has its costs.

Everything considered, the extra weekly food costs in money and time that an average working person incurs comes to something like $50 and 3 hours. Of course, that's just an average. Your figures may be higher or lower.

> **Take a few minutes now to estimate the extra food and drink costs you incur as a result of your work life. Again, you should arrive at both a dollar figure and an hourly figure.**

Decompression

I don't know what state of mind you are in when you arrive home from work or finish with tasks you do at home for income, but most people aren't exactly eager for creative play or deep sharing with their spouses or other loved ones. More often, people are exhausted, want to be left alone, crave a glass of wine or a beer, and are not capable of doing much except staring at the TV or the computer. As Vicki Robin perceptively points out, "If it takes a while for you to 'decompress' from the pressures of the job, that 'while' is a job-related expense." She hazards a guess that this might amount to, on average, 5 hours a week, and $30 a week for alcohol and/or other recreational substances.

What about you? How many hours a week and how many dollars a week do you spend decompressing from your work life? After you get home, how much time does it take before you are able to work productively and/or have quality time with your family or housemates? And what do you spend on alcohol or other recreational substances to enable you to relax?

> **Take a few minutes to come up with and write down figures, in dollars and hours, that seem like an accurate estimate to you.**

Other Work Life-Related Expenses

How much of your time and money go to work life–enhancement expenses, such as educational programs, tools, and conferences? How much time and money do you spend on activities and toys that you consider your just reward for staying in an income-producing situation that drains you? Do you pay dues to a professional organization that you wouldn't belong to if it weren't for your job? Is there stress at work that is undermining your health? Are there chemical exposures or other environmental factors at work that are dangerous and that could lead to expensive illness? Are you paying for help around the house (a house-keeper? a gardener? a handyman?) that you wouldn't need if you had the time to take care of these things yourself? If you have children, how much are you paying for day care that you wouldn't need if you weren't working? Are you paying for a therapist or taking antidepressants to help you deal with the stress of your work life?

There are so many possible types of work life–related time and money expenses that it is impossible to be 100 percent accurate in accounting for them. No one expects you to do a perfect job in determining these costs. For the sake of example, I am hypothetically estimating the combined costs in this category, per week, at 10 hours and $100. If you are paying for significant amounts of child care that you wouldn't have to otherwise, your dollar figure will undoubtedly be higher.

Do the best you can to come up with an estimated weekly cost for these other work-related expenses, in dollars and in hours.

Now you're ready to find out what you are actually making per hour. Now is when you will put to use the actual numbers you've written down for each category. As an example, here's what happens when I plug in the hypothetical numbers we've generated for each category.

Let's say you work 40 hours a week, for which you get paid $800 pre-tax, which apparently comes to $20 per hour. However, now let's factor in the time and money you spend on work-related expenses. Here are the hypothetical figures we've come up with:

Commuting:	7.5 hours/week	$180
Clothes:	2.5 hours/week	$23
Meals:	3 hours/week	$50
Decompression:	5 hours/week	$30
Other:	10 hours/week	$100
Total:	**28 hours/week**	**$383**

When you add these extra 28 hours a week to the 40 hours you spend on the job, you see that your work life actually costs you 68 hours a week. And when you subtract these extra financial costs of $383 from your weekly pay, you see that you are actually making $417 (and that's before taxes, which need to be paid on the full $800 in income!).

If you're getting health insurance and other benefits as part of your job compensation, that's certainly a plus, and they need to be factored into the equation.

Of course, what's important are *your* actual numbers, but according to these hypothetical numbers, you would actually be making, not $20 per hour, but just over $6 per hour.

Take a moment now to plug in your numbers, taking into account all your work-related expenses.

Now, you have your real hourly wage. Now you have a sense of how much of your life you've been trading for money.

Doing this exercise may produce an unpleasant sinking sensation in your gut. You may feel embarrassed, angry, helpless, ashamed, frightened, sad, and/or betrayed. You may not like this one bit.

I don't blame you. But hang in there for a moment. This could be a moment of true significance. Even if you have discovered that, when you factor in taxes, you've actually been paying for the privilege of working, this could be a real opportunity. Sometimes our finest moments aren't when we feel great. Sometimes they occur when we feel deeply uncomfortable or frustrated. Sometimes it's not until we feel the depth of our discontent that we are able to step out of ruts and find new ways of thinking and living.

Here's why it's so important to factor in all your job-related expenses and thus to know your true hourly wage: If you think you're making $20 an hour, then when you consider spending $20 for something, you think, well, that's an hour's work. But if you realize you're actually making more like $6 an hour, then you grasp that the $20 item is actually costing you more than three hours' work! That's quite a difference, and it puts a whole different light on your spending patterns. Grasping the truth will make it much easier for you to resist the pull of advertising and to hang on to your hard-earned dough.

These calculations also allow you to assess current and future employment possibilities more realistically. They help you to recognize the hidden but very real costs of taking an intensely stressful job, or taking on work that requires extensive commuting. You will think twice before accepting a job that comes between you and your family, or that so drains your joy that you compensate by buying stuff you don't really need in an effort to feel better.

Some of us pay quite a price for being "normal." As journalist and author Ellen Goodman put it: "Normal is getting dressed in clothes that you buy for work, driving through traffic in a car that you are still paying for, in order to get to the job that you need so you can pay for the clothes, car, and the house that you leave empty all day in order to afford to live in it."

STEP NUMBER THREE:
KNOWING WHERE YOUR MONEY IS GOING

A lot of us are in rebellion against money. We resent the dominant role it can play in our lives. We hate how much it controls us. Most of us have done things to get money or to hold on to it that we aren't exactly proud of.

As a result, we avoid looking squarely at our money issues. We don't know how to talk to our families about money without getting into arguments. We don't really have a grip on our financial lives.

But, for you, this is all about to change, with this next step.

This step is about keeping track. It's actually pretty simple. Here's what you need to do:

Keep Track of Every Dollar
That Comes into or Goes out of Your Life.

At this point you may want to take a deep breath. Please recognize that keeping track of your money isn't giving it more power; it's taking your power back. It's not about becoming obsessive. It's about becoming more in charge of your economic destiny.

Keeping track of every dollar that comes into or goes out of your life will give you the knowledge you need to take effective, clear, and potent action on behalf of your fiscal future. It's a path to financial intelligence.

Keeping track of every dollar can seem like a daunting task, and you may wonder if it's worth it. Well, I'm here to tell you that it is. At first, it may seem cumbersome, but I promise you, the longer you do it and the more you get the hang of it, the easier it will get.

Set Up a System to Track Your Household Spending.

You can do this any way you want. Some people create their own methods; others use the latest budgeting websites, such as mvelopes.com, wesabe.com, or mint.com. Some people use spiral-bound notebooks, or pocket-size memo books. Some track their money on their computers. Some people use electronic spreadsheets. Many banks allow you to download your transactions into a number of computer accounting programs. This permits you to place the data into the categories you select. There are even accounting applications for smart phones.

However you keep track, it greatly helps to get in the habit of obtaining a receipt for every purchase you make, regardless of whether it's large or small. Save all your receipts, keep them in one place, and then go through them once a week or once a month, recording the expenditures in whatever manner you're using. This way, you won't have to rely on your memory to know where you spent your money or how much of it you spent. It's particularly helpful when keeping track of expenditures made by more than one person in your family.

If you have a credit card, debit card, or checking account, then when you get your monthly statements you can crosscheck to make sure a) that you haven't been charged for anything you didn't buy, and b) that all your expenditures have been recorded in your tracking system.

This may sound time-consuming, but once you've gotten organized, it takes only an hour or so per month.

Part of the education comes from developing your own categories. For starters, you might want to use the categories I've listed below. Of course, not all of these categories will apply to you—just use those that are relevant. And, just as certainly, there will be categories that you, in all your glorious eccentricity, will need to add.

Food
Groceries for home consumption
Restaurants
Takeout meals for home consumption

Home

Mortgage or rent payments
Homeowner's or renter's insurance
Property taxes
Home and yard maintenance and repair
Improvements
Household furnishings
Household supplies

Transportation

Car:

Monthly payments
Registration
Gas
Maintenance
Insurance
Parking
Tolls
Moving violations and parking tickets
Car rental
Carpooling contributions

Public transportation:

Cabs or shuttles
Buses

Health Care

Wellness care:

Vitamins and other supplements
Massages and bodywork
Exercise (bicycles, gym membership, dance classes, etc.)
Dental cleanings

Illness care:

Insurance
Prescription and other pharmaceutical drugs
Doctors visits
Dental procedures
Eye care
Other

Utilities
   Electricity
   Gas
   Water
   Cable
   Internet
   Phone
   Cell phone
   Garbage pickup/recycling

Education
   Books
   Tapes
   Courses/tuition
   Workshops
   Student loans

Personal Grooming
   Clothes
   Shoes
   Cosmetics, toiletries, and other personal care products
   Dry-cleaning
   Personal services (hair, nails, waxing, facials, and so forth)

Children
   Child care
   Toys and games
   Clothing and shoes
   Activities and outings

Entertainment
   Concerts
   Movies
   DVD rental
   Theater

Gifts
   To individuals
   To organizations (charitable contributions)
   To political causes

Hobbies

Professional Services
Therapist
Accountant
Lawyer
Landscaper
Housekeeper

Pets
Food
Vet bills
Cat litter
Dog bones and treats
Toys

Holidays, Vacations, and Travel

Magazine and Newspaper Subscriptions

Taxes
Federal income tax
State income tax
Payroll/self-employment taxes

Retirement Plan Contributions

Miscellaneous

Remember, these categories are only suggestions. The idea is to create a set of spending categories that reflect the uniqueness of your life and provide a portrait of your lifestyle from a monetary perspective. If you buy a lot of clothes, you might want to subdivide the clothes category into clothes you wear at home, clothes for work, and clothes for recreational activities; or into clothing that is necessary and clothing that is unnecessary—or whatever your brilliant mind comes up with in order to give you as much information as you want and need in order to be truly financially literate. *Working with and developing your own categories for your expenses takes time and effort in the beginning, but the time you spend doing this will more than pay for itself, even in the short run.*

If you smoke, you'll want to add a category for cigarettes, and you'll soon see how much this habit is costing you, which might give you added motivation to stop. If you're paying interest on a credit card balance, you'll want to add a category for that interest. If you're paying a high interest rate, you'll soon see how rapaciously that eats away at your financial security. At the same time, you'll see where you can cut back on nonessentials so that you can pay off your debt.

Remember, the idea is to track every expenditure that you or any other family member makes. Record every purchase, be it a box of paper clips or a new car. *For each expenditure, record the date, the amount, to whom it was paid, and what was purchased.* For cash expenses, you can round off to the nearest dollar. When you've paid with a check, credit card, or debit card, it helps to record the exact amount. (This makes it easy, when you get your monthly statement, to ensure that the bank hasn't made an error to your detriment.)

There are many benefits to tracking all your expenses. It won't take long before you start to get a clear picture of where your money is going. Certain expenses may be fixed, at least for the time being, such as your mortgage or your rent. But others are more easily reduced. Most likely, you will see areas in which you can cut back almost immediately.

Keep Track of Every Dollar of Your Income.

For most of us, this doesn't require nearly as many categories and is a much simpler thing to do. Be sure to distinguish among wages, tips, and any interest or dividend income you might have. If your income derives from several different sources, create a different category for each one. Note any items or things of monetary value that you sell. Tracking your income as well as your expenses is an indispensable part of knowing your financial reality, and it will be of immense value around April 15, when you do your taxes.

Some people—usually Savers or Vigilants—find tracking their money to be easy and enjoy every step of the process. Others are almost allergic to the idea. My experience is that the people who have the hardest time at first are the ones who eventually get the most out of it, if they stay with it. If you are someone who initially abhors the idea of tracking every dollar that comes into or goes out of your life, I'll bet you can find creative ways to do it, and that you will experience enormous satisfaction from feeling in control of something that has so much power in your life and that has up until now been shrouded in mystery.

One of the key insights in Thomas Stanley and William Danko's best-selling book *The Millionaire Next Door* is that there is a key difference between people who have achieved a high net worth relative to their incomes and those who haven't. Those who have achieved a high net worth know where their money is going. They know how much they are spending on housing, clothes, transportation, and so forth. Those who haven't achieved a high net worth despite a high income typically have little grasp of how much they spend. The contrast is dramatic.

We all have blind spots—areas where we aren't conscious. Most likely, your blind spots are the very places where your money leaks are most debilitating to your fiscal well-being. Since these areas are, almost by definition, the areas where you are most unconscious, it can be hard to get a grip on them. That's where tracking the money that moves in and out of your life shines. It's the best way to become conscious of how money actually comes and goes in your life, as opposed to how you think it comes and goes.

You may be afraid that tracking your money will expose things about your spending patterns that you'd just as soon keep hidden. But what you are confronting is simply the truth about the choices you've been making in your life—choices you may choose to continue or you may choose to alter.

The more thorough you are in tracking your money, the more benefits you will get. The path from avoidance to awareness is a powerful one. It means respecting your life energy enough to become conscious of how you spend it.

As the practice of recording any and all movements of money into or out of your life becomes a habit, you will no longer wonder where your money is going. You will see it in front of you, in black and white. You will have awareness and consciousness where before there had been fog. You will have clarity where before there had been confusion.

And you will have freedom where before there had been compulsion.

STEP NUMBER FOUR:
KNOWING THE VALUE OF YOUR LIFE

When you know both your net worth and what your real hourly wage is, and can see your actual spending patterns, you are in a position to do something immensely powerful and liberating. You are on the verge of a whole new level of fiscal sanity.

You can now accurately assess whether the spending you engage in is worth the amount of life energy that you must expend in order to do it. As Thoreau put it, "The cost of a thing is the amount of what I call life which is required to be exchanged for it, immediately or in the long run."

A few pages back, I gave a hypothetical example of how you might think you are earning $20 per hour, but when you take into account job-related expenditures of your money and your time, it turns out that you are actually earning more like $6 per hour. That, of course, was just an example. What matters to you are your actual numbers. Knowing your true hourly wage allows you to look at the dollars you spend and see how many hours of your life they represent.

For example, if you spend $60 a month to get premium channels on your television, and if you've calculated that your actual hourly wage is $6 an hour, you can ask yourself whether the fulfillment and pleasure that you get from having access to premium channels is worth 10 hours a month of your time. If you are contemplating a purchase of a car, and a snazzy new model has caught your eye, you can look at the additional $10,000 it would cost to buy that car and translate that into how many hours of your life energy it would take for you to make that much money. At $6 per hour, it would take 1,667 hours, or about 10 months of working 40 hours a week.

Whatever your actual hourly wage is, the principle remains the same. You can—and I strongly suggest you do—look at every one of your expenditures and ask whether they do or do not warrant the amount of your time and life energy that they, in fact, are costing you. As you track your expenses, you can reflect on each one from this point of view, questioning whether the value in terms of your life that you received from the purchase was worth the number of hours and the amount of your life energy that it actually cost you.

You might find that in one category, your spending has been unconscious and automatic, even addictive, and that the quality of your life isn't being enhanced by these purchases, at least not in proportion to the life energy they cost. Maybe you realize that buying a new pair of shoes every few months is costing you more than you realized—even if they were on sale. Maybe the next time you want to lift your spirits you'll decide it would be a better idea to exercise than to participate in what one of my shopaholic friends calls "retail therapy."

One woman I know didn't want her husband to know how much she spent on clothes. When she felt lonely or depressed, or when she wanted to celebrate, she would go shopping for clothes, but she hid them from him. When she bought new clothing, she would cut the tags off and put the newly acquired items in the back of her closet. Then she would wait at least a month to wear them. That way, if her husband asked, "Is that new?" she could reply, "No." She told me years later that by keeping track of every expenditure, she began to realize that her "innocent" subterfuge was actually a form of dishonesty and was damaging the relationship.

Eventually, she was able to confide in her husband about her struggles with shopping, and even to talk with him about the inner emptiness she sometimes felt that she tried to fill up with new clothes. As they developed better communication, they were able to experience a level of marital harmony that could never have occurred when they weren't dealing openly with their conflicts around money.

Most families have issues over money from time to time, and some have them chronically. Couples commonly take on oppositional attitudes, since we tend to gravitate toward those who possess complementary characteristics. One is a Saver and the other is a Sensualist, or one is a Vigilant and the other is an Innocent. When couples have conflicting money styles there are likely to be frequent communication breakdowns. But what if, instead of getting caught in cycles of polarization or deception, you were to ask your mate or family member—with as much curiosity and as little judgment or accusation as possible—whether he or she actually got fulfillment, satisfaction, and value corresponding to the amount of life energy spent? Might this be a key to addressing your differences more thoughtfully and with more respect? Might this be a step toward developing real empathy for each other?

When I first did this exercise, I discovered certain areas where my spending was, in fact, providing me with only fleeting pleasure. I found, for example, that I had a long-standing habit of buying books on a whim, because I liked the idea of reading them, even though the reality of my life was that I would never have the time to absorb the number of books I was buying annually. Many of these fine works ended up donated to the library, unread. I didn't want to give the habit up, despite the time and energy it took to acquire the books, find space for them on my overcrowded bookshelves, watch them sit there for months, then finally realize I wasn't going to read them. Each time I bought yet more books I had to make space on my bookshelves by hauling a bunch off to the library, only to repeat the process with the next set of books. Of course, since I didn't want to give up the habit, I had no trouble finding a way to justify these repeated purchases. I told myself that buying books was important to keeping myself well-informed, and so it was an act of self-respect. The solution, I rationalized, wasn't to be more careful in my spending. It was to buy more bookshelves.

But as I stared month after month at the amount I was spending on books that I knew I hadn't read, several questions slowly began to dawn on me. How, exactly, was buying books that I didn't read helping me to be better informed? And was spending money in this way really an expression of self-respect? No, I came to see, because it wasn't valuing the life energy it cost me. I wasn't only wasting money, I was wasting my precious life energy.

It helps, as you reflect on how much you've spent in each category and subcategory, to translate the dollar figure into "hours of life energy," using your actual hourly wage. Then you will be better able to assess whether the expenditure provided you with sufficient satisfaction and value to warrant the life energy you paid for it. Of course, this is a determination that you and you alone can make. No one else can—and no one else should—tell you where to draw the line. That is your choice to make, based on what you truly value.

Remember, though, that there are enormous forces in our society that profit from each of us remaining unconscious around money and that depend on us remaining slumbering in the assumptions of the old good life. It's no accident that corporations spend hundreds of billions of dollars on advertising designed to get us to "buy, buy, buy." If we fall prey to their hypnosis—and the vast majority of people do—we will surely watch our money go "bye, bye, bye."

We are taught to measure our self-esteem by what we buy and own.

But how self-respecting is it to waste minutes and hours and even years of our irreplaceable life energy through unaware consuming? We live in a society that promotes instant gratification. We aren't taught to ask whether our use of the money that flows through our lives is bringing us lasting satisfaction.

How many lives have been crippled by people's unconsciousness around their money? You find this not only among uneducated minimum wage earners with little more than the clothes on their backs, but also among multimillionaires with private planes and teams of accountants. When people don't pay attention or take responsibility for the money in their lives, the results aren't pretty. This is true regardless of the amount of money they make.

Latrell Sprewell is a former professional basketball player who starred for many years at the highest echelons of the sport, earning nearly $100 million playing in the NBA. Late in his career, he was offered a three-year $21 million contract from the Minnesota Timberwolves but turned it down, saying, "I have a family to feed." In 2005, Sprewell refused to play for $5 million a year. His agent called that amount "a level beneath which Sprewell would not stoop or kneel." In 2007, Sprewell's seventy-foot yacht was repossessed by federal marshals after he failed to maintain payments and insurance for the vessel, for which he reportedly still owed $1.3 million. In 2008, his Milwaukee home went into foreclosure. By then, he was facing a $200 million lawsuit from the mother of his four children, another suit (by a bank) alleging failure to pay credit card bills, and efforts by government to collect more than $70,000 in allegedly delinquent taxes.

Latrell Sprewell is an example of what can happen, even to the wealthiest and most talented of us, if we aren't honest with ourselves, if we don't pay attention and take full responsibility for our money lives. His story is extreme, but I'm sure you've seen plenty of other unfortunate examples of what can happen to people who buy deeply into the "more is better" mentality around money. It's a sickness that some call "affluenza."

"Affluenza" is a word that combines "affluence" and "influenza." It has been defined as a painful, contagious, socially transmitted condition of overload, debt, anxiety, and waste resulting from the dogged pursuit of more. Its symptoms include the bloated, sluggish, and unfulfilled feeling that results from an epidemic of stress, overwork, waste, and indebtedness. It is, in short, a disease that stems from pursuing the old good life.

Our society has developed many strange attitudes around money. We love it and we hate it. We crave it and we waste it. But few of us actually know what we are doing with it. Sadly, there often seems to be something about the way we relate to money that separates us from our hearts.

What makes our times so interesting is that now it's up to each of us to create our own vision of the good life, and then, living within our means, to embody it as fully as we can in our lifetimes. What's new about the new good life is that it takes as many forms as there are people who want to be aware and free, and it has as many variations as there are people waking up from the sleep of unthinking consumption. What makes the new good life so exciting is that it has as many expressions as there are people who want to define prosperity in their own ways, and it is represented in the choices of each and every one of us who wants to be free and to thrive, who wants to live a life that is unique, sustainable, joyous, and worthwhile.

Living the new good life doesn't require that you forgo anything that genuinely gives value and beauty to your life. You can interact with the world around you in any way you choose. You can have lots of friends, be connected to the Internet, have a MySpace page and a Facebook page, use an iPod, and go out dancing. But instead of being ruled by cycles of consumption and debt, and being caught up in an overworked and underslept world of personal and planetary unsustainability, you can create your own definition of wealth based on what truly matters to you.

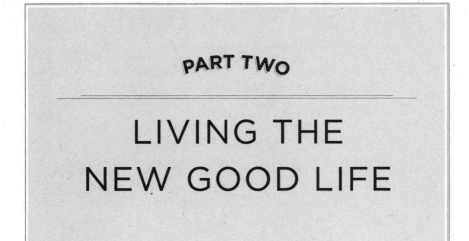

PART TWO

LIVING THE
NEW GOOD LIFE

FOUR

Wherever You Live Is Your Temple—
If You Treat It Like One

Social status is important to human beings. There are healthy ways of attaining it, and there are not-so-healthy ways.

One of the defining features of the old good life was that many of us sought to enhance our social standing and gain feelings of self-worth by consuming more lavishly and conspicuously than others. Underlying the desire to own flashier household appliances, bigger sport-utility vehicles, and ever larger suburban homes was often the desire to feel a sense of wealth and importance.

In the process, our homes, our cars, and even our watches became status symbols. It may have felt good to live as though we could freely indulge our whims, but in many cases we were actually becoming less free as we did so, because we were going deeper and deeper into debt.

Housing is the single largest expense category for most people and families. We take large mortgage payments so for granted today that many people would be surprised to learn that as late as 1950, two-thirds of American homeowners actually owned their homes free and clear. Now the number of U.S. homeowners who own their homes outright is less than 20 percent. And a growing number of U.S. homeowners are carrying not one, but two or even more mortgages on their houses.

HOUSEHOLD DEBT AS PERCENTAGE OF ANNUAL AFTER-TAX INCOME	
1949	33.2
1959	61.5
1973	66.7
1979	73.5
1989	86.7
2000	102.2
2005	131.8
2009	170

SOURCE: The Economic Policy Institute: The State of Working America, http://www.stateofworkingamerica.org/tabfig_05.html.

Today, mortgages of thirty or even forty years are common. But mortgages of that length are a recent phenomenon. Six months before the stock market crash of 1929, *Better Homes and Gardens* magazine advised readers it was foolish to take out a mortgage longer than five years. That was a long time ago, but the article's counsel remains eerily prophetic of our times, when the pace of foreclosures is at historic highs. The magazine warned readers about "rascals who like to sell people houses they can't afford, then deprive them of them when they can't meet the payments."

Why have we been willing to take on ever larger mortgages with ever longer terms? One of the reasons has been the belief that the houses we live in provide tangible proof of our social status. It is our homes, more than any other category of expense, where we so often fall prey to the unexamined assumption that bigger is better.

BUT IS BIGGER ALWAYS BETTER?

Today, newspapers, magazines, television shows, and Internet sites are filled with practically salacious articles about the size of celebrities' houses. In 2008, for example, *The New York Times Magazine* ran a feature article that described Rush Limbaugh's secluded beachfront property in Palm Beach, Florida. The property has five separate homes, all of them Limbaugh's. The one in which he lives, alone with his cat, is twenty-four thousand square feet. Limbaugh, who has no children and isn't married, designed much of the home, intending it to be as impressive as the world's grandest hotels. The massive chandelier in the dining room is a replica of the one that hangs in New York's Plaza Hotel. And the guest suite is an exact replica of the presidential suite in the Hotel George V in Paris.

Rush Limbaugh's house may strike some as pretentious, but it's actually rather unassuming compared to another home that has gotten a lot of press lately, one built by producer Aaron Spelling in Holmby Hills, California. The fifty-six-thousand-square-foot house (seventy thousand if you count the attic) has 123 rooms, including a bowling alley, wine cellar, beauty salon, humidity-controlled silver storage room, rooftop rose garden, library, gym, tennis courts, pools, and sixteen carports.

Do large homes create an environment for family harmony? Evidently not in Limbaugh's case, for he has been, as he puts it, "unlucky in marriage." And also apparently not in Spelling's case, because the Spelling family life has become in recent years a soap opera that few would envy. After Aaron Spelling's death in 2006 at the age of eighty-three from a stroke, his widow, Candy Spelling, publicly blamed their daughter, Tori, for killing her father because she hadn't been responding to his phone calls. Candy didn't mention that at the time of his death, Spelling was being sued by a former nurse for sexual harassment, sexual battery, and assault. Nor did she mention the friendship with another man that Tori has publicly referred to as an affair. In her subsequent memoirs, however, she did describe the many rooms of her mansion in laborious detail, including the rooms that housed her candy collection, her luggage collection, her doll collection, and her wrapping paper collection.

There are, of course, many reasons why people are drawn to larger homes. Michael Frisby, a former White House correspondent for *The Wall Street Journal,* has a home in Fulton, Maryland, that is eleven thousand square feet. Frisby grew up poor, as did his wife, and now they are pleased to show themselves and the world that this is no longer the case. "I always wanted a house big enough," Frisby told National Public Radio correspondent Margot Adler in 2009, "that my kids could be in

In 1950, percent of U.S. homes with 2.5 bathrooms or more:
1 percent

Today, percent of U.S. homes with 2.5 bathrooms or more:
50 percent

their room screaming, and my wife could be in a room screaming, and I could be somewhere else and not hear any of them. And I think I have accomplished that with this house."

Michael Frisby may have the home he desires, but for me the vision he describes sounds a little lonely. If my children or wife were screaming, I would want to hear them so I could go to be with them and if at all possible help them with whatever pain or frustration they were feeling. I've always found there to be truth in the adage that, among friends and family, joys that are shared are doubled while sorrows that are shared are halved.

Nevertheless, there are more homes in the United States today with five or more televisions than there are homes with one or none.

Some people say they need a bigger house because they have children. I agree completely that more space can be helpful when you have kids. The question is, how much more?

I've asked many people about their childhoods. I've heard from those who had good childhoods and those who had difficult ones. I've yet to hear anyone say they remember their childhood fondly because they lived in a big house, and I've yet to hear anyone speak of pain that their home was too small. I've spoken with people who grew up in grinding and debilitating poverty, and who lived in buildings that were so unsanitary and so unsafe that they really were unsuitable for human habitation. When people from even such challenging backgrounds reflect back on their childhoods, however, the size of their homes does not appear on their list of complaints.

Larry Dossey, M.D., is one of the leading lights in the nation today in scientifically demonstrating the healing powers of the mind, spiritual practice, and prayer. Speaking of his childhood, he says, "We were as poor as church mice. We had no running water and no electricity, [but]

I never felt deprived. I believe that as long as kids have love, they don't care if they live in a palace or a hut."

Ironically, since big houses cost more, they often entail more work hours and financial stress for the parents, which can leave kids home alone more. And children, being small themselves, often find smaller spaces cozier and more appealing, particularly if it means Mommy and Daddy are closer and with them more often.

There is a balance to be found here, in what Shay Salomon, author of *Little House on a Small Planet,* calls "the delicate dance of need and greed." Sometimes we want a larger home because of what we think it will say about us—that we are successful, that we have made something of ourselves, that we are a person of stature and significance. We don't want to admit to such crass motives, so we pretend we are doing it for our children.

I have known my friend Jim since we were both children, and I've watched him do a great deal of work to become the person he is today. When we were little, he lived in a large home, with parents who were dedicated to the old good life. His father was rarely home, working long hours to make money, and his mother seemed to be constantly stressed as she participated in an array of social events and prepared elaborate meals for the family.

What I remember most about Jim's house was an oversized formal living room that the children were not allowed to enter and a large dining room that as far as I could tell was only used for formal occasions. There were many rooms that we weren't supposed to play in and fancy furniture that we weren't permitted to touch. There were tall ceilings and marble floors, but there was something about it all that felt sterile and empty.

Jim's childhood was very lonely, and he told me that neither of his parents ever seemed to have any time to talk with him or play with him. One day, in his anguish and despair, Jim ran away from home, leaving a note that said, poignantly, "I would rather eat peanut butter sandwiches for breakfast, lunch, and dinner, and live all together in just one small room with no furniture if it meant I could have time with you. But I know that isn't possible, so I'm going to try to find some parents who will play with me."

I wish I could say that reading this note awakened his parents to what young Jim was needing from them, but that's not what happened. I am glad to say, though, that Jim has grown up to become a wonderful father who has made it a point to create a lifestyle where he can spend a lot of time with his children. He takes the responsibilities of parenthood quite seriously and didn't become a father until his late forties because he didn't feel mature enough until then. Now, his home is simple, modest, and family-centered, and he says that fatherhood is the most enriching and elevating experience of his life. I've been to his house often, and I can tell you that his children are among the happiest kids I know. And there's nothing formal or ostentatious about the way they live.

When I remember the note Jim wrote so many years ago, I realize that he and his wife, Amy, have actually become the affectionate and caring parents he was looking to find. Although Jim and Amy are far from monetarily wealthy, their children live in a safe, warm, and loving home.

HOMES FOR HUMANITY

Does everyone who attains wealth feel a need to display that fact with a large home? Certainly not. Warren Buffett is today the second richest person in the world, with a financial net worth of approximately $37 billion. Yet he still lives in the same home in Omaha, Nebraska, that he bought in 1958 for $31,500. In 2006, Buffett showed the world that his heart was as big as his wallet when he gave more than $30 billion to the Bill and Melinda Gates Foundation.

But perhaps even more remarkable than the story of Warren Buffett is that of Millard Fuller. If the old good life was measured in the accumulation of wealth and the things money can buy, then Millard Fuller certainly met the criteria. But when he saw what his financial accomplishments were truly costing him, he reversed course and became a stellar exemplar of the new good life.

A successful businessman and lawyer, Fuller had become, by the age of twenty-nine, a self-made millionaire. His business partner was Morris Dees (who later became the cofounder of the Southern Poverty Law Center, a chief fund-raiser for four presidential candidates, and a nationally recognized civil rights lawyer). Together, they had set out with a single goal, to get rich. They sold tractor cushions, cookbooks, rat poison, candy, toothbrushes—anything and everything they could sell to make money—and they were massively successful in accomplishing their goal. By the time Fuller was thirty, he owned an expensive home, a cabin on a lake, luxury cars, speedboats, and thousands of acres of land. But there was a problem. Although he didn't know it at the time, even as his financial fortunes were rising, his marriage was disintegrating.

The day that shook Millard Fuller to his core was the day his wife, Linda, told him that she no longer felt she had a husband, and that she didn't know if she loved him any longer. At first he was shocked and bewildered. How could she not love him when he had given her everything money could buy? But then the reality sank in. "The week that followed was the loneliest, most agonizing time in my life," he later recalled.

Linda had by now left him, and he had to beg her to see him again. Reluctantly, she agreed, and after many tears and profound heart sharing, they agreed to start over again and to change their lives radically. To prepare for this new life, whatever it was to be, they agreed it was necessary to dispense with the very things they had allowed to get in the way of their relationship with each other and with God. Accordingly, they sold everything they owned—the businesses, the houses, the boats, the cars, and the land—and then donated the proceeds to churches, colleges, and charities.

Now what?

In 1968, the Fullers visited Clarence Jordan, who had started a Christian interracial farming community called Koinonia 140 miles south of Atlanta, Georgia. Jordan took them on a tour of the dilapidated shacks, often without heat or plumbing, that lined the dirt roads in the area. The Fullers knew, of course, that such living conditions weren't confined to southern Georgia, but in fact were replicated throughout the United States and the world. A quarter of the world's population, about 1.5 billion people, live in deplorable housing or are without homes at all.

As an expression of their Christian faith, Millard, Clarence, and a few coworkers began to build houses for people in the area who were in need. Sadly, Clarence Jordan died of a heart attack early on, but Millard and his associates continued for the next five years to build houses for impoverished families in the areas around Koinonia.

Deeply moved by the enormous impact that having basic but decent houses had on the lives of the families who received them, Millard wondered if the same thing could be done in other parts of the world. He and Linda moved to Zaire (now the Democratic Republic of the Congo), where they spent the next three years building homes throughout the country. Much of their work took place in a city of the most extreme poverty, Mbandaka.

Convinced now that the concept could work just about anywhere, the Fullers returned to Georgia in 1976 and launched Habitat for Humanity International. Their motivation was simple: "Everyone who gets sleepy at night," Millard said, "should have at the very least a simple, decent, affordable place to lay their heads."

The plan was and continues to this day to be straightforward: the building of simple, decent houses for low-income families using volunteer labor and donations. The families that receive the homes participate fully in the construction and pay only for the costs of the materials. Unlike conventional mortgages, no interest is ever charged and no profit is ever made.

Skeptics, of course, said it wouldn't work, but it did and it continues to, even though most of the volunteers have little or no experience in construction. Cash and materials are donated by individuals, churches, corporations, and many other kinds of organizations. People from all walks of life give freely of their time and skills. At first there were legitimate questions about whether houses built in this fashion would be sufficiently sturdy. These were answered, at least in part, in 1989 when Hurricane Hugo hit South Carolina with ferocious force. The hurricane left nearly one hundred thousand people homeless and was the most damaging hurricane in U.S. history to that date. Yet every single one of the hundreds of Habitat homes in the state survived the storm.

Habitat for Humanity's goal is to eliminate homelessness everywhere. Measured by the number of homes built, Habitat for Humanity is today the largest homebuilder in the world by far. With devoted support from former U.S. president Jimmy Carter and many others, Habitat for Humanity has built more than three hundred thousand homes in more than one hundred countries, providing an enormous number of people with safe, decent, affordable housing. As Cynthia Kersey explains in her book about perseverance and triumphs small and large, *Unstoppable,* "Habitat for Humanity builds more than houses. It builds families, communities and hope."

Millard Fuller was a force of nature who did an enormous amount of good on this earth until the day he died in 2009. Forty-one years earlier, he and his wife, Linda, had left material wealth behind for something they felt was of far greater value: a chance to serve and make a difference to others. By the measure of the old good life, where the goal is to have as much money and the things that money can buy as possible, what they did made little sense. But by the values of the new good life, they became two of the richest people alive.

WHAT MAKES A HOUSE A HOME?

I grew up in a wealthy family and lived during my teen years in an expensive home complete with its now-famous ice cream cone–shaped swimming pool. But when I was twenty-one, I left behind that way of life and the money it represented, making it clear in both my words and in my actions that I did not want to depend on my father's financial achievements nor follow in his footsteps.

The cabin that my wife, Deo, and I built in 1969 when we moved to a Canadian island was a simple and rustic dwelling, 320 square feet, located deep in a cedar forest. When I remember the ten years we lived there, I feel fondness and gratitude, for it was the first time in my life I ever felt truly at home.

During those years I would sometimes visit my parents in their various homes. On one such occasion, my father said something to me that I will always remember. "What bothers me the most about you," he said solemnly, "is that you are the only person I've met who can't be bought. Everyone else has their price, except you." I took this as a compliment, although I'm not at all sure he intended it that way.

The contrast between my parents' homes and our little cabin was so great it could at times be startling. Our life was about making conscious choices to live simply and honor the earth. Their life was quite different.

Their primary residence, located in Rancho Mirage, California, was a formidable display of architectural opulence. My mother's clothes closet alone was more than twice the size of our entire cabin. On one occasion, I decided to count the number of televisions in their home. I found thirty-four, although there might have been a few that I missed.

The house had a sophisticated alarm system, designed to protect its valuable contents as well as its inhabitants. On those rare instances that I stayed there while my parents were away, I was told to make sure that all the windows and doors were closed and locked at night, and to be certain the alarm system was turned on. Once it was, if any door or window should be opened even a crack, an earsplitting alarm would go off. If that happened, I was told that I should immediately press a particular button that would turn the system (and the noise) off. Otherwise, an armed response would be there within minutes. Okay, I said, I can handle it.

But things didn't work out quite the way they were supposed to. One quiet morning I woke up and ambled outside to greet the day and get a breath of fresh air, forgetting about the alarm system. Immediately after I opened the door, however, a shrill alarm as loud as an ambulance siren began to blast. In a state of shock from the intense noise, I remembered there was a button I was supposed to push to shut it off. Holding my hands over my ears in an attempt to lessen the overwhelmingly loud alarm, I raced to where I had been told the button would be, whereupon I discovered two buttons, not one. Which was I to push? One of them was marked "emergency." The noise was so intense that it felt like an emergency to me, so I pushed that button, whereupon the earsplitting noise not only didn't stop, but if anything became even more incessant. It turned out this was not the button I was supposed to push if it was a false alarm. This was the button, instead, that was supposed to be pushed in the event an intruder had broken into the house. It automatically locked all the doors, imprisoning me within, and summoned security.

Sure enough, within minutes armed guards arrived, sirens blaring and guns drawn. There followed some very awkward moments with me still in my pajamas, feeling utterly confused and no doubt blabbering like an idiot. It took me awhile to explain who I was and that I had set off the alarm by mistake and then had compounded the error by pushing the wrong button. In retrospect, I think the whole thing is rather funny, but my father was not amused when he learned of it.

It's so easy to become prisoners of our possessions. Here were my parents, living in one of the hottest places in the United States, just outside Palm Springs, California, and they had to have their windows shut in order for their alarm system to work, so no fresh air flowed through the home at night. Instead of cooling the house with the evening air, they kept the air-conditioning on virtually all the time. They could afford it, but still this didn't strike me as the best example of living in harmony with nature.

Although houses in the United States have been getting bigger for some time, I believe the houses of the future will not be as large as those we've grown accustomed to seeing, and many of those larger homes already in existence will be shared. People will look for houses that are designed to welcome rather than to impress, that feed their spirits while costing less to buy, to rent, and to maintain. They will want homes in which every room is used every day and in which there are no wasted spaces—homes less like furniture stores or warehouses and more like nests.

In the days to come, I believe that the homes that will be most cherished will be human scale, chosen to enhance not our egos but our connection with those we love. Smaller homes free up our time and energy to do things other than work to pay the rent or the mortgage. By having lower housing costs and less house to clean and maintain, we can spend more time with our children, our friends, and our partners. We have more time to write poems or paint pictures, to plant gardens or bake bread, to play tennis or build bunk beds, to make love or volunteer for Habitat for Humanity.

For many reasons, including the increased costs of many resources, the need to reduce waste, and the need many people feel to simplify their lives, our living spaces will get smaller. If at the same time we can make them more beautiful, more humane, more energy efficient, and more supportive of our spirits, we will have taken an important step into the new good life.

SMALL IS BEAUTIFUL

Small Is Beautiful: A Study of Economics as If People Mattered is the title of an influential and prophetic book written in 1973 by the economist E. F. Schumacher. The fundamental principles of the prevailing economic ideology at the time were that the faster and bigger the economy grew, the better off we would be; and that rapid economic growth could and should continue without limits indefinitely into the future.

We are now, of course, seeing the environmental and fiscal consequences of such thinking, but in the 1970s Schumacher's ideas were considered radical, for he had the temerity to suggest that infinite economic growth was neither possible nor desirable. Challenging the whole idea of measuring our standard of living by the amount of our consumption, he pointed out that this entailed "assuming . . . that a man who con-

sumes more is better off than a man who consumes less." But if consumption is merely a means to human well-being, he said, then "the aim
should be to obtain the maximum of well-being with the minimum of
consumption."

I am with Schumacher in this regard, and in particular when it comes
to housing, where I believe the goal should be to the highest possible
quality of life at the lowest possible economic and ecological cost. Smaller
homes cost less to rent, less to buy, less to build, less to heat, less to furnish,
less to light, less to clean, and less to maintain. They save money from
every direction—on mortgage principle, mortgage interest, property
taxes, insurance premiums, electric bills, gas bills, and upkeep costs.

Besides, with less space to put things, there is less inclination to buy
excessive furnishings and accumulate clutter. Possessions have a way,
after all, of expanding to fill the available space, so with less space there
is less temptation to spend money on unnecessary stuff.

I have a friend who lives alone and has gone into considerable debt in
order to afford a large four-bedroom home. Before he bought the home,
I got in his face and challenged him about wanting such a big place, but
he replied that he needed the extra bedrooms because he needed somewhere to put his furniture. He freely admitted that he rarely used the
furniture, so I asked why he didn't sell some of it and get a smaller
home, thus saving a great deal of money. He replied that he had spent a
fortune for the furniture, and if he sold it now he couldn't recoup anything like what it was worth. The sad reality is that now he is having to
work sixty hours a week in order to make his mortgage payments.

In contrast, Kate Kaemerle is the owner of EnTech, a Seattle public
relations company that helps green businesses create and market products and services. At one point in her life, she explains, "I thought I
needed the new car, the fashionable clothes, the perfectly furnished
home. . . . It was the fantasy of happiness through more stuff, spurred by
the advertising industry that I knew only too well." But then she came to
the realization that "life was important, not things." She sold most of her
possessions, keeping only "the basics and what was important to me."
When she went house hunting, she stumped real estate agents because
"instead of looking for the biggest house I could afford, I looked for the
smallest house that could fit my needs. Less home to maintain and clean
means more time for my passions. . . . Less house, less stuff and less
work means more time to enjoy life, create community and just be."

I'm not saying that everyone must live in a tiny house to be happy. You have to find what works for you, what enhances your life the most, what gives you the highest quality of life, and, of course, what you can afford. The new good life doesn't ask you to give up anything except what isn't in accord with your true well-being.

When you think back over your life and the places you have lived, where have you lived that you were the happiest? Has it been in the largest homes in which you've resided? Or has it been the ones where, for whatever reason, there was the most love and the most time to enjoy your life?

As I've pondered the ever-growing size of American houses and the similarly ever-expanding nature of our waistlines, I've wondered if there isn't something gluttonous that has arisen in the American personality. What price are we paying for the belief that bigger is always better?

The extravagant amount of energy consumed by large houses is on ironic display in the home of environmental advocate Al Gore. The day after the former vice president's film about global warming, *An Inconvenient Truth,* won an Academy Award for Best Documentary, the Tennessee Center for Policy Research released a report stating that Al Gore's Tennessee home uses more than twenty times the energy of the average U.S. home. The Gore mansion uses nearly $30,000 worth of electricity and natural gas a year and consumes more electricity per month than the average American household uses in an entire year.

A spokesperson for the Gore family pointed out that the Gore home isn't an average house—it's about four times larger than the average new American home. But that's just the point. Larger homes use vastly more energy than smaller ones.

OBESITY RATES FOR U.S. ADULTS 20–74 YEARS OF AGE		AVERAGE SQUARE FOOTAGE OF A NEW SINGLE-FAMILY HOME	
1950	10 percent	1950	983
1970	16 percent	1970	1,500
1990	24 percent	1990	2,080
2005	35 percent	2005	2,488

SOURCES: National Association of Home Builders and National Center for Health Statistics

THIRTY-FIVE WAYS TO REDUCE YOUR HOUSING COSTS WHILE INCREASING THE QUALITY OF YOUR LIFE

One-third of the money American households spend goes to housing costs. Shrinking that bill can produce substantial savings. Here are ways that you can begin to realize those savings.

Heat Your Home—Not the Whole Planet

In areas that have cold winters, heating costs can quickly tear a hole in a family's budget. With prices for heating oil, propane, and kerosene on the rise, taking steps to reduce your heating costs can make a huge difference, particularly if you have an older home.

Older homes often have wonderful character, but the bad news is these houses can cost two to three times as much to heat compared to today's newer energy-efficient homes of the same size. The good news is that improvements to these homes can literally save you thousands of dollars a year.

- If your home is poorly insulated, add additional insulation. It will pay for itself quickly.
- If you have an old furnace, consider replacing it. Replacing a twenty-year-old furnace with a newer high-efficiency model would save the average U.S. household $800 a year in heating costs, because furnaces from the 1980s and early 1990s are only 50–60 percent as efficient as today's Energy Star–qualified furnaces.
- Check for drafts around windows, doors, and fireplaces, in order to locate any areas where heated air is escaping. Then use caulk, weather stripping, door sweeps, and other appropriate means to block the leaks.
- In the winter, limit your use of ventilating fans, such as those found in bathroom ceilings and kitchen hoods. These fans can suck all the heated air out of the average house in an hour or two. Their regular use during the winter adds a surprising amount to heating costs.
- There's never any point in turning your thermostat above your desired temperature. Your home won't heat up any quicker. The

only result will be that the furnace or heating system will be on longer, leading to overheating and higher bills.

- Turn down the heat at night and when you're out for the day, but not too much. If the house gets too cold, it can actually cost you more to get the contents and the air up to the desired temperature than it would have to have kept them reasonably warm. Anything below 55 degrees Fahrenheit (13 degrees Celsius) starts to be self-defeating.
- If there are rooms in your house that you don't use regularly, don't heat them except when needed. Close the heating vents or turn down the thermostats in those areas. This can save a lot of energy and money.
- Do conscientious maintenance on your furnace, heat pump, or other heating equipment. Keeping filters clean will improve the efficiency of your heating system and help it to last longer.
- If your windows are single pane, consider replacing them. Replacing aluminum frame single-pane windows with double-pane, low-E, wood or vinyl frame windows will save 32 percent of the average home's annual heating energy cost. (Low-emissivity windows, also called low-E, have an ultrathin metallic coating in the glass that reflects heat back to its source, thus keeping homes warmer in the winter and cooler in the summer.) This represents more than $600 a year for an average two-thousand-square-foot home. It will also increase comfort.

Lowering the Cost of Running Your Refrigerator

The refrigerator is the household appliance that consumes the most energy and costs the most to run. The average American household spends several hundred dollars a year for the electricity to run its fridge. Here's how to save more than half of that money:

- Twice a year, vacuum the coils and filter on the back of your fridge. When you remove the dust that has accumulated, you improve your fridge's efficiency as much as 25 percent.
- Don't put hot things in your fridge. Let them cool to room temperature first.
- Think before you open the door. Keep items well organized and easy to locate. This will reduce the amount of time you stand there

staring, with the door open. By minimizing the amount of time the door is open, you keep cold air in and warm air out.

- If you are going to defrost items from your freezer, think ahead by a day and put them in the fridge rather than on the counter. It will take them longer to defrost this way, but as they do they will be cooling the items in the fridge, which saves energy and money, rather than cooling the air in your home—air that most of the year you may pay to heat.
- Keep refrigerated food items covered. The moisture in uncovered foods tends to evaporate, making the foods less palatable and putting an extra burden on the compressor.
- If you have an old fridge, consider getting a newer one, preferably one with an Energy Star label. Old fridges are electricity hogs. The most efficient newer ones use only a tenth as much energy as those produced before 1993.

Lowering or Eliminating the Cost of Air-Conditioning

In warmer climates, air-conditioning accounts for 15–20 percent of annual electricity use, and as much as 60–70 percent of summer electricity bills. Fortunately, the same insulation and caulking steps that lower winter heating bills also keep a home cooler in summer, thus substantially reducing air-conditioning costs.

As recently as 1960, only 12 percent of U.S. homes were air-conditioned. Today, with three-quarters of homes and businesses chilling their air, the United States may be the coldest nation on Earth each summer—indoors.

Happily, it's quite possible to virtually eliminate air-conditioning in most climate zones. This would save the average household $200–$1,000 a year in electricity, plus the costs of purchasing and servicing the air-conditioning units. Here's how:

- Install and use ceiling fans. Ceiling fans are elegant, energy efficient, and can greatly reduce or eliminate air-conditioning costs. The gentle air circulation they create evaporates moisture from the skin and makes a hot room feel 10 degrees Fahrenheit (6 degrees Celsius) cooler, while using less than one-tenth the electricity of a medium-sized room air conditioner. As a warm-blooded creature, you generate substantial body heat. Clothing keeps you warm primarily by trapping your body heat. Even when you're naked, though, your body heat creates an envelope of hot air around you. Ceiling fans push the hot air surrounding you out of the way. (This is the same principle that is at play when you blow on hot food to cool it. Your breath—at 98.6 degrees Fahrenheit or so—isn't particularly cool. Blowing on hot food cools it because you're blowing the heat off the food.)

- Turn ceiling fans off when you aren't in the room. They don't do any good without the presence of warm-blooded humans. In fact, without anyone there, fans that are turned on actually add a slight amount of heat to the room.
- Make sure your ceiling fans are blowing in the right direction in summer—downward. If they're blowing air upward, they are ineffective. Most fans have a switch to change the fan direction, although it's often unlabeled.
- Turn off electric lights except when necessary, especially in the summer. Not only will you save money and energy, but your home will be considerably cooler. It actually would be more accurate to call incandescent lightbulbs "heat bulbs" rather than "lightbulbs," because they emit 10 percent of the energy they consume as light and 90 percent as heat.
- Don't use halogen floor lamps, particularly in the summer. Operating at temperatures of up to 700 degrees Fahrenheit (400 degrees Celsius), they emit only 5 percent of their energy as light and have been implicated in more than two hundred fires. Halogens have many good uses, but in floor lamps (also known as torchieres), they are energy and money hogs.
- Plant deciduous shade trees on the southwestern and western sides of your home. Well-positioned shade trees can reduce indoor temperature by as much as 15 degrees Fahrenheit.
- In hot weather, keep your windows and blinds or curtains closed during the heat of the day, and open at night.
- If you must have an air conditioner, be sure it's shaded. An air conditioner that's in the sun is 20 percent less efficient than one in the shade. And if you're using an older model, consider replacing it. Today's units use 30–50 percent less electricity than models from the midnineties.

- A refreshing way to keep your hair and clothes damp and create a cooling effect as the water evaporates is to use a spray bottle (such as a plant sprayer) that can be adjusted from a fine mist to a heavier stream. Spray your face, hair, neck, arms, clothes, and, of course, your friends.
- When it's really hot, keep your hair wet and wear a wet wrung-out shirt. Before you dismiss this one as eccentric or not worth what you might think is a fashion mistake, consider that wearing wet clothes is amazingly effective at cooling the body, especially in dry climates. I've lived in a home that wasn't insulated at the peak of scorching summer heat, where indoor thermometers registered well over 100 degrees Fahrenheit, and been totally comfortable with wet hair and wearing wet clothes. My clothes would dry fairly quickly, so I needed to rewet them frequently. For modesty's sake, some people prefer to wear two shirts—the inner one wet, and a looser, outer dry one. My son used to call this a secret air-conditioning system.

In very hot weather, I've even worn a wrung-out wet T-shirt underneath formal clothes, in order to stay cool while being presentable. In the mid-1990s in southern Florida, I used this technique to help me deal with a rather heated situation that turned out to be plenty embarrassing.

I had been invited to give a presentation at a Unity church in West Palm Beach. It was a very hot day.

I don't remember all the themes I spoke of that day, but I vividly recall saying that there is in each one of us a little bit of Donald Trump and a little bit of Mother Teresa. Each of us has within our natures the ability to compete and the ability to cooperate. It is when these forces are in balance that we are happiest and most productive. But we're paying a price for the extent to which we've become a more competitive culture than a cooperative one. Many of us have come to follow the hyper-individual path, the Donald Trump path, and have lost touch with the powers of nurturing, kindness, and cooperation.

At the time, I didn't think I was saying anything terribly controversial, but as I said these things, the minister, sitting in the front row, seemed to become distressed and began whispering intensely to a well-dressed and beautiful woman sitting next to him. I had been introduced to her briefly prior to my talk, and she was apparently some important person involved with the church. Her name was Marla.

Eventually I finished, and the audience was appreciative enough to give me a standing ovation. That helped me to feel better, but underneath I still had an uneasy feeling that there was more to what was happening than I yet knew.

And there was. As I was autographing books following the talk, the minister approached awkwardly along with the elegant woman who had been sitting next to him. The woman handed me several copies and asked if I would please sign them. "Of course," I said. "To whom would you like me to make them out?"

"Please sign this one to me. I'm Marla," she replied. "And sign this one to my husband, Donald." She looked at the minister, paused, and then continued deliberately: "Donald Trump."

If I hadn't been wearing a cool inner shirt I would have broken into a sweat right then! I had spoken of Donald Trump as a symbol of ego and excess, while unbeknownst to me, his wife was sitting in the front row.

I was mortified, but fortunately it turned out that Marla had enjoyed my presentation, and no harm was done. In a later conversation with her I learned that after the event, she went home and told her husband that the speaker at the church had mentioned his name. "Probably as the epitome of evil," he had grumbled. "Basically," she had replied.

I was sad but not surprised when, a couple years later, I learned of their divorce.

In 2008, Donald Trump sold his sixty-two-thousand-square-foot home in Palm Beach for $100 million. At the time, it was the most expensive single-family home ever sold in the United States. I don't know what the air-conditioning costs were for the home, but somehow I doubt Trump used the wet T-shirt technique to bring them down.

Lowering the Cost of Water Heating and Clothes Washing

Water heating accounts for 20 percent of the energy consumed in the average U.S. home. Solar hot water is one of the most widely used and energy-efficient green technologies. With federal tax incentives and an increasing number of qualified installers, solar hot water is worth considering if you own your home. In the meantime, these steps will save the average household $100–$250 dollars a year.

- Set your hot water heater no higher than 120 degrees Fahrenheit (50 degrees Celsius). If you have a tank hot water system, wrap it in an insulation blanket.
- Wash clothes in cold water. This step alone will save most homes $100 a year or more. Ninety percent of the energy used in washing clothes goes to heating the water. Water that is hot generally doesn't get clothes any cleaner. It's just harder on them.
- If possible, use a front-loading washer. They use only about one-quarter as much hot water as top loaders. Their agitation systems use less energy, are more efficient, and are less prone to breaking down. And they leave the clothes much drier during the final spin cycle, saving energy if you use a clothes dryer. All this, while using significantly less energy and being gentler on your clothes.
- Enjoy your hot showers, but stay conscious. Hot showers are a pleasure and a privilege that not everyone in the world gets to enjoy, which is a pity because they are wonderful sources of cleanliness, relaxation, and pleasure. Don't make the mistake of lingering so long that the additional time costs energy and money without providing much in the way of stress release or cleansing.

Lowering the Cost of Drying Your Clothes

Electric clothes dryers are a stupendous waste of energy and money, drawing as much as 6,000 watts and costing an average of $200 per year to run. That's why they require 240-volt current, twice the strength of ordinary household current. Gas dryers are much more efficient, costing an average of $100 per year to operate. But by far the most energy-efficient way to dry clothes is to use the sun's radiance.

If you don't have the time or patience required to hang up each single sock, handkerchief, or other small article, try this "best of both" solution: Use your dryer for socks and underwear and other small articles that are labor intensive to line dry, but use your clothesline for larger items such as sheets and towels, which are quick and efficient to hang up. You'll save a lot of energy, with minimum effort.

If you miss the soft feel of fabrics dried in a dryer, you can use the air fluff setting (which uses no heat) on your dryer for ten minutes to fluff them up after line drying. Air fluffing also helps remove lint.

In 1960, only 15 percent of U.S. households had dryers. Today, only 15 percent of households even occasionally line dry their clothes. So out of fashion have clotheslines become that some apartment buildings and homeowner's associations have banned them, deeming them unsightly. In 2007, a unique condo building in Los Angeles received the U.S. Green Building Council's gold LEED rating for environmentally con-scious design. Considered to be all green and ultrachic, the condos fea-ture sustainable bamboo flooring but forbid line drying. I appreciate people wanting to work together to keep their neighborhoods tidy, and I think some people might want to be discreet with their underwear, but what exactly is it about the appearance of sweet-smelling, freshly washed clothes billowing in the sun that is so offensive as to warrant banning?

- When sunshine is lacking, use indoor clothes-drying racks. In winter, the air in many houses becomes excessively dry due to the extensive use of forced air and other heating systems. This can ir-ritate and harm nasal membranes, lungs, eyes, and skin. In addi-tion to saving money, drying clothes on a rack adds moisture to the indoor air, thus making it healthier to breathe and better for your hair and skin.

Lowering the Cost of Lighting

There has been a tremendous push in the United States recently toward replacing incandescent lightbulbs with compact fluorescents. The rea-son? These bulbs use only one-third as much electricity and last ten times as long. However, there is a problem. While compact fluorescents are undeniably more efficient, many people find them less than appeal-ing. Dissatisfaction with the color of the light, poor dimming, slow warm-up times, and shortened bulb life because of high temperatures inside enclosed fixtures are the most common complaints. Plus there are problems with disposal, due to the mercury content in the bulbs.

The technology exists to solve many of these problems, but it comes at a cost. Meanwhile, there's been a lot of pressure by government agen-cies and retailers to lower the prices in order to increase market penetration. The result has been that many manufacturers have been cutting corners, putting compact fluorescents of lesser quality on the market. Some wear out early, others fail to work at all, and few seem to provide the color or dimming features that people want. Suppliers, many of them in China, are using substandard components. Lightbulbs that don't work don't save energy or money.

In the average U.S. household, 20 percent of the cost of electricity goes to lighting. Fortunately, there are steps that can reduce that cost considerably, including the appropriate use of quality compact fluorescents.

- Whether using incandescent or fluorescent bulbs, use just the amount of light that is needed. Brighter is not always better. Bright lights are used in retail stores because they have been shown to make people buy more, but there are many occasions for which they aren't helpful. They aren't conducive to romantic moods, to deep relaxation, and to many of the feelings and interior experiences that make for a rich inner life. Once in a while, try turning off all the lights and dine only by candlelight.
- Use dimmers. Dimmer switches, if used frequently, easily pay for themselves through reduced electrical use and extended bulb life. And they let you calibrate exactly the amount of lighting you want to have, rather than always being obligated to the full wattage of the bulbs you have installed. If you use halogen bulbs and dim them, you can get nearly the same amount of light as with incandescents while saving 30 percent on energy. The savings isn't as great as with compact fluorescents, but the light quality is superior and you have the option to choose how much light you want at different times.
- Use compact fluorescents in fixtures where dimming isn't an issue because you always want the full brightness capacity. A single high-quality compact fluorescent bulb can save twenty dollars in electricity over its lifetime. How do you know you're getting a high-quality bulb? GE Energy Smart compact fluorescents are widely available and have placed the highest in consumer reviews. Like all compact fluorescents on the market today, however, their dimmable models get low marks from consumers.
- Turn off the lights when you leave a room. Some people believe it's cost effective to leave them on if you will be out of a room only briefly. This is true only if your absence will be very brief—under

one minute for incandescents, and under ten minutes for compact fluorescents.

Save Money Doing Nothing

Americans spend more money to power home audio and video equipment when turned off than when actually in use. That's because many idle electronic devices—including cell phone chargers, microwaves, TVs, stereos, cable boxes, DVD and CD players, cordless phones, burglar alarms, and home computers—continue to consume energy even when switched off. Lawrence Berkeley National Laboratory, the oldest of all the U.S. Department of Energy's national laboratories, calculates that these energy leaks account for 5 percent of the nation's electricity—as much as refrigerators. Some experts call them energy vampires, because they cost the unsuspecting average household $100 annually.

- To save money on your energy bill while also prolonging the life of your equipment, get a Smart Strip LCG3 Energy Saving Power Strip with Autoswitching Technology. This power strip uses very little energy and automatically shuts down devices that aren't in use. Unlike regular power strips, you don't have to crawl around to locate the power button. Once you install it, you save money and energy continuously, without doing anything more.

CHOOSING WHERE YOU LIVE:
TWELVE KEYS FOR MOVING INTO THE NEW GOOD LIFE

We often give great thought to questions of which college (if any) to attend, what career to pursue, and whom to marry. These are, of course, immensely important choices, but joining them as a fundamental question today is the determination of where to live. Here are some considerations that I think are worth contemplating to help you prepare for the times to come.

Think Twice About Living in a Hurricane Zone

Mike Tidwell predicted the 2005 Hurricane Katrina disaster in vivid detail in his 2003 book, *Bayou Farewell: The Rich Life and Tragic Death of*

Louisiana's Cajun Coast. Many have called him a prophet, but he rejects the label, claiming that signs were obvious to anyone who bothered to look. Now, he says, the signs are indicating that "Katrina-like disasters could become commonplace along vast stretches of U.S. coastlines in the not-so-distant future." He and many other experts note that hurricanes have been becoming more ferocious along America's Atlantic and Gulf coasts. Tidwell fears that stronger storms, coupled with rising ocean levels, could turn some of America's coastal cities into places resembling New Orleans. "In 2003," he says, "I declared with complete confidence that Katrina was coming. I argued that below-sea-level New Orleans would soon fall prey to a major hurricane because of human actions. Now I beseech readers to trust me when I say Houston and Tampa and New York and Baltimore and Miami are in equally deep trouble."

It's tempting to dismiss such doomsday scenarios, but there is no question that we are already seeing a disturbing pattern of increasing hurricane damage. Whether Tidwell's dire predictions will occur ten years from now, seventy-five years from now, or not at all, remains to be seen. But already the climate is changing and insurance companies are refusing to put their capital at risk. In 2010, for example, State Farm Insurance abruptly cancelled the policies of 125,000 of its Florida customers. And Allstate insurance is no longer issuing new policies to homeowners in coastal Maryland, parts of Virginia, and parts of New York State. Does this mean the company will need to change its name to "Somestates"?

Live Close to the Places You Need to Go

Driving is a lot more expensive, in both time and money, than most people realize. In coming years, as oil production declines and oil prices increase, it will become even more so, reducing property values in areas that are dependent on extensive commutes. You will save a great deal of money if you don't need a car to get to work and to the other places you need to be. The more you can reduce the amount of driving you do, the more money you'll save and the less stress you'll feel. If you can get around town on foot or on a bicycle, you'll have a decided advantage over those who can't.

There is one guaranteed way to save a ton of money, and that is to not own a car. Most likely, this is a realistic possibility only if you live in a city where there are many services within walking or cycling distance, and/or if you live close to viable transportation alternatives such as reliable buses, subways, or bicycle lanes. It's also easier if you don't have small children.

If this might be a possibility for you, it's worth considering because the financial implications are enormous. According to AAA, the average American spends $8,410 per year, per vehicle. If instead of having a car you put $8,410 a year into a retirement account where it was invested with a 3 percent return, in twenty years you'd have more than $232,000, enough to pay for a lovely home in most parts of the country. If you saved that same amount—$8,410 a year—and invested it at 5 percent, in twenty-five years you'd have more than $421,000, enough, perhaps, to pay for a lovely home and your retirement.

If there are two of you in your household who can get by without cars the savings are even more striking. If two of you were each to put $8,410 a year in a retirement account that was invested at 4 percent, after thirty years you would have close to $1 million.

Of course, you would still incur some transportation costs, but they'd be small compared to the cost of owning and driving even the least expensive car.

Look for "Walkability"

A friend of mine used to live in a cozy little home where he could walk or jog happily from his doorstep through a neighborhood that felt safe, interesting, and enlivening. He was basically happy. After inheriting money, he moved to a large house on a hilltop with a commanding view, but the roads are steep so he now has to drive miles to get to a place where he can comfortably walk or buy a loaf of bread. He hasn't been able to befriend his neighbors, and he feels isolated and depressed. He recently told me that he was happier before.

How walkable is your neighborhood? Are the places you like to go close enough to walk to, or do you have to get in the car to go anywhere? These might be questions you want to keep in mind the next time you are thinking about moving. Walking is healthy, costs nothing, and allows you to engage with the world around you in a way that speeding by in a car does not. Life spent enjoying the richness of a community is far more soulful than life spent alone behind the wheel.

Human beings are designed to walk. If you want a quick test for the quality of living in a particular area, look for the number of people out walking. Studies have shown that when urban neighborhoods become more heavily used by cars rather than pedestrians, people there experience a drop by more than half in the number of friends and acquaintances they have in the area.

Look for Parks

Another indicator of the quality of life in a town or city is the ratio of parks to parking lots. This provides a clue to whether the area was designed for people or for cars.

In 1998, when Enrique Peñalosa became mayor of Bogotá, Colombia, he began transforming the quality of urban life with a vision of a city designed for people. Under his leadership, the city established or renovated 1,200 parks, introduced a highly successful rapid transit system, built hundreds of miles of bicycle lanes and pedestrian paths, reduced traffic congestion by 40 percent, planted one hundred thousand trees, and involved local citizens directly in the improvement of their neighborhoods. Even though Colombia is a strife-torn country wracked by decades of civil war and a devastating poverty rate, the streets of this city of eight million inhabitants became safer than those of Washington, D.C.

Peñalosa's views aren't applicable only in Latin America. They are deeply relevant to the quality of life in towns and cities in the United States, too. "High quality public pedestrian space in general, and parks in particular," he says, "are evidence of true democracy at work." The reason that parks and public spaces are important to a democratic society, he says, is "because they are the only places where people meet as equals. . . . Parks are as essential to the physical and emotional health of a city as the water supply."

Most city and state budgets, of course, allot infinitely more money and other resources to roads than to parks. "Why," Peñalosa asks, "are the public spaces for cars deemed [so much] more important than the public spaces for children?"

Look for Water

In the future, the growing scarcity of water and the increasing costs of transporting water will impact both quality of life and property values in many areas. Los Angeles, for example, draws much of its water from the Colorado River, some six hundred miles away. With water shortages, will cities in arid areas such as Los Angeles, Las Vegas, Phoenix, and many other locations in the Southwest be able to provide sufficient water for the number of people that currently call them home? If not, property values will plummet.

Meanwhile, the irrigation of U.S. lawns and landscapes claims an estimated eight billion gallons of water a day. That's a lot of water being used for nonessential purposes. It's enough water, in case you're interested, to make more than three hundred bottles of beer a day for every person in the United States.

Look for Cities and Towns with Stable Populations

When the population of a city decreases significantly, for whatever reason, property values invariably plunge. This can be severe. Consider, for example, what has happened in recent years in the city of Detroit, still the nation's eleventh largest city although its population is less than half of what it was in 1960. In 2009, the *Chicago Tribune* reported that the median price for a home sold in Detroit in December 2008 was $7,500. That's not a misprint. It's less than the lowest-priced new car in the country. And quality of life for renters in Detroit is pretty tough, too.

It's entirely possible that Detroit will be the first major American city to go bankrupt. Already 50 percent of the city's children live below the poverty line. In Detroit's case, of course, the decline of U.S. automobile manufacturing is primarily responsible for this economic debacle. In the future, though, a changing climate and an unstable economy may lead to natural disasters, job losses, and challenges with water and food availability in towns and cities across the country. Those areas hit hardest by these events will suffer precipitous population decline, which invariably leads to strapped municipal budgets and plummeting property values.

Be Near Farmland

We've grown accustomed to strawberries that travel three thousand miles to our supermarkets, but increasing fuel costs may make locally grown food a far more economical choice in the future. The most fortunate locations will be those where small-scale agriculture is still possible. If you can grow food on your property or close by, all the better.

If Necessary, Move to a Less Expensive Area

I love San Francisco, but in that extraordinary city today, only 3 percent of the teachers, 6 percent of the police officers, and 4 percent of the nurses can afford to buy a home. Regrettably, these kind of disheartening statistics seem to reflect the reality in many large cosmopolitan cities. Author Shay Salomon notes a trend among those seeking less costly places to live: Coastal Californians are moving inland; inland Californians are moving to Oregon; urban Oregonians are moving to rural Oregon; rural Oregonians are moving to New Mexico; and New Mexicans are moving to Mexico. (Of course, millions of Mexicans—both documented and undocumented—are moving to California, but that's another matter.) This kind of migration can be damaging to community connectivity and sense of place, and it is surely not without its costs. But some people are finding that they can improve their quality of life significantly in a new location, so it may be worth considering.

Maybe Rent

It's long been a lynchpin of conventional financial advice that you should buy a home as soon as you can. Renting, according to this thinking, is just throwing your money away. That may have been true when property values were appreciating rapidly, but whether it will be true in the coming years is uncertain. In the long run, real estate is probably still a good investment. The trouble is, reality often intervenes, forcing us to make decisions in the short term. And in the short term, as recent years have graphically shown, property values can and sometimes do go down.

Renting has a number of advantages. You can pick up and move with far less difficulty. This added flexibility may be at a premium in the years to come, if unsettling events take place. When you own, if you want or need to find a new job, you're essentially restricted to looking in the area proximate to your home. When you rent, if you get a job offer in another area you can make the move far more easily.

Owning a home is more expensive than most people realize. There is maintenance, there are repairs, there are property taxes and insurance. Renter's insurance, in contrast, is far cheaper, because you aren't insuring the dwelling itself but only your belongings.

Is it cheaper to rent or to buy? This depends on a great number of factors, but unless property values appreciate, it's usually cheaper to rent. An exception might be for people who have high annual incomes, because for people in the highest income tax brackets, the mortgage interest deduction can make the net cost of owning less expensive.

It rarely makes sense to buy a home unless you plan to live in it for five or more years. The costs involved in buying and selling a home are such that you will almost certainly lose money if you own for less than that length of time.

Consider Home Sharing

Many of us feel that having housemates is something that's fine for college students, but we should have outgrown it by the time we are truly adults. Well, maybe—and maybe not. Many people today are finding that the savings and increased sense of community more than make up for the loss of privacy. The key, obviously, is to find housemates whose lifestyle and values are congruent with your own.

I have a number of friends who rent the home in which they live, and then rent out or sublet some of the bedrooms in the home. Although they must deal with finding new tenants each time one leaves, overall the experience seems to be workable and quite viable financially. One friend actually rents a four-bedroom home for the amount she is able to get in rent from the tenants who rent the three bedrooms she doesn't occupy. In effect, she gets free rent in return for being the property manager. Another friend rents out the "master" bedroom (I don't like that terminology), and has converted the garage into her office space, enabling her to live and work at home for far less than it would cost her otherwise. Of course, you can do this only if your own rental agreement with the owner allows for it.

Don't Take On Too Much Mortgage

If you are going to buy, a prudent rule of thumb is not to carry a mortgage greater than two years' income. I violated this rule only once and lived to regret it deeply. After our grandchildren were born with special needs, I mortgaged our home to the maximum to take advantage of what my financial adviser said was a safe investment with returns somewhat higher than the interest we were paying for the mortgage. But when that investment turned out to be handled several steps down the line by one Bernard Madoff, and the money was completely lost, I found myself in quite a pickle. Our home came frighteningly close to foreclosure. I certainly hope that you won't ever have to deal with the kind of sudden financial disaster that the Madoff fraud visited upon my family, but life is uncertain and there can be surprises. Hence the wisdom of not carrying a mortgage beyond two years' income, even if banks or other lenders will provide it to you.

Mortgages have become such an accepted part of our economic lives that most of us consider ourselves fortunate if we are able to qualify for one. If we do qualify, and if we are able to make the necessary down payment, we then say that we own our own homes. But that's not entirely true. Having a mortgage is not the same thing as owning a home outright.

Having a mortgage means that you are obligated not only to pay property taxes, but also to pay a specified sum every month for a certain number of years to the lender, a sum that often exceeds the property's rental value. And if you fail to make that payment even for a few consecutive months, the bank or other financial institution that holds the mortgage can foreclose, causing you to lose all rights to the home.

Typically, banks begin the foreclosure process if a homeowner is four months behind in making payments, but some types of loans go into foreclosure if even two months are missed. If a bank forecloses upon your home, you must move out. The home you thought was yours will then be sold on the steps of the county courthouse to the highest bidder. If the bid amount is less than the total amount owed on the mortgage, the bank can seek what's called a deficiency judgment. If that happens, you not only lose the home, you also owe the bank an additional debt!

In order to reduce monthly payments and make a home purchase seem more affordable, people have been taking on longer and longer mortgages. But this is usually penny-wise and pound-foolish, because the longer the term of your mortgage, the more you pay over time in interest. Most people understand this concept in the abstract but aren't aware of the staggering sums of money that are involved. Studies have shown that consumers typically aren't able to answer basic questions about compound interest and inflation. Research by economists Victor Stango and Jonathan Zinman has found that people making monthly payments often underestimate how much interest they will pay over time.

But the numbers are enormous, as the chart below (based on a $300,000 mortgage at a fixed rate of 7 percent) shows. The shorter the term, the better the long-term reality—by a colossal margin.

What about adjustable rate mortgages (ARMs)? Economists Karen Pence and Brian Bucks found that most people with adjustable rate mortgages don't know how much their rates could change, which almost always means they have taken on a great deal more risk than they realize. This explains why foreclosure rates on adjustable rate mortgages are 50 percent higher than they are for fixed rate mortgages. This, by the way, isn't the case only for subprime borrowers with shaky credit. Even prime rate borrowers who are well qualified end up in foreclosure far more often when they have adjustable rate mortgages than when they have fixed rate mortgages.

People who take on adjustable rate mortgages are attracted by the initial lower monthly payments, but they typically don't grasp how bad things can get with this type of loan. When the index on which your adjustable rate is based goes up, so will the interest rate on your loan. This can be costly. For example, if you have a $300,000 adjustable rate loan

Mortgage	Interest Rate	Length of Mortgage	Montly Payment	Interest Paid Over Life of Loan
$300,000	7% Fixed	10 years	$3,483.25	$117,990
$300,000	7% Fixed	15 years	$2,696.48	$185,366
$300,000	7% Fixed	30 years	$1,995.91	$418,528
$300,000	7% Fixed	40 years	$1,864.29	$594,859

and start out paying 5 percent, but it adjusts to 8 percent, you have to pay an additional $591 per month. If it adjusts to 10 percent, your monthly payment goes up by more than $1,000. No wonder adjustable rate mortgages end up in foreclosure so much more often than fixed rates.

Avoid Toxicity

After Hurricane Katrina, many displaced Gulf Coast residents were temporarily housed in about 140,000 trailers provided to survivors of the disaster by the Federal Emergency Management Agency (FEMA). The trailers, whose interiors were fabricated largely from composite wood and particleboard, were subsequently found to have indoor air with elevated formaldehyde levels. Trailer residents reported acute to severe respiratory problems; children suffered chronic coughing, burning eyes, nosebleeds, and sinus infections; and there were deaths attributed to the formaldehyde. Hearings before the House Committee on Oversight and Government Reform focused on who would bear the responsibility for so many severe health problems—the government or the companies that manufactured the homes. Though formaldehyde is a known carcinogen, there are no federal regulations governing the amount of formaldehyde that is allowed in trailers or mobile homes.

Similarly, several months after FEMA provided trailers to residents displaced by the Iowa floods of 2008, occupants reported violent coughing, headaches, asthma, bronchitis, and other serious problems.

Of course, it's not just trailers and manufactured homes where indoor air quality can be a problem. Any home in which there is substantial use of particleboard, medium-density fiberboard (MDF), vinyl flooring and siding, and other unhealthy materials can pose a health hazard. As the Environmental Protection Agency (EPA) puts it, "A growing body of evidence has indicated that the air within homes and other buildings can be more seriously polluted than the outdoor air in even the largest and most industrialized cities."

I have friends who, when they became pregnant, created a room for their baby-to-be. Wanting only the best for the new arrival, they installed new vinyl flooring and bought new furniture for the room. Unfortunately, they made an all-too-common mistake. They didn't know that new furniture made with particleboard and MDF is high in formaldehyde, nor that formaldehyde and vinyl can be hazardous to human health. Sadly, their baby developed a long list of health problems. We may never know whether they were caused by chemical exposures in the home, but according to many experts in environmental health, there is a strong possibility that they were.

How concerned should we be about formaldehyde? According to the EPA, formaldehyde at levels commonly found in homes where cabinets and furniture are made from particleboard and MDF can cause "watery eyes, burning sensations in the eyes and throat, nausea, and difficulty in breathing." Higher levels can cause cancer.

What about lower levels? In 2007, despite enormous pressure from the companies that sell particleboard and MDF, the California Air Resources Board ruled that "exposure to low or moderate levels of formaldehyde can result in eye and upper respiratory tract irritation, headache and rhinitis."

And the vinyl flooring? The magazine *Parents* is a popular publication that is not particularly known for rocking the boat. Yet in 2005, the magazine published an article titled "The Hidden Toxins in Your Home" by Rebecca Kahlenberg. "When children breathe in fumes from a new vinyl shower curtain or a new vinyl floor," she wrote, "they are exposed to toxic materials called phthalates. . . . Vinyl contains chemicals that can put kids at higher risk of developing asthma, cancer and organ damage." The article mentioned a 2002 study of more than ten thousand Swedish children that found that when a vinyl floor was damp, children who were exposed to it experienced increased asthmatic symptoms.

What if your home has vinyl flooring, particleboard furniture and cabinets, and other suspect materials? What if you reside in a trailer or manufactured home? With older homes, thankfully, most of the chemical outgassing has probably already occurred. But still, it's important to have good cross-ventilation, particularly if there are children or people with respiratory difficulties in the home. Avoid bringing in new materials (including synthetic carpets and paints with high levels of volatile organic compounds, or VOCs) that might emit additional toxic gases. Old solid wood furniture is far superior from a health point of view, and often less expensive, than new furniture, which is almost always made from particleboard and other wood products high in formaldehyde.

Until recently, no large builder of manufactured homes had taken on the challenge of creating and selling green, healthy, and affordable housing. But that changed in 2009, when Clayton Homes, a company owned by Warren Buffett and the largest provider of manufactured homes in the United States, came out with the i-house.

The i-house is ingenious. The butterfly roof is designed for a rainwater catchment system as well as to carry an optional solar photovoltaic system. Amenities include dual-flush toilets, bamboo flooring, decks made from recycled materials, climate control in each room, and low-E double-pane windows. The wood that is used comes from sustainable forests, and the exterior walls are formaldehyde free.

Extremely energy efficient, the i-house will be far cheaper to live in than other manufactured homes. According to Warren Buffett, "Estimated costs for electricity and heating total only about one dollar per day when the home is sited in an area like Omaha, Nebraska."

Whether it will succeed in the marketplace remains to be seen, because people purchasing trailers and manufactured homes have traditionally not been willing to pay extra for green and nontoxic features. With many innovative attributes, the i-home carries a price tag above that of most other manufactured homes. The i-house II—with two bedrooms and 1,023 square feet—carries a price tag of $93,000. The i-house I—with one bedroom and 723 square feet—sells for $74,900. Though priced somewhat higher than conventional trailers and manufactured homes, the i-home is still inexpensive compared to homes that are built on-site, particularly given the amenities it features. Some industry analysts believe that it will jump-start a trend toward housing that is more affordable, energy efficient, and nontoxic.

Many people know the environment is in danger and would love to help save it, but they believe that going green is a luxury that is essentially reserved for the wealthy. But there are a great many actions that save money while reducing our exposure to toxins and reducing our carbon footprint.

Reducing our consumption of fossil fuels and shifting to renewable nonpolluting sources of energy may be the most important challenge we collectively face in our lifetimes. In the old good life, the American home became an oversized expression of our addiction to consuming fossil fuel energy. Our task, now and in the future, is to become as free from that addiction as we possibly can. Thankfully, there are many steps we can take that are green squared—they make sense both ecologically and economically.

Next to housing, transportation is the largest expense incurred by most people and households. It is also an arena with phenomenal environmental implications. And so it is to transportation that we now turn.

FIVE

Life Is Too Short for Traffic

For the vast majority of humanity's time on this planet, we've moved around on foot. We've walked. We've walked a lot. Once in a while, we've run. When we learned to harness horses, we rode.

But things changed dramatically with the advent of the motorized vehicle. Indeed, that invention massively altered the course of human experience. Now, the average person in the United States walks less than three hundred yards on a typical day, while traveling more than thirty miles in a car or truck.

We see this as progress and take pride in how fast our cars enable us to go. Even cars marketed as "family sedans" often come with speedometers that indicate speeds of up to 160 miles per hour, though no county or state in the United States permits driving speeds above 80. The manufacturers have found that the higher the top speed indicated on the speedometer, the more money people will pay for the car.

We pay extra for fast cars and love their ability to take us swiftly to our chosen destinations. But nowadays there's another reality that compromises the fun: traffic congestion. Drivers in the United States collectively spend eight billion hours a year stuck in traffic jams. That's forty hours a year, per driver—one full week of work time sitting in traffic, not moving at all.

It seems as though with each passing year our cars are taking over an ever larger share of our time and money. The level of traffic congestion that used to be called "rush hour traffic" has in many cities become an all day phenomenon that gets even worse at certain hours. Isn't it a little odd to still call it "rush hour" given that it's a time when cars are slowed to a snail's pace?

Freeways and expressways have been built to make things better, but in New York, for example, commuters now refer to theirs as the "Long Island Distressway."

Today, the average American adult spends seventy-two minutes a day behind the wheel of a car. That's 437 hours a year spent driving, an amount equal to fifty-four eight-hour workdays. I'm not sure what this says about our priorities, but this is more than twice as much time as the average American father spends with his children.

To top it off, according to the U.S. Bureau of Labor Statistics, nearly 20 percent of our income goes to the costs of owning and maintaining our cars. (If you have undertaken the calculations I recommend in chapter 3, you may already know this to be true for you, too!)

This means that each year, we're spending the time equivalent of nearly three work-months driving our cars, and more than two months of our income paying for our cars. All told, we're spending the equivalent of close to five work-months a year either driving our cars or working to pay for them.

A 2009 ad for a Toyota truck proclaimed "236 horsepower at your service." But a closer look makes you wonder whether our vehicles are serving us or the other way around.

MARKETING AN AUTOMOBILE OBSESSION

If any one company has epitomized the transportation policies of the old good life, it's General Motors. Not that long ago, the company represented 10 percent of the U.S. economy and was a symbol, perhaps the preeminent corporate symbol, of the American way of life. In fact, General Motors may have been responsible, more than any other single entity, for consumerism as we know it today. It was General Motors' longtime chairman Alfred Sloan who developed the idea of "planned obsolescence," the business strategy of making annual cosmetic changes in cars in order to make last year's model seem unfashionable, thus driving people year after year to want the new and improved model. When Sloan came up with the idea, one astute observer, Vance Packard, warned of the consequences. He defined planned obsolescence as the "systematic attempt of business to make us wasteful, debt-ridden, permanently discontented individuals."

But the idea took hold. In 2009, Dan Neil, the automotive columnist for the *Los Angeles Times,* reflected that Sloan's program "put Americans on the acquisitive treadmill they are panting on yet today."

Another of Sloan's grand ideas was the "Ladder of Success." The company spent more than a billion dollars a year promoting the idea that its brands—Chevrolet, Pontiac, Oldsmobile, Buick, and Cadillac— corresponded to ascending social status. As Neil explained, "The Ladder of Success was in fact an automotive caste system, a program of class stratification. Armed with the power of modern scientific marketing and advertising, General Motors was able to weld an existential link between who we are and what we drive."

THE REAL COST OF CARS

In an ideal world, we would drive a lot less. Our cities and our lifestyles would be designed so we could easily walk to the places we need to go. We'd be far less dependent on cars and trucks, and those we used would use renewable nonpolluting energy for fuel. We'd reverse the decades-long government policies that have squelched public transportation, and would instead build high-speed rail, bike trails, elegant and efficient bus systems, and pedestrian-friendly environments. City maps would show bike paths and walking routes. Our air would be cleaner and our time would be more our own. Our cities would be quieter and more welcoming. Our climate would be more stable and our bodies healthier.

I hope we get there, but that's not the world we live in now. In the world we've got, there are choices for each of us to make, some of which involve rethinking our basic attitudes about cars.

Automobile advertising, of course, has gone to great lengths to paint driving as a joyful and sexy experience. An Infiniti advertisement launched ironically on the twenty-fifth anniversary of Earth Day announced "It's not a car. It's an aphrodisiac." A Chevrolet Camaro ad introduced "A car that makes you wish the whole world was paved with concrete."

Some of these ads are almost comical in the way they represent the assumptions and values of the old good life. Yet nearly all of us have been influenced by the billions of dollars car companies spend on advertising each year. Studies show that more than 98 percent of people consistently underestimate how much it costs to own and drive a car.

Get-out-of-debt specialist Dave Ramsey may be exaggerating, but he has a point when he says, "The worst auto accidents you'll ever see occur on the showroom floor." He's talking about the damage people incur when they sign up for years of debt by buying cars they can't afford.

According to the U.S. Bureau of Labor Statistics, car ownership costs are the second largest household expense, behind only shelter (home mortgage or rent). The average American household spends almost as much on their cars as they do on food and health care combined.

David Leonhardt is an economics journalist with *The New York Times*. In 2008, with help from Jake Fisher, a senior automotive engineer at the *Consumer Reports* test track in Connecticut, he calculated the costs of owning various cars and trucks. Assuming the vehicle is driven fifteen thousand miles a year, he found a number of mass-market vehicles, including the fully loaded Ford F-450 pickup truck, the Lincoln Navigator, and the Lexus LX 570, that over a five-year period cost near or above $100,000. Of course, that's not merely the price tag at a dealership. It's the actual cost, which includes insurance, interest, depreciation, repairs, maintenance, taxes, tires, oil, gas, and other miscellaneous expenses inherent in car ownership and use.

The website Edmunds.com has a handy feature called "True Cost to Own." You can look up any car, new or up to five years old, and get a pretty good idea of what it would cost to own and drive that car for five years.

In my opinion, such calculations, as useful as they are, still underestimate the real costs you may have to pay in the coming years. For one, they can't predict how the price of gas might change. If gas prices rise, the costs of owning and driving will increase, and for some cars quite substantially. They don't include the costs of parking. And they assume that you have a good driving record. If your driving history is less than optimum, you'll pay more for insurance than they provide for in their calculations.

They also don't take into account the physical health costs of being in an accident. In the United States, there are more than six million auto accidents each year, at a purely financial cost of $230 billion. Tragically, more than twice as many people have died in car accidents in the United States since 1900 than have been killed in all the wars in U.S. history. That's a sobering fact you're not likely to see mentioned in today's car ads.

Still, for most people, owning a car feels like a necessity, not an option. Fortunately, there are many ways you can lessen the costs and risks, decrease pollution, and add to the quality of your life.

NEW GOOD LIFE STRATEGIES TO REDUCE YOUR TRANSPORTATION COSTS

Buy Used

A lot of us have gotten into the habit of buying or leasing a new car every two or three years. But what makes more sense, economically, is to buy a used car every ten or twelve years, or even longer, particularly if we maintain it well.

Buying used instead of new means forgoing the excitement we've come to associate with "new" cars. But it's worth it. By buying used, you greatly reduce the depreciation and insurance costs you'll incur over the course of the time you own the car. From a purely financial point of view, buying a used car is always less expensive, in both the short and the long run.

My suggestion, if you can afford it, is to buy a car that is several years old and isn't too big or too costly, take care of it well, and keep it for a very long time. This may seem obvious, but it's amazing how many otherwise intelligent people do otherwise. It's more important than it might appear to buy one that gets excellent gas mileage, because the price of fuel is likely to rise over the years and could increase a great deal. Of course, cars that have been maintained regularly will be more reliable and have fewer unexpected problems.

When does it stop being cost-effective to keep an old car running? According to Tom and Ray Magliozzi, longtime car mechanics with ad-

> Never, ever, buy a salvaged car. The potential for problems is huge. Salvaged cars may look pretty, but they are just cosmetically reconditioned wrecks. If a car is salvaged, it will say so on the certificate of title.

vanced degrees from MIT whose radio show *Car Talk* is broadcast weekly on National Public Radio stations: "As long as you can get inexpensive parts, and don't have to go to the dealer for repairs, a good car can be made to run economically for a very long distance, as much as four hundred thousand miles."

That might seem like an exorbitantly long time to keep a car, and not that long ago it would have been. Twenty-five years ago, sixty thousand to eighty thousand miles was considered high mileage for a car. But mileage expectations have increased greatly over the past few decades. Why? The Japanese started making cars that were more reliable and longer lasting than those that were coming out of Detroit. Eventually, American car companies realized they had to improve quality in order to catch up.

There's also a health advantage to buying a used car: eliminating your exposure to something not many people realize is a health hazard—"new car smell." Some people find the smell of vinyl and plastic outgassing attractive and even seductive, but they probably wouldn't if they knew what it really is: a mixture of VOCs, including benzene (a carcinogen), acetone and ethylbenzene (central nervous system toxins), formaldehyde (a carcinogen), toluene (causes widespread cellular damage), and xylene isomers (fetal toxins). Riding in a brand new car is, essentially, like continuously sniffing bad glue.

In 2001, a two-year study by an Australian government research organization found that the gases from vinyl and plastic materials in new cars cause headaches, lung irritation, nausea, and drowsiness, and can even cause cancer. The study by the Commonwealth Scientific and Industrial Research Organisation found the emissions to be toxic within a matter of minutes and likely to be responsible for many accidents.

When it comes to cars, as with so many things, "new" is not always "better." Sometimes it's actually more toxic. And almost always, it's a lot more expensive.

Avoid Leasing

There is a good reason that most dealers encourage you to lease. They make more money if you do. But you end up paying more.

The lure, of course, is "no money down," but over the course of time you actually come out behind, particularly if you end up driving more than twelve thousand miles a year (as most people do), if you return the car in less than perfect condition (even a few minor dents can count against you), or if your circumstances change and you need to turn the car in early—all of which will result in substantial fees and penalties.

There are some who recommend leasing because of tax advantages. But these benefits are minimal for most people and don't make up for the added risks of leasing. If you lease a car and an unforeseen crisis occurs leaving you unable to make your lease payments, you're stuck with few options, all of which will cost you a lot of dough. If you own a car and this kind of thing happens, you can sell it. With a lease, though, you are obligated to continue making the payments.

Don't Pay for Premium Gas

Some people believe that premium gas gives you more miles per gallon than regular gas, but it's not true. To increase the octane rating of gas, companies include additives that slightly increase your mileage. They also add ethanol, however, which has the opposite effect. Premium gas does contain extra detergents, but the gasoline that's sold today by the major gas companies already has plenty of detergents to keep your engine clean. Except in the case of a few highly specialized cars, premium gas is not worth the extra cost—it's mostly just another marketing gimmick. And the difference in price, over time, is considerable.

Consider "Hypermiling"

"Hypermiling" is the practice of adjusting your driving habits to maximize fuel economy. By staying within the posted speed limit, accelerating gently, and mastering the arts of minimizing braking and preserving momentum (by coasting to stoplights in hopes of timing green lights, leaving a substantial buffer zone between yourself and the car ahead, and picking up extra speed going downhill so you can coast on the way back up), you can increase your miles per gallon by 50 percent or more. Although this might mean slightly longer travel times (and putting up with aggravation from a few aggressive drivers), you'll also minimize wear and tear on your car and reduce maintenance and repair costs.

Practice Good Maintenance

In a worsening economy, there is a tendency to cut costs wherever you can. But there are certain expenses that you shouldn't cut if you can avoid it, because they could end up costing you much more in the long run.

Your motor oil needs to be changed regularly, every five thousand miles (or less). Otherwise it turns to sludge and is bad for your car's engine. And take care of your tires. When tires aren't properly inflated, you burn more gas. What's worse, a lot of accidents are caused by insufficient air pressure. And if your tires are bald or your brake pads are worn out, you need to attend to the problem so that you don't place yourself and others at serious risk.

Keep Insurance Costs Down

One way to save money is by raising your deductibles. An even better way is to buy a smaller and less expensive vehicle. It costs less to insure vehicles that are less likely to be stolen and are less expensive to repair or replace. As your car ages and declines in value, you can lower your comprehensive insurance. And, of course, drive carefully. Traffic violations and accidents raise your premiums.

Consider a Hybrid

Hybrids are the fastest growing segment of the car market and are showing excellent resale values. If and when gas prices spike, their resale value will improve even more. Their repair costs, thus far, are about the same as traditional cars.

Don't be misled, though. Just because a car is a hybrid doesn't mean it's fuel efficient. Some car manufacturers are using hybrid technology to add power to their vehicles rather than to increase fuel economy. In effect, they're just greenwashing their overpowered vehicles. BMW's 2010

X6 Hybrid, for example, gets only 16 miles per gallon in city driving and not much better on a highway.

And then there are cars that are sold as hybrids but just barely qualify as hybrids and certainly do not live up to the real intent for a hybrid vehicle. These cars have been slightly modified so that they shut off at idle and get a tiny bit better gas mileage, but to put them in the same category as a Toyota Prius or a Honda Insight should be considered false advertising.

Real hybrids such as the Toyota Prius and Honda Insight are a different story altogether. They were designed as hybrids from the ground up and can run on either the gas engine or the electric motor, or both. Real hybrids are amazing inventions and are probably the cars of the future. If you drive fifteen thousand miles a year, and gas costs $3 a gallon, the difference between getting 50 miles per gallon, as you might in a Prius, and 20 miles per gallon, as you do in many other cars, is $1,350 annually. If gas costs $4 a gallon, you save even more, about $1,800 a year.

Real hybrids also save you money on maintenance. While conventional cars with automatic transmissions require new brake pads every twenty thousand to thirty thousand miles, there is virtually no brake maintenance in the full hybrids because they use electrical regenerative braking.

Some people have been deterred from hybrids out of fear of having to replace the battery packs, which could cost several thousand dollars. Toyota says their batteries are expected to last the lifetime of the vehicle, but only time will tell. Lab tests show they can go up to 180,000 miles with no deterioration, but the real world might be a different story. Honda, Ford, and Toyota all warrant their battery packs for at least 80,000 miles. If you drive a hybrid long enough, it's likely that you'll eventually need to replace the battery pack, but if you've gotten 150,000 miles out of it, you'll still come out way ahead.

Some car buyers feel it's hard to justify the extra cost of a hybrid, especially when gas prices are low. But the price of gas is likely to rise in the future, and the financial savings hybrid cars bring their drivers go beyond the gas pump. Many tax incentives and other benefits are granted to hybrid owners. Some areas allow hybrids without passengers to drive in high-occupancy vehicle lanes. Many cities offer free or discounted parking to hybrid owners. Some universities provide special parking rates for faculty- and student-owned hybrids, and some hotels reward hybrid drivers with free parking. A number of car insurance providers, including Farmers Insurance Group, Geico, and Travelers, offer discounted insurance rates to hybrid drivers in some states. And there is a growing list of employers who are encouraging their workers to commute in hybrid vehicles. At companies including Google, Bank of America, Patagonia, and Clif Bar, employees receive up to $5,000 for purchasing or leasing a hybrid. A list of businesses that offer hybrid employee benefits can be found at http://www.hybridcenter.org/employee-incentives.html. And all kinds of information about hybrids can be found at HybridCars.com.

Carpool

Carpooling offers many advantages beyond sharing the cost of gas. There are obvious environmental benefits, and ride sharing offers opportunities for social interactions that can counter the isolation of many hours spent driving alone.

Green America is a national nonprofit consumer organization promoting environmental sustainability and economic justice. In 2009, the organization's newsletter told a remarkable story of what can happen when people carpool.

When Anne Benson joined a long-standing daily carpool from Shirlington, Virginia, to downtown Washington, D.C., she wasn't expecting romance. She simply wanted to share gas costs with several other colleagues, to take advantage of Virginia's faster highway lanes reserved for cars with more than one passenger, and to benefit from her employer's reserved parking spaces for carpoolers. But after many enjoyable drives, she and one of her carpool-mates, Andrew Miller, ended up falling in love, marrying, and creating a family.

Of course, joining a carpool isn't typically going to lead to true love. But it does promise a win-win-win combination for your social life, for the planet, and for your pocketbook. And newer online tools make it easier than ever.

Zimride.com uses Google maps, networks such as Facebook, and a matchmaking algorithm to connect riders and drivers. The free service

In the San Francisco Bay area, a phenomenon has emerged called "casual carpooling." Every weekday morning, a stream of cars and a flow of pedestrians converge at a Safeway supermarket in the Rockridge neighborhood of Oakland, California. These people don't know one another and nothing's been organized or arranged. Nobody sticks out a thumb to signal that they would like a ride. Those on foot simply take the empty seats in the waiting cars. As soon as a car is full, it takes off for San Francisco. Meanwhile, the same thing is continuously happening at about thirty other East Bay locations. Thirty to forty-five minutes later, the cars arrive at the intersection of Fremont and Mission streets, in downtown San Francisco's central financial district, whereupon the passengers disembark and proceed to walk to work or hop on city buses.

The drivers get to use the fast, toll-free high-occupancy vehicle lane, thus arriving at their destinations faster and cheaper. The passengers get free rides. And a lot fewer cars are driven, which means a lot less gas is burned, a lot less pollution is emitted, and a lot less oil needs to be imported.

There are two things that make San Francisco's casual carpooling outstanding. One is that it is entirely unregulated. There is no governmental or organizational oversight whatsoever. The other is that it is enormous. According to Randy Rentschler, a spokesperson for the Metropolitan Transportation Commission for the Bay Area, "Free carpools are the single largest category of vehicles passing the bridge in the morning—more than [other] cars, toll payers, buses, everyone. It just works and it's a good thing for everybody. . . . The single largest transport resource not just in the Bay Area, but in the entire country, are the empty seats in everyone's car." He says that carpools now account for 46 percent of morning traffic on the Bay Bridge. And half of that 46 percent is "casual." This means that casual carpool vehicles make up nearly a quarter of the total morning traffic across the San Francisco Bay Bridge.

Could this kind of thing be replicated in other cities? Adam Starr, who wrote a fascinating 2009 article about this phenomenon for *Good* magazine, thinks it's possible. "While the Bay Area's layout makes it especially conducive to casual carpool, other cities may soon see the advantages of developing their own casual carpool culture, especially as the realization broadens that being eco- and econo-conscious are increasingly the same thing."

offers options for one-way trips, round-trips, and daily commutes. You also learn details about a potential driver or passenger, such as preferred driving speed and music preferences. "The real goal is to build a community around this," says John Zimmer, Zimride's founder. "A community empowers trust relationships. On top of that, it saves money and gas mileage." Last year, he used Zimride.com to catch a series of rides from New York City all the way to Palo Alto, California.

Other websites include AlterNetRides.com, carpoolworld.com, NuRide.com, Rideshare.com, eRideShare.com, and DivvyMyRide.com. Plus, there are many local ride-sharing resources that serve particular metropolitan areas. Do an Internet search for your town or city and "ride sharing" or "carpooling," and you'll probably find a host of possibilities.

Share a Car

Many people have found that as they alter their lifestyles to drive less, they are able to share cars rather than own them exclusively. With thoughtful coordination and good communication, many couples and families have found they can cut down on the number of vehicles they own.

In an increasing number of cities, Internet-based car-sharing cooperatives and companies are helping people share access to cars. This enables the costs of owning, insuring, and maintaining a car to be shared with others, and you get the flexibility of getting an appropriate-sized vehicle for particular trips and errands.

Zipcar (zipcar.com) is a membership-based car-sharing company providing car rental to its members, billable by the hour or day. Currently operating in fifty U.S. cities, Vancouver, Toronto, and London, Zipcar represents a new business model in car rental. The concept is to provide simple, fast, and inexpensive Internet-based car sharing on an hourly or daily basis. Unlike traditional car rental companies, the Zipcar rental price includes gas, insurance, parking, and 125 miles per day. There are no lines or waiting because you reserve your car online, and it's waiting for you instead of the other way around. Rather than being housed at a car rental agency, the cars are located in parking lots and garages throughout the cities where the company operates. You go online, find a car near you, and then reserve it for when you need it. Prices seem to be generally cheaper than typical car rental agencies, except for long trips and extended rental periods.

Pedal Your Motor

If you want to reduce your reliance on cars, there is a mode of transportation that can play a helpful role—the electric bicycle. Electric bikes are quiet, speedy, and fun to ride. They are a green alternative to driving that, unlike a typical bicycle, doesn't require you to travel entirely on your own foot or pedal power. They aren't terribly expensive and are in many cases a wonderful choice for errands and short commutes. You can get kits and convert a conventional bike, or you can buy them ready to go. The electricity they use to charge up costs only a few pennies a day.

Electric bikes often look very much like conventional bikes. In some cases, the motor is hidden discreetly within the frame. In other cases, it's attached to the frame. Many models allow you to choose, with a twist of the handlebar, between 1) an all-electric ride, 2) an entirely pedaled ride, or 3) a ride combing electric with pedal power.

One friend of mine used to ride his bicycle only a few times a year, but now he uses it for errands several times a week. What made the difference? Using a kit, he added a rechargeable electric motor to his old bike. He still pedals for power, but now he gets motorized help whenever he wants with the flick of a wrist. This enables him to go farther and faster than he would without the power assist. He can easily keep up his speed and even accelerate when going up hills, which feels safer. The extra power assist also enables him to easily pull a bike trailer, so he can even make large shopping trips.

He still has a car but uses it less. "I used to drive to the store to get a bar of soap," he says. " I knew it didn't make a lot of sense to burn expensive gas and drive three thousand pounds of car a half mile to the store and back, but that's what I did. But not anymore. Now that I've got the electric assist on my bike, I ride it a lot more."

Depending on the model, electric bicycles can go anywhere from fifteen to sixty miles between charges. Some models actually recharge while riding downhill, which not only extends the battery range, but also prolongs the life of the brake pads and gives the rider more control and safety going down steep hills.

Most electric bikes ride along quite easily at 15 to 25 miles per hour. For short trips, riding an electric bike can actually be faster than driving a car, because you are far less likely to get stuck in traffic and you don't have to waste time driving around looking for parking. In most states, they don't require a license plate or vehicle insurance. And they are always quiet.

There are also larger electric bikes and scooters that run entirely on electricity without any pedal power from the rider. Bigger and faster, these electric motor scooters are more expensive and don't have the health benefits of pedal power, but they are extraordinarily fuel efficient, and some can attain speeds up to 45 miles per hour.

In my household, we have an electric bike that we use whenever possible for errands. My adult son rides it to work and back—about eight miles round-trip—three or four times a week. Having the electric bike reduces the miles we drive and spares us having to own an additional car, thus saving us many thousands of dollars a year.

Electric bikes emit no carbon dioxide or other pollutants. Even when you factor in the pollution generated in producing the electricity used to charge their batteries, electric bikes are still only about 5 percent as polluting as driving a car the same distance. Plus, the price you pay for the electricity to recharge the battery is minimal compared to what you'd pay for gas.

You do need to have a safe place at home to park your electric bike, such as a covered porch or a garage, where the bike can plug in to a standard outlet to recharge its battery. And a word of caution: The electric scooters and bikes available today vary in quality. You might want to purchase one at a store that will service them. Or, if you buy online, choose a company that guarantees it will provide spare parts if the bike needs them.

Ride a Bicycle

Many Americans tend to think of bicycles as only for children, but in much of the world bicycles are the primary mode of adult transportation. In the Netherlands, for example, bicycles account for nearly 30 percent of all urban trips. Not only does every city in the country have bike lanes and trails, but cyclists are often given many advantages over motorists. Cyclists are permitted, for example, to move out before cars at many traffic lights. In 2007, Amsterdam became the first major city in the industrialized Western world where more trips were taken by bicycle than by car. Is it a coincidence that, adjusted for population size, the rate of obesity in the Netherlands is less than a third what it is in the United States? And that the amount spent on health care *per person* is about half as much?

Since most of us remember loving riding our bikes as kids, why can't we have some of that happiness now? I know many people who have taken up bike riding again in their forties or fifties, and are finding that it offers many advantages for their bodies as well as their spirits.

The health benefits can be major—just ask anyone paying $1,000 a year or more for a gym membership so they can ride a stationary bike. Riding a bike is good cardiovascular exercise. It's kind to your joints. It provides a wonderful aerobic effect. It builds strength in your legs. And it strengthens the muscles in and around your body's core.

Weather issues and public policy decisions make some environments far more bike friendly than others. Different cities, of course, have different approaches to bikes. Many, unfortunately, ignore them. I think it's time for that to change.

Here are three U.S. cities where it has:

- Davis, California, has great bike weather and wonderfully progressive bike-friendly policies. Nearly 20 percent of the residents of this Northern California city commute on bikes. So many school kids walk or bike to school that there is no need for school buses. The city recently spent $2 million building a tunnel under a surface street, just for bikes. Now that's showing respect for cyclists! The city actually has more bikes than cars.
- Boulder, Colorado, doesn't enjoy the mild weather of Northern California. But by ensuring that 90 percent of arterial roads have bike lanes, they've greatly reduced traffic congestion and air pollution.
- Portland, Oregon, gets a lot of rain. Yet the city has built more bike paths than any other city in the United States and has given bikes, helmets, lights, locks, and other essentials to low-income adults in order to increase their ability to enter the workforce.

In most U.S. cities, though, there are safety concerns for bicyclists. In areas with inadequate cycling infrastructure (bike paths and so forth), cyclists are at higher risk. Car drivers cause more than 90 percent of all accidents involving a car and a bicycle.

The next time you're driving and see a cyclist, show them the respect they deserve. In terms of social responsibility and carbon footprints, they are going many steps further than Prius drivers.

Paris, France, boasts a successful bicycle rental program called Vélib', or "bike freedom." The program began in 2007, and two years later more than twenty thousand bicycles were distributed across the city at 1,800 locations. In its first two years of operation, Vélib' bikes were used more than fifty-three million times, making this the greenest form of public transportation in Paris. Even though problems with theft were serious (many of the bikes were showing up on black markets in eastern Europe and northern Africa), as of 2009, one million trips were taken weekly for commutes around the city.

CARS—THE NEXT WAVE

Plug-in Hybrids

Plug-in hybrids have the potential to make a quantum leap over current hybrids. They were first made available to the public in 2010 and were initially quite expensive. It is hoped, though, that models will be available within a few years that will be cost competitive with regular cars. They get 100 miles per gallon or more, but the advantages go way beyond fuel efficiency. It is not an exaggeration to say that plug-in hybrids could help save us from oil dependence, air pollution, and a deteriorating atmosphere. By dispensing with 80 to 90 percent of the gasoline used by conventional cars, these vehicles could play a key role in our getting unhooked from fossil fuels.

It's not just tree-hugging environmentalists and fans of Al Gore who are agog about plug-ins. One of the foremost advocates in the country for these vehicles is R. James Woolsey. A former director of the Central Intelligence Agency who spent three years as a member of then–defense secretary Donald Rumsfeld's Defense Policy Board, Woolsey drives a hybrid with a "Bin Laden Hates This Car" bumper sticker. In 2008, he coauthored an op-ed in the *National Review* in which he wrote of ending our reliance "on the whims of OPEC's despots, the substantial instabilities of the Middle East, and the indignity of paying for both sides in the War on Terror."

Woolsey is on the board of directors for the electric vehicle advocacy group Plug In America. He is also a founding member of the Set America Free Coalition, whose support for plug-ins recognizes the national security problems of our current oil dependence: "Ninety-seven percent of the fuel used in U.S. transportation is petroleum-based, and two-thirds of our oil is imported. With gas prices on the rise and no end in sight, our cars' addiction to foreign oil is bankrupting us. And because so much of the oil we import comes from countries that hate us, we're actually helping to bankroll terrorists that hunt us. As long as our cars can only run on gasoline, we'll continue to be held hostage."

A commonly raised question about plug-in technology is whether you are simply trading one form of pollution for another—tailpipe emissions for power-plant smokestack emissions. In 2007, the Natural Resources Defense Council and the Electric Power Research Institute conducted the definitive "wells-to-wheels" life-cycle analysis to find out. The study found that a shift by the United States to plug-in vehicles would reduce pollution spectacularly. The reduction in carbon emissions alone is prodigious—it would surpass five hundred million tons annually—and other exhaust pollutants would similarly decline.

The study also found that the existing U.S. power grid could easily handle the load of three-quarters of Americans switching to plug-ins. These vehicles will generally recharge at night, using excess electricity from power plants that can't shut down completely, so they won't add to the peak load. In fact, plug-in hybrids may one day actually reduce the demands on our electrical grid. After being charged at night (when the demand for electricity, and its cost, is lowest), the batteries of parked plug-in hybrid vehicles could—if hooked up for this purpose—provide electricity for a multitude of uses during daylight hours (when the demand for electricity, and its cost, is highest). A significant amount of daytime household electrical needs could be met by a plug-in hybrid parked outside the home. This would be useful and save money on a daily basis, and in the event of power outages it could be lifesaving.

A large-scale shift to plug-in hybrid cars would massively reduce gasoline use, totally eliminate our dependence on imported oil, and dramatically decrease air pollution and carbon emissions. If we were, at the same time, to build thousands of wind farms across the country to feed renewable, nonpolluting energy into the electrical grid, we could run our cars entirely on energy from the wind. This would rejuvenate farm and ranch communities, shrink the U.S. balance-of-trade deficit, and reduce automobile carbon emissions to nearly zero. Assembly lines that formerly made cars and trucks could be used to produce wind turbines, revitalizing Detroit and other cities while producing many jobs. "Recharging batteries with off-peak wind-generated electricity," says Lester Brown, president of Earth Policy Institute, "costs the equivalent of less than $1 per gallon of gasoline."

All-Electric Cars

Looking a bit farther into the future, the prospects for all-electric vehicles look bright. Already Tesla Motors has produced an all-electric sports car, the Tesla Roadster, that can travel 244 miles on a single charge of its lithium-ion battery pack. The car is very expensive and incredibly fast, capable of accelerating from 0 to 60 miles per hour in 3.9 seconds, making it literally one of the fastest cars in the world. *Motor Trend* said the car is "undeniably, unbelievably efficient" and would be "profoundly humbling to just about any rumbling Ferrari or Porsche that makes the mistake of pulling up next to a silent, 105 miles-per-gallon Tesla Roadster at a stoplight."

The "105 miles-per-gallon" figure cited by *Motor Trend,* by the way, is an interesting number, because in actuality, all-electric vehicles use no gasoline whatsoever. The Roadster has a fuel cost of about three cents a mile based on the Pacific Gas and Electric Company's retail electricity price, which corresponds, in cost, to about 105 miles per gallon. Hence the figure used by *Motor Trend.* However, PG&E offers a discounted rate for owners of electric vehicles who recharge at home overnight, which is what almost anyone owning one would do. Based on this more accurate rate, called the E-9, the Tesla Roadster, which can outrace a Ferrari, a Lamborghini, and a Corvette, comes in at an astounding 350 miles per gallon.

The Roadster is a limited-edition specialty vehicle and is priced beyond the reach of most people. But it clearly demonstrates that an all-electric ultra-high-performance car can be produced. In time and with the economies of mass production, we could see all-electric vehicles that are affordable, next to which today's Prius will look like a gas guzzler.

All-electric vehicles will have the added advantage of not needing tune-ups and of requiring little in the way of service. There will be no transmissions or clutches to repair, no fuel injection systems or radiators to maintain, and no timing belts to adjust. Some people feel that this suggests the real reason U.S. car companies didn't get behind electric cars until recently. Car dealerships have traditionally depended on their parts and service departments for much of their income.

Hydrogen-Powered Vehicles: Going Nowhere Quickly

The idea that hydrogen might one day displace fossil fuels has been around since the science fiction writings of Jules Verne in the nineteenth century. Most recently, the dream focused on cars powered by hydrogen fuel cells, with water vapor as the only waste product coming out of the cars' exhaust pipes.

Up until around 2005, it looked like hydrogen cars were about to burst onto the horizon. In 1997, the German automaker Daimler-Benz declared that it would start selling a minimum of one hundred thousand hydrogen fuel cell vehicles by 2005. In 1998, General Motors CEO Jack Smith told the Detroit auto show that GM would have a production-ready hydrogen fuel cell vehicle ready "by 2004 or sooner." In 1999, Ford's CEO, Jacques Nasser, said that he saw fuel cell cars becoming a viable alternative to gasoline cars for many people during the course of his career (he was replaced in 2001). In 2003, U.S. president George W. Bush launched his Hydrogen Fuel Initiative, providing more than $1 billion for hydrogen research. And in 2004, California's governor, Arnold Schwarzenegger, promised a "hydrogen highway" all across the state by 2010.

The effort, however, turned out to be far more costly and fraught with difficulties than the hydrogen hopeful envisioned. Today, the promise of hydrogen-powered personal transport seems as elusive as ever, despite the billions of dollars governments worldwide have poured into the effort to make hydrogen cars a reality.

In 2009, the Pulitzer Prize–winning automotive journalist for the

Los Angeles Times Dan Neil wrote that "hydrogen fuel-cell technology won't work in cars. It's a tragic cul-de-sac in the search for sustainable mobility. . . . Any way you look at it, hydrogen is a lousy way to move cars."

What makes hydrogen such an ineffective fuel? Part of the problem is that hydrogen is so light. Even when the gas is condensed under pressure, there is still no known material that can hold enough of the gas to give a car the kind of range consumers want. Another part of the problem is lack of infrastructure and consumer demand. Yet another difficulty is that hydrogen is produced by the electrolysis of water, and the amount of electricity that would be needed to create enough hydrogen to fuel all the cars in the United States is four times greater than the current capacity of the national grid.

By 2009, with no hydrogen-powered vehicles publicly available and almost no demand for the volatile gas, the state of California had closed several of the hydrogen fueling stations it had built, and California's Air Resources Board had rescinded the financing it had pledged to build more. And Ballard Power Systems, a leading developer of hydrogen vehicle technology, had pulled out of the hydrogen vehicle business, concluding that the industry was going nowhere.

In 2009, the Ford Motor Company dropped its plans to develop hydrogen cars, and the French automaker Renault-Nissan canceled its hydrogen car research efforts. A few months later, U.S. energy secretary Steven Chu announced that the government was cutting off funds for the development of hydrogen vehicles, because they would not be practical over the next few decades. Dr. Chu, a Nobel Prize winner for his work in physics, said the U.S. government preferred to focus on projects that could bear fruit in the foreseeable future.

WHATEVER HAPPENED TO PUBLIC TRANSPORTATION?

In 2009, *National Geographic* conducted an annual study measuring and monitoring consumer progress toward environmentally sustainable consumption in seventeen countries around the world. The resulting "Consumer Greendex" found that Americans ranked as the world's least green consumers. Not only did we score the lowest percentage on public transit use every day, but we also scored the highest percentage of people who never, ever, take public transit.

How did this happen? Are we Americans that antisocial? I don't think so. It's more a product of public policies that have had unintended consequences.

The Interstate Highway Act of 1956 produced an enormous network of highways across the United States. The largest public works project in American history to that date, it paid for a vast suburban road infrastructure, making commutes between the suburbs and urban centers much easier and far quicker. In part, the system was justified for reasons of national defense. It provided roads big enough to carry our tanks, in case the Russians invaded.

But it also had several unanticipated results. It furthered the flight of citizens, businesses, and investments from inner cities. It led to huge increases in the population of suburbs and a decline of walkable cities with good public transit systems. It greatly increased the use of petroleum and consequently the amount of air pollution. And it ushered in an auto age in which almost every transportation decision has been oriented around private cars and trucks driving on public highways.

The bias is built into our language. We speak of "investing" in highways and "investing" in freeways and parking spaces. But we "subsidize" trains and buses. Officials criticize bus, rail, and other public transportation alternatives for "losing money." Lost in this language is the fact that public transit is a civic necessity. Buses, railroads, and other forms of public transportation can no more "lose money" than roads and highways.

Today, with the exception of a few of our larger cities, most notably New York, U.S. public transit systems have been profoundly neglected. A third of all mass transit users in the entire United States use the New York City system, which is why New York is the only city in the country where more than half of the households don't own a car. There are a few other cities with significant systems—including Portland, Oregon, Washington, D.C., Chicago, and San Francisco—but even these are beset by serious problems. Most of the U.S. civic transportation systems are poorly functional at best and abysmal at worst. Even New York, widely acknowledged to have the best public transit system in the United States, falls far short compared to systems in Tokyo, Moscow, Taipei, London, Seoul, Paris, Hong Kong, Berlin, and Copenhagen.

Unfortunately, the lack of financial support for public transit in the United States has made us far more dependent on the automobile than is healthy or sustainable. And it has hurt, in particular, those among us who are the most vulnerable.

Who do you see standing by the bus stops of the nation, waiting without shade in the heat of the summer and without shelter in winter, for buses that may or may not come on time? You see people who are dependent on public transit to get to work, to markets, to school, to health care. You see those who are too young, too old, too sick, or too poor to drive. You see the elderly, the disabled, and the working poor. You see, disproportionately, people of color.

When Rosa Parks refused to sit at the back of a Montgomery, Alabama, bus in 1955, she sparked one of the greatest social changes in American history. We can all be grateful that people of color are no longer physically relegated to the back of the bus. But it's unfortunately true that today, thanks to a pattern of continually shorting public transportation in favor of the private vehicle, Rosa Parks might find bus service to be unreliable or even nonexistent in her community. Or she might find the bus passengers to be only people of color.

Public transit in the United States has not always been so neglected. In the 1920s and 1930s, almost every town in the country had a light-rail system trolley service. Mass transit was convenient, cheap, and plentiful.

But in the years between 1936 and 1950, there took place one of the sorriest events in our nation's history—what has become known as the "Great American Streetcar Scandal." A number of large corporations, including General Motors, Firestone Tire, Standard Oil of California, and Phillips Petroleum, operating secretly through front organizations, conspired to purchase streetcar systems in forty-five major U.S. cities, including Detroit, New York City, Oakland, Philadelphia, Phoenix, St. Louis, Salt Lake City, Tulsa, Baltimore, Chicago, Minneapolis, and Los Angeles. The consortium then proceeded to completely dismantle the trolley systems, ripping up their tracks and tearing down their overhead wires.

For this, General Motors and its corporate allies were indicted in 1947 on federal antitrust charges. For two years, the workings of the conspiracy and its underlying intentions were exposed in federal court. Eventually, despite being represented by the best attorneys money could buy, the defendants were found guilty by the federal jury.

Amazingly, the executives who secretly contrived and carried out the demolition of America's light-rail network were fined a grand total of one dollar each. Having destroyed the mass transit network that would otherwise have been their competition, the auto and oil companies quickly acquired dominion over the transportation policies of the country. The subsequent rise of the car culture and the abandonment of public transit in the United States were made possible by a series of public policy decisions that benefited the very industries—big oil and big auto—that had conspired to destroy the country's light-rail service.

To cite one prime example: Lobbyists from the oil and auto industries persuaded state and federal agencies to assume responsibility for the tremendous expenses involved in building and maintaining roads. This created the illusion that driving was much less costly than using public transport. If the auto and oil companies had been required to pay even part of the cost of roads, just as trolley companies had to pay to lay and maintain track, the true cost of the private automobile would have been more apparent, and public transportation would never have been suppressed.

Another example: Governments at every level have required businesses, as a condition of their licenses and permits, to provide ample parking spaces. What if instead local zoning ordinances required workplaces to be located within walking distance of public transit?

One final example: It has long been considered a basic legal principle that if a product causes harm by design, the producer may be held legally responsible. And it's well known that rates of cancer, asthma, emphysema, and other lung diseases are higher in smoggy cities and worse yet in neighborhoods that include heavily trafficked highways. Why, then, has no car or oil company ever had to pay a cent to cover the medical costs their products have caused? Instead, points out the Pulitzer Prize–winning author Edward Humes, "Consumers and, ultimately, taxpayers have always footed that bill—a subsidy worth trillions of dollars" to the car and oil industries.

In the last fifty years, the federal government has invested more than $1 trillion in auto-dominated transportation, and the states have invested considerably more. Today, construction of a single mile of freeway can cost as much as $130 million.

In the old good life, cars and highways reigned supreme. For almost a century, General Motors acted as a corporate champion of the old good life, and so nothing could have signaled more powerfully the crumbling of the way of life it came to represent than the company's descent into bankruptcy in 2009. It marked the end of an entire era.

Now we're seeing where our obsession for the private car and truck has taken us—into gridlock, pollution, and dependence on imported oil. We've come to a turning point in history, in which serious questions are ours to answer. How can we best support alternative modes of transportation that are better for the environment and for public health? How can we create climate- and community-friendly transportation systems?

What if we created public policies that made plug-in hybrids and all-electric cars affordable? What if we built truly high-speed rail systems, including magnetically levitated (maglev) trains that can travel at half the speed of airplanes while burning far less fuel and generating much less pollution?

We could develop cities that are walkable and bicycle friendly, and we could create public transit systems that are efficient and enjoyable. We could become a society that no longer leads the world in producing greenhouse gases and no longer leads all other industrialized nations in neglect for public transit. Instead, we could lead the way toward transportation policies and behaviors that support a thriving economy and quality of life, while contributing to healthy communities, clean air, and a stable climate.

MOVING FORWARD

The bus system in Curitiba, Brazil, provides a splendid example of what is possible when a government truly gets behind public transportation. Residents of Curitiba say the bus system plays a huge role in making their city livable and joyful. The buses run reliably and frequently, in some cases as often as every ninety seconds. The stations are convenient, well-designed, comfortable, and attractive. As a result, the city of Curitiba, with a population of more than two million, has one of the most heavily used yet lowest cost public transit systems in the world. Nearly three-quarters of the city's commuters use the bus system to get to and from work. The city's streets are stunningly free of congestion, and the air is nearly pollution-free.

Another example is the subway system in Hong Kong. It's so well designed that it attracts 90 percent of all the city's travel. Seven million daily riders take advantage of this clean, speedy, and economical way to move around the city.

In Japan, bullet trains traveling at speeds up to 190 miles per hour carry almost a million passengers a day. On some of the most heavily used intercity lines, trains depart every three minutes. Late arrivals are rare, and when they occur the average delay is only six seconds. Over the last four decades, Japan's trains have carried billions of passengers in great comfort without a single casualty.

In London, England, concerns about traffic congestion and air pollution led officials in 2003 to institute a charge on vehicles entering the city center. By 2007, trips into the city by personal vehicle had dropped 36 percent, while those by bus had increased 31 percent. Trips into the city on bicycles had increased a staggering 66 percent.

What can be done in the United States? Even though public transit has been so often neglected, there is still a platform to build on as we go forward. At present, fifteen U.S. cities have subway systems, thirty-two have light-rail systems, and many thousands have bus service. Greyhound connects 3,700 U.S. cities, and Amtrak operates more than one thousand U.S. stations. Mass transit use is beginning to rise, fueled at least in part by the volatile price of gasoline. In 2008, the number of U.S. passenger vehicle miles driven fell 3.6 percent, while the number of trips taken on mass transit increased by 4 percent, reaching 10.2 billion—its highest number in fifty-two years.

It remains unfortunately true that public transportation often takes longer than driving a private automobile, particularly in regions where public transportation spending has not been made a government priority. But mass transit may be more enjoyable than many of us realize. One family I know relies almost entirely on bus service for all their transportation needs. The mom told me that she has wonderful conversations with her children while riding the bus. They talk about whatever they want to, including the people and things they see along the way. She said she enjoys these conversations far more than she did when she was driving because her attention isn't split. And she has been highly encouraged by how her kids have responded to having her undivided attention.

Mass transit may also be more available than many of us think. A service from Google makes public transportation more accessible than ever for residents of more than four hundred cities in over thirty-one countries. By logging on to http://maps.google.com you can click on the "Get Directions" button, click on the "By car" tab, and scroll from there to "By public transportation." Then just type in your starting point and intended destination, click on "Show options" to enter your intended departure or arrival time, and if you are in one of the covered regions, you will be given multiple public transportation options for the journey, with precise timing data. In many areas you will also be told the total cost of the trip and how this compares to what you would have spent driving it, based on the average per-mile cost of driving a private automobile. In most cases, you will find that the total cost is only a fraction of the driving cost.

The U.S. automobile obsession has taken a terrible toll, but the new good life presents opportunities to create more satisfying and beautiful lives. When you walk, bike, use public transit, carpool, drive fuel-efficient vehicles, and/or arrange your life so that you drive less, you save money, get more exercise, and are able to interact socially with your fellow human beings. You restore vital connections with people, nature, and community. And you participate in something much bigger. You join the effort to reduce our national dependence on foreign oil, to cut down on air pollution, and to slow global warming.

More than forty years ago, Dr. Martin Luther King, Jr., described one of the foremost problems with the old good life. "We are prone," he said, "to judge success by the index of our salaries or the size of our automobile rather than by the quality of our service and relationship to mankind."

The cost of such thinking has been staggering. But we are now truly at a turning point in history. Our task and our adventure is to learn how to live within our means and within the means of nature. Our calling is to learn how to walk—and ride—lightly on the earth.

SIX

Eating Better, Spending Less

After housing and transportation, food is the largest expense incurred by most people. And as you will soon see, food is also an area with far greater environmental implications than most people recognize.

In the face of ever escalating food costs, is there anything you can do to reduce what you pay for food? You bet there is. I'll show you how in a moment. And what's more remarkable is that you can lower the price you pay for food while eating more healthfully and without sacrificing flavor or enjoyment. You don't need to be rich to eat well.

If you're perplexed about just which foods are healthiest, you aren't alone. We are all constantly bombarded with the latest diet of the month, with each passing fad claiming to have The Answer. Meanwhile, we're also barraged by food ads from companies all wanting us to eat more of the products they sell. The results are costly on many fronts: a great deal of confusion, ever-expanding waistlines, and ever-growing rates of heart disease, cancer, high blood pressure, and diabetes. These chronic diseases—and the enormous suffering and financial costs they carry—are classic illustrations of why the old good life wasn't really so great.

We all know that there are diseases of poverty that take a heavy toll among people with inadequate nutrition and poor sanitation. Less often recognized is that there are also diseases of affluence that afflict people who eat too much of the wrong foods. In fact, these afflictions—which include obesity, cancer, heart disease, and diabetes—are so tightly linked to eating habits that they are now being referred to in the scientific literature as "diseases of nutritional extravagance."

Beyond a certain point, there actually seems to be an inverse relationship between the amount of money we spend on food and the health we experience as a result. This inverse correlation is so telling that you could argue that money could be considered an enabler, something that permits and even encourages unhealthy lifestyle choices. This includes rich desserts, highly processed foods, and meat products high in saturated fat. Money can enable addictions to high-fat and high-sugar foods that provide far more calories than they do nutrients.

One of my relatives is a good example of this problem. He is clearly overweight, and he spends a great deal of his money on foods that aren't healthy. When I've asked him about this, he answers that through his employment he has excellent health insurance. I'm glad he does, and I hope he is able to retain his job and his benefits in the coming years. But isn't it part of the old thinking to believe that we can consume more than is healthy, and if we become ill, then a doctor will make it all better? If we believe, as my relative seems to, that doctors and modern medicine will be there to rescue us when we become sick, I'm afraid we may be in for a rude and painful surprise. There is not a pill for every ill. And "MD" does not stand for "medical deity."

Some people try to save money on their food bills by collecting coupons from newspaper ads and other sources and basing their purchases on them. I don't do this myself, and I don't recommend it as a rule, for a reason. Most of these coupons are for brand-name products and highly processed foods (that have been highly marked up in the first place), and these are not healthy choices. And besides, there are far better ways to save money on food—ways that steer you toward the healthiest of foods rather than those that compromise your commitment to taking care of yourself.

Some of the steps I'm about to recommend may be familiar to you. Others may be new. Some of them may seem simple to accomplish; others may take more effort. You don't have to implement all of them at once in order to save dramatically on your food bills and your medical bills. Just use the ones you can. The important thing isn't how large the first steps you take are. It's that you keep moving in the right direction.

PRINCIPLES OF HEALTHY AND INEXPENSIVE EATING

If you follow these principles, you can cut your food bills, maximize flavor and nutrition, and contribute to a longer and far healthier life.

- **Eat low on the food chain.** There are so many advantages to eating low on the food chain that this is truly one of the fundamental keys to the new good life. A plant-based diet with an abundance of vegetables, fruits, and whole grains typically costs 25 percent less than a diet that revolves around meat. Plus, when you eat more plant foods and fewer foods derived from animals, there is less saturated fat in your bloodstream. This results in cleaner and more open arteries, a happier cardiovascular system, higher levels of oxygen and nutrients getting to your brain and other organs, and a much lower incidence of heart disease. As well, when you eat fewer animal products you expose your cells to fewer environmental toxins, since these chemical evildoers build up in increasingly higher concentrations as they work their way up the food chain. People who eat plant-based diets are slimmer and healthier than the norm. They save money on food and have greatly reduced medical bills.
- **Avoid food that travels the globe.** When you select vegetables and fruits that are in season and locally grown, you will be eating produce at its tastiest, freshest, most nutritious—and least expensive. Depending on where you live, you probably won't eat cherries in January or watermelon in February, but that's not a great loss because even the most expensive fruits taste poor when they're not in season because they've been picked unripe. Transported thousands of miles, they carry a fat carbon footprint along with their higher price tag.
- **Shop on the outside aisles of your grocery store.** That's where you'll generally find the freshest and healthiest foods. And that way you'll avoid the highly processed foods that are typically found in the center aisles of supermarkets.

- **Don't buy foods with too many ingredients.** The longer the list of ingredients on a package, the more likely it is to be expensive and unhealthy. This is particularly true if the list includes chemicals you don't know how to pronounce.
- **Don't buy foods that are advertised.** Food companies advertise most heavily those products with the highest profit margins, and almost without exception these turn out to be the most highly processed foods.
- **Beware of fake "health" foods.** As the health food movement has grown, many packaged products have appeared that are highly processed and are not particularly good for you. Just because a product is made with soy, or sold in a health food store, or claims to be "all natural," doesn't mean it is truly wholesome. Many such processed food products are quick, tasty, and convenient ways to empty your wallet and undermine your health.
- **Bulk is best.** Most natural food stores, and increasing numbers of supermarkets, now have bulk bins. You can often save more than 30 percent by buying in bulk rather than purchasing prepackaged items. Grains, seeds, nuts, dried fruit, and nutritional yeast are just some of the many foods that are often available in bulk bins. This may seem like an unusual way to shop, but, in fact, it's the way people have shopped throughout most of shopping history. It's only fairly recently that we started packaging so many food products, a practice that has been to the great detriment of the environment and our bank accounts.
- **Defend yourself from end-of-aisle and checkout displays.** Supermarket executives know that impulse buys make up about 60 percent of total purchases. They also know that end-of-aisle displays are particularly effective in generating impulse buys, and checkout displays (typically for candy and magazines) generate even higher rates of impulsivity. They bank on the knowledge that the more often we walk past these displays, the more likely we'll spend more than we intended. Analyzing our habits and recording our purchases, they've made a science out of luring us to buy things we don't need. You'll be less vulnerable to their efforts if you're aware of what they're doing and if you eat before shopping. If you shop for food when you're hungry, you're more susceptible to their pre-

dations. Making thoughtful shopping lists also helps to curb impulse buying. If you like to experiment with new products, try limiting yourself to one or two per shopping trip. This works very well with children, too. If they know they can buy something up to a few dollars, they stop their endless requests for everything that looks bright and colorful. Parents can simply say, "If you want to get this, then you have to put the other one back."

- **Reduce the number of trips you make to the store.** For some families, a trip to the grocery store is a daily activity. They don't realize how costly this can be—in time spent waiting in line, in gas, and in increased rates of impulse buying. If you plan ahead, and particularly if you have and make good use of a freezer, you can trim your food shopping to once a week or less. The less frequently you shop, the less you'll spend.

  On the other hand, if you happen to live within close walking distance of your food store, you can adopt the European way of shopping almost every day for just what you'll be eating that day, which enables you to use produce that is as fresh as possible. Of course, the Europeans who use this shopping strategy are either walking, biking, or taking public transportation to their markets.

- **Shop at farmers markets.** By buying direct from the growers you save money, and you just about guarantee that your food purchases are at their peak of freshness, flavor, and nutritional value. To save even more money, shop at the end of the market when many farmers will give you a great price on whatever they have left. (They don't want to take their unsold produce back home with them.) Just ask if they have any "end of market" specials.

- **Prepare more of your meals at home.** This is a cornerstone of the new good life. It's a great way to save money and become more self-reliant. The average person in the United States spends more than a third of their food dollars on restaurants and fast food. If you eat most of your meals at home, you'll typically spend 40 percent less on your overall food expenditures compared to people who eat out frequently. Plus, you'll have more connection to your family, and maybe even smarter kids. According to Barbara Kingsolver, "A survey of National Merit scholars—exceptionally successful eighteen-year-olds crossing all lines of ethnicity, gender, geography, and class—turned up a common thread in their lives: the habit of sitting down to a family dinner table."

Of course, people can also have meaningful dinner conversations and feel connected to their families sitting at a restaurant table. But there seems to be something about the process of cooking for yourself, and possibly preparing the meals together with other family members, combined with being in the comfort and privacy of your own home, that helps families to feel their bonds with one another.

- **Leftovers are great.** Somehow we have developed a cultural stigma against eating leftovers. Perhaps that stems from the days before refrigeration, when leftover food could quickly spoil and become a health hazard. Today, though, it makes no sense to waste food. Rather than squandering leftovers, make something original from them. Look upon them as saving you time and money. In fact, you can create leftovers deliberately by making extra when you prepare a meal. In our family, we sometimes make a triple-sized recipe, and then have several meals ready to go. We also make big, hearty, and delicious stews using all the various leftovers in the fridge. The stew provides some ready-to-go food that we can keep in the fridge for the next few days. Or we can freeze a few meals' worth that we can later reheat for meals any time we need them. When fruit is getting overripe, we make smoothies, stale bread can get cubed into a soup or casserole, and overripe tomatoes make good tomato sauce.
- **Take a free lunch.** They say there's no free lunch, but when you take your lunch it almost is. Even a cheap fast food lunch can cost five dollars; packing up some leftovers from last night's dinner costs almost nothing.
- **Spice it up.** Herbs and spices are wonderful ways to add a rich variety of interesting flavors and aromas to foods that you prepare. In many traditional cultures, spices serve as an inexpensive way to turn basic, economical ingredients into appetizing fare. In the Western diet, we've been able to afford to use large quantities of fat and sugar as our primary spices. But what a cost we've paid in terms of our health! Many herbs and spices, in contrast, have remarkable medicinal value. Turmeric (an ingredient in most cur-

ries), for example, is a marvelous anti-inflammatory, rivaling ibuprofen and aspirin. Some herbs and spices may be costly per ounce, but you use only small amounts so it doesn't amount to that much (unless you buy saffron, which I don't, because this is one spice that can be ridiculously expensive).

- **Plan ahead.** If you head off to a day at work without packing lunch, chances are you'll be eating out within a few hours. If you wind up having to get dinner on the table in five minutes, you'll tend toward convenience foods that are ready to go, and most of these are less nutritious and more expensive than traditional foods. Putting a pot of whole grain rice on the stove, or some potatoes in the oven, doesn't take long, but it has to be done an hour before you plan to eat if it's going to be ready when you want it. Some ovens, rice cookers, and slow cookers have timers that let you set the cook time in advance. Or food can be cooked a day ahead and stored in the fridge so it is ready with a few minutes of warming.

- **Eat out consciously.** Preparing your own food is a huge money saver, yet you may still choose to dine out occasionally. When you do, you can cut down on appetizers, fancy desserts, and expensive wines. This will cut your dinner bill in half and still allow you to enjoy the pleasures of a delicious meal prepared for you by a talented chef and served by friendly staff. Keep your money circulating in your community by dining at family-owned restaurants rather than chains. Choose to eat at restaurants that use fresh, nutritious, locally grown ingredients.

- **Avoid fast food—it costs more than you think.** Most people know that fast food is unhealthy, but they underestimate just how bad it can be. In the documentary film *Super Size Me,* Morgan Spurlock ate all his meals at McDonald's for a month. He underwent extensive medical testing before, during, and after the experiment, and the results were horrible. Three weeks along, his physicians implored him to stop because he was risking permanent damage to his liver and his heart. Fast food is cheap, but only in the short term. The long-term health implications are beyond expensive. A Harvard study found that medical bills are the leading cause of bankruptcies.

- **Eat the way gourmets around the world eat.** It can be an adventure to experience gourmet cuisines from other cultures, and it's often a cost-effective and healthy way to go. Most of the world can't afford to destroy their health with an American-style diet. Almost no one else eats as high on the food chain as Americans do, which is one of the primary reasons the United States spends far more on health care than any other nation.

- **Watch the booze.** When a team of researchers from the University of Utah analyzed how ten thousand people in the United States spent their food dollars, they found that 7 percent spent more than a third of their food budget on alcohol. I love a bottle of beer or a glass of wine as much as anyone, but too much is as bad for your wallet as it is for your liver. A close friend of mine has a strong family history of alcoholism. She has created two rules to limit her consumption: She never drinks alone, and she never drinks when she's upset or unhappy.

- **Steer clear of soft drinks.** The average American today drinks about fifty-five gallons of soda pop a year, at a cost of more than $500 annually. And that's just the obvious cost. What are the hidden costs? A single twelve-ounce can of soda pop contains thirteen teaspoons of sugar (usually in the form of high-fructose corn syrup). Fifty-five gallons—the average American's annual consumption—contain more than seventy pounds of sugar. How bad is this? The sugar in soft drinks supplies 7 percent of the calories Americans consume. That is more than we get from vegetables.

- **Think outside the bottle.** Bottled water is one of the greatest marketing coups of the last hundred years. The next time you are tempted to shell out two dollars to quench your momentary thirst, you might remember that most bottled water (including Aquafina, Dasani, and many other brands) is just filtered tap water that's been put in a bottle.

  If your tap water smells or tastes bad, or if you have reason to be suspicious about its safety, you can invest in a point-of-use filter, the kind you install on your faucet or under your sink. Then rather than buying bottled water, you can filter it yourself and carry a water bottle, sparing the environment in the process. How fast will that pay for itself? Based on the average cost of tap water in the United States, eight glasses a day comes to about forty-nine cents a year. Buy that water in Evian or Fiji bottles and you'd be spending $1,400. (If ever again you're tempted to buy a bottle of Evian, remember that Evian spelled backward is "naïve.")

In many ways, bottled water strikes me as symbolic of the old good life and illustrative of why we so urgently need to put it behind us. Like many aspects of the old good life, bottled water is expensive, it's environmentally destructive (think of billions of nonbiodegradable plastic bottles being shipped all over the planet), and it's mostly hype. The bottled water industry promotes an image of purity, but in 2008 the Environmental Working Group released a comprehensive study that found a surprising array of chemical contaminants—including cancer-causing chemicals, disinfection by-products, fertilizer residue, and pain medication—in every bottled water brand tested.

- **Grow your own.** Growing some of your own food can be as straightforward as putting a parsley plant and a few green onions in pots near a sunny window, or as elaborate as planting a garden. If you have space, consider planting dark green-leafed vegetables such as chard, kale, and collards. They are among the easiest vegetables to grow, don't require much fertilizer, and deliver an amazing amount of nutrients per square foot.

  During World War II, twenty million Americans planted home vegetable gardens—called "victory gardens"—that produced 40 percent of all the vegetable produce consumed nationally. People dug up lawns to plant vegetables and planted food crops in backyards and in vacant lots. In 2009, with the assistance of elementary schoolchildren from Washington, D.C., Michelle Obama broke ground for the first vegetable garden at the White House since World War II. As per the First Lady's instructions, the garden was entirely organic.

THE GOOD LIFE DOESN'T HAVE TO COST THE PLANET

It's important to be thrifty and save. But a truly fulfilling life requires more than frugality. It also requires, I believe, a sense of purpose that is connected to something greater than ourselves. For me, this means living with gratitude and respect for all life, caring for others, and being part, if I can, of restoring the earth.

For the ten years that my wife, Deo, and I lived on an island off the coast of British Columbia, we grew 90 percent of our own food. Everything we grew was entirely organic. Although the phrase "carbon foot-print" didn't exist back then, ours was very small.

We had no livestock because we didn't want to kill animals for food, since there was other food we could grow or buy that provided all the nourishment we needed. Some may think I am overly sentimental, but I've known too many animals who've felt like family to me. When I see a wild bird in flight, my instinct is not to grab a gun to shoot and kill it. My desire is to appreciate its beauty and understand its place in the web of life.

In the years since our time on the island, I've learned a great deal about how animals are treated in modern factory farms, and what I've learned has changed me yet again. I won't describe it in gory detail, because you've probably seen pictures or heard stories of how bad it is—of the concentration camp conditions these animals are forced to endure. But I will tell you that in reality it's every bit as bad as—or worse than—you've heard.

All of the animals involved in modern meat production—cattle, pigs, chickens, turkeys, and so forth—are kept in conditions that violate their essential natures, that frustrate even their most basic needs, that cause them incomprehensible suffering. You don't have to be a vegetarian, nor even a particularly compassionate person, to be disgusted by the level of cruelty that takes place every day in modern meat production. Julia Child, the famous chef, author, and TV personality, used to dismiss vegetarians as sappy. But when, late in her life, I took her to visit a veal production facility, she was horrified by what she saw. "I had no idea it was so severe," she told me.

All this leaves me with a question that I think we need, as a society, to ask: How is it that we call some animals "pets," lavish our love on these animals, and get so much in return—and yet then we turn around and call other animals "dinner" and feel justified, by virtue of this semantic distinction, in treating these animals with any level of cruelty so long as it lowers the price per pound?

The cruelties inherent in modern meat production are so intense that it's hard to eat these products and honor compassion at the same time. If you eat any kind of meat, you might want to purchase products that you know to be truly free-range and organic, such as those with the "Animal Compassion" logo from Whole Foods Market.

Because I so deeply deplore cruelty to animals, and I've been publicly active in bringing attention to the systematic cruelty in modern meat production, people often ask me if my reluctance to eat meat stems from ethical reasons. Yes, it does, and yet over the years I've learned something else that has also affected me greatly. As a concerned citizen of our beautiful but endangered planet, I want to do whatever I can to help protect the fragile biosystems on which so much depends, so that your children and mine, and all generations yet to come, might have a chance for a viable future.

What does that have to do with eating meat? A lot more than you might think. In 2006, the Food and Agriculture Organization (FAO) of the United Nations released a seminal report titled *Livestock's Long Shadow.* The report states that meat production is the second or third largest contributor to environmental problems at *every* level and at *every* scale, from global to local. It is a primary culprit in land degradation, air pollution, water shortage, water pollution, species extinction, loss of biodiversity, and climate change. Henning Steinfeld, a senior author of the report, stated, "Livestock are one of the most significant contributors to today's most serious environmental problems. Urgent action is needed to remedy the situation."

As Ezra Klein wrote in *The Washington Post* in 2009, "The evidence is strong. It's not simply that meat is a contributor to global warming; it's that it is a huge contributor. Larger, by a significant margin, than the global transportation sector."

In his influential documentary *An Inconvenient Truth,* Al Gore presents a compelling argument for the seriousness of human-induced global warming. But for some reason he asks us to change our lightbulbs while never asking us to change our diets. Seeing this omission, I've realized how deeply we are conditioned to think of meat eating as the reward for affluence and how difficult it can be to question it. Meat eating has held such a central place in the old good life that it can just slip by, unquestioned.

But question it we must if we are going to take seriously our responsibility to the planet. Cattle are notorious for producing methane, which is one of the four primary greenhouse gases. You may find it difficult to take cow burps and flatulence seriously, but livestock emissions are no joke. Methane comes from both ends of the cow in such enormous quantities that scientists seriously view it as one of the greatest threats to our earth's climate.

And there's more. The FAO report states that livestock production generates 65 percent of the nitrous oxide (another extremely potent greenhouse gas) produced by human activities. The FAO concludes that overall, livestock production is responsible for 18 percent of greenhouse gas emissions, a bigger share than all the SUVs, cars, trucks, buses, trains, ships, and planes in the world combined.

Similarly, a 2009 report published in *Scientific American* remarked that "producing beef for the table has a surprising environmental cost: it releases prodigious amounts of heat-trapping greenhouse gases." The greenhouse gas emissions from producing a pound of beef, the study found, are fifty-eight times greater than those from producing a pound of potatoes.

Some people thought the Live Earth concert handbook was exaggerating when it stated that, "Refusing meat is the single most effective thing you can do to reduce your carbon footprint," but it wasn't. This is literally true. Even Environmental Defense, a group that was called George W. Bush's favorite environmental group for its less-than-radical stands, calculates that if every meat eater in the United States swapped just one meal of chicken per week for a vegetarian meal, the carbon savings would be equivalent to taking half a million cars off the road.

People have begun comparing eating little or no animal products with driving a Prius ("Vegetarianism is the new Prius") and likewise compared eating meat with driving a Hummer. But this comparison, as striking as it is, actually understates the amount of greenhouse gases that stem from meat. In 2006, a University of Chicago study found that a vegan diet is far more effective than driving a hybrid car in reducing our carbon footprint. Scientists who have done the calculations say that a Prius driver who consumes a meat-based diet actually contributes more to global warming than a Hummer driver who eats low on the food chain.

Then, in late 2009, Worldwatch Institute published a seminal report that took things further. The thoughtful and meticulously thorough study, written by World Bank agricultural scientist Robert Goodland, who spent twenty-three years as the Bank's lead environmental adviser, and Jeff Anhang, an environmental specialist for the Bank, came to the conclusion that animals raised for food account for more than half of all human-caused greenhouse gases. Eating plants instead of animals, the authors state, would be by far the most effective strategy to reverse climate change, because it "would have far more rapid effects on greenhouse gas emissions and their atmospheric concentrations—and thus on the rate that the climate is warming—than actions to replace fossil fuels with renewable energy."

I often see very well-intentioned people going to all sorts of lengths to live a greener lifestyle. It's sadly ironic that they sometimes ignore what would be the single most effective thing they could be doing. If we are really committed to saving the environment we need to know where our leverage is. We need to focus on where we can get the most benefit. Eating lower on the food chain is a real boon to the whole earth community. The good life doesn't have to cost the planet.

The question we will collectively answer with our lives in the coming years is this: Are we going to take the earth's needs into account, or are we going to indulge our appetites without regard for the impact we're having on the environment?

The Fourth Assessment Report of the Intergovernmental Panel on Climate Change, which was released at the end of 2007, was the largest and most detailed summary of the climate change situation ever undertaken. Its authors included thousands of scientists from dozens of countries. It unequivocally predicted serious risks and damages to species, ecosystems, human infrastructure, societies, and livelihoods in the future unless drastic action to reduce warming was taken.

Summarizing our current predicament, the Worldwatch Institute says that if we do not radically change course, "Children born today will find their lives preoccupied with a host of hardships created by an inexorably warming world. Food supplies will be diminished and many of the world's forests will be destroyed. Not just the coral reefs that nurture many fisheries but the chemistry of the oceans will face disruption."

And one more thing: We all know that everyone needs to eat, but we tend to overlook the fact that it's not efficient to cycle grain through animals. The production of a pound of feedlot beef requires sixteen pounds of corn and soybeans. That's why the noted author Frances Moore Lappé called modern meat production "a protein factory in reverse." From the point of view of world hunger, if you feed corn and soybeans to livestock, you're actually wasting most of the protein and other nutrients that you've grown. If you think about the vast numbers of people who are starving on our planet, it begins to look like a crime against humanity to take 80 percent of the corn and soybeans grown in the U.S. today and feed it to livestock. But that is exactly what we are doing, so we can have cheap meat. Cheap, that is, if you don't count the human suffering that is and will be caused by climate deterioration, the cruelty to billions of animals, and the unmet food needs of hundreds of millions of people.

It's striking to me how much correlation there is between the food choices that are the healthiest, those that are the least expensive, and those that are most socially and environmentally responsible. It is a fact of singular significance today that eating lower on the food chain— eating more plants and fewer animals—addresses all of these goals in a positive way.

While efforts to use government as an agent of social change don't have the best reputation, this could be an instance in which such an approach might be useful. Since we have taxes, why don't we tax the things that are bad for the world and use some of that money to lower the price of things that are good? This would be a revenue-neutral way of fostering a better world. For example, what if we taxed agrochemicals and used the revenue to subsidize organic and other safe forms of growing food? What if we taxed junk food and used the income to subsidize fresh fruits and vegetables? What if we taxed white bread and used the revenue to lower the price of whole wheat bread? What if we taxed products that are responsible for a disproportionate share of greenhouse gases, such as meat, and used the money to subsidize vegetable gardens and fruit orchards in every school and neighborhood in the country?

The results would be impressive: We'd have genuinely happy meals, because we'd be eating far better and at far less expense. We'd be so much healthier as people that what we'd save in medical bills would go a long way toward solving the crisis in the health care system. And we'd dramatically reduce our emissions of greenhouse gases and thus have a more stable climate.

TWELVE NUTRITIONALLY RICH AND INEXPENSIVE FOODS

Most lists of the healthiest foods feature wild salmon and blueberries. That's great if you're an Alaskan bear and you find them in the wild, but for most humans such foods are quite expensive.

Here are twelve foods that can give you much pleasure, that can bring you vibrant wellness, that can be produced without cruelty to animals or harm to the earth, that don't require excessive resources, and that don't cost an arm and a leg.

Since many of us have never learned (or have forgotten) how to prepare and enjoy these wonderful foods, I've provided some recipes. And I've made sure that all the ingredients in each recipe are both nutritious and inexpensive.

Popcorn: Surprisingly Healthy

Popcorn was originally discovered by Native Americans, but it didn't become fashionable as a snack food in the United States until the Great Depression, when its low cost and high nutritional value made it popular. Countless businesses failed during the 1930s, but the popcorn business thrived and helped to save many family farms as it became a source of income for struggling farmers.

Air-popped popcorn is an inexpensive whole grain product that is low in calories and a great source of fiber. It's also a good source of protein, vitamins B1 and B2, and iron. Weight Watchers recommends popcorn as a snack for the weight conscious; the American Dental Association endorses this sugar-free snack; and the American Cancer Society recognizes the benefits of the high fiber content of popcorn in helping to prevent several types of cancer.

Popcorn is a healthy food, but you need to beware of the large amounts of fat, sugar, and salt often added to commercial popcorn. In the mid-1990s, the Center for Science in the Public Interest analyzed the popcorn served in movie theaters. They found that most used coconut oil to pop the corn and then topped it with butter or margarine. "A medium-size buttered popcorn," the report concluded, "contains more fat than a breakfast of bacon and eggs, a Big Mac and fries, and a steak dinner combined."

Has commercial popcorn improved since then? Hardly. Today, a *small* popcorn from Regal Entertainment Group (the largest theater chain in the United States) contains as much saturated fat as three Big Macs.

There are two other caveats regarding popcorn. It's not a good food to serve children under the age of four because of the risk of choking. And microwaveable popcorn often contains various artificial flavoring agents, including the chemical diacetyl, which is commonly used to impart a buttery flavor. Diacetyl has been implicated in causing respiratory ailments and linked to severe lung disease.

This is not a problem, of course, if you pop your own popcorn using an inexpensive air popper, for then it's your choice what to add. Go easy on the fat; try adding nutritional yeast (see more on this below), cayenne, cumin seed powder, or other spices along with salt. Eat it fresh from the popper, and you'll have a fun, tasty, and healthy whole grain food that is so inexpensive it's sometimes used (such a waste) as packing material.

Quinoa: The Mother of All Grains

Pronounced "keen-wah," quinoa is the most easily digested of all whole grains and the least mucus forming, and it cooks quickly (in about twenty-five minutes). A cup of cooked quinoa has as much calcium as a quart of milk, in a more digestible form.

Quinoa is higher in protein than wheat, barley, corn, or rice. Among grains, only oats rival its protein content. And it's uniquely high in the particular amino acids that are often low in plant foods. It's a good source of lysine, for example, as well as the essential sulfur-bearing amino acids methionine and cystine. Quinoa is also an excellent source of phosphorus, vitamin E, several B vitamins, and minerals. It's gluten-free, which is a disadvantage in making bread but an advantage for those who are sensitive to gluten.

How is it, you may wonder, that quinoa is not better known in the modern Western world? The Incas held quinoa as sacred. They called it *chisaya mama,* the "mother of all grains," and used it as part of their religious ceremonies. When the Spanish colonists conquered South America, they actively suppressed quinoa as part of their efforts to stifle native spirituality and spread Christianity. But now it's making a comeback.

Cooked quinoa is a great ingredient in hot casseroles, soups, stews, stir-fries, or in cold salads. Dry-roasting quinoa in a pan or in the oven before cooking will add a toasted flavor.

Always store quinoa in your refrigerator. It's oils are uniquely nutritious, but they are also subject to spoilage if left too long in a warm envi-

QUINOA WITH WALNUTS

2 tablespoons olive oil

1 medium onion, chopped

1 celery stalk, chopped

1 medium carrot, chopped

6 button mushrooms, sliced

2 cups water

1 cup quinoa, soaked 5 minutes, rinsed, and drained

$\frac{1}{2}$ teaspoon black pepper

$\frac{1}{2}$ teaspoon dried rosemary

2 tablespoons soy sauce

$\frac{1}{2}$ cup chopped walnuts

$\frac{1}{4}$ cup chopped parsley

Heat the oil in saucepan over medium-high heat. Add the onion, celery, and carrot and cook, stirring, for about 5 minutes. Add the mushrooms and continue to cook, stirring, for 1 minute. Stir in the water, quinoa, pepper, rosemary, and soy sauce. Cover and bring to a boil, then turn down the heat and simmer for 25 minutes. Toss the cooked quinoa in a bowl with the walnuts and parsley. Serve hot or cold.

SERVES 4

ronment. If I had to choose one food to survive on for any length of time, it would probably be quinoa.

Flaxseeds: The "New" Wonder Food

Flaxseeds are getting a lot of press lately as the new wonder food. But they've been eaten by people for thousands of years. In fact, flax was one of the original "medicines" used by Hippocrates. By eating flax, you aren't conducting a risky, novel experiment. You're consuming one of the world's oldest, healthiest, and least expensive foods.

If flax is such a marvelous food source, how did it come to be so forgotten in the Western diet? It fell out of favor for the very reason it's so nutritious. The same nutrients that make flax so remarkable—its

FLAX 'N' CORN BREAD

½ cup frozen apple juice concentrate

½ cup flaxseeds

1½ cups soy milk

1 cup cornmeal

½ cup whole wheat pastry flour

½ teaspoon salt

1½ tablespoons baking powder, sifted

Allow the apple juice concentrate to soften at room temperature. Preheat the oven to 325 degrees Fahrenheit. Oil a 9 x 9-inch square or 10-inch round pan. Grind the flaxseeds in a coffee grinder. Empty the flaxseeds into a mixing bowl, whisk them thoroughly with the soymilk and apple juice concentrate, and set aside. In a separate bowl, mix the cornmeal, whole wheat pastry flour, salt, and baking powder. Pour the flax mixture into the dry ingredients, stirring well. Transfer into the oiled pan and bake for 1 hour, uncovered. Remove from the pan and cool before slicing.

SERVES 8

unique essential fatty acids—also give it a short shelf life. Oil manufacturers found other oils, with longer shelf lives, to be more profitable.

Among all foods, flaxseeds are the best source of a type of phytoestrogen called lignans, which have been shown to help prevent not only breast cancer, but also cancer of the prostate, uterus, and ovaries.

Among all the plant foods in the world, flaxseeds are also the richest source of omega-3 fatty acids. Why is this so important? Because most of us don't get nearly enough of this crucial nutrient.

There are two classes of fatty acids, omega-3 and omega-6 fatty acids, which must be in balance for you to be healthy. Before we relied so heavily on processed foods, human consumption of these two classes of fatty acids was roughly equal. But just about everyone eating a Western diet today gets far too much of the omega-6s and not nearly enough of the omega-3s. Many experts believe this imbalance to be at the root of a vast array of problems, including asthma, coronary heart disease, and many forms of cancer, autoimmunity, and neurodegenerative diseases.

The imbalance between omega-3 and omega-6 fatty acids is also believed to contribute to obesity, depression, dyslexia, hyperactivity, and even a tendency toward violence. Bringing the fats into proper proportion may actually help to relieve those conditions.

Eating wild salmon, at about fifteen dollars a pound, is one way to get your needed omega-3s. The other is to eat flaxseeds, at about two dollars a pound.

Keep flaxseeds refrigerated or frozen. Whole flaxseeds stay fresh for up to a year if stored correctly. In our household, we grind a few tablespoons in a designated coffee grinder every few days and keep the meal in the refrigerator. (Once the seeds are ground into a meal, they can go rancid quickly.) Sprinkle ground flax meal on cereals or salads, or mix them into casseroles.

Nutritional Yeast: A Nutrient Powerhouse

Nutritional yeast is a terrific addition to anyone's diet. It's an excellent source of protein, both because it contains more than any meat product and because it contains all of the essential amino acids. Particularly rich in lysine and tryptophan, it is an excellent complement to most grains.

Nutritional yeast is considered to be a "primary grown" yeast, which means that it is cultivated specifically for its nutritive value. It's also an "inactive yeast," which means that it has no leavening ability. People who have difficulty digesting yeasted or fermented foods usually have no problem with this product. It is gluten-free and *Candida albicans* negative, which means it is generally considered safe even for those with wheat allergies and those prone to yeast infections.

Nutritional yeast is not the same as baking yeast, which is used to leaven breads. Nor is it the same as brewer's yeast, which is a by-product of the beer industry. While brewer's yeast contains many nutrients, it carries the bitter flavor of the hops used in the brewing of beer. Nutritional yeast is also different from yeast extracts, which have strong flavors and typically come as dark brown pastes.

Nutritional yeast is an excellent source of B vitamins. It's also a great source of the trace mineral chromium, a nutrient the body requires to regulate blood sugar. For this reason, nutritional yeast can be very helpful to diabetics and to those with a tendency toward low blood sugar.

Nutritional yeast has long been popular with the health conscious,

PASTA AND YEAST "CHEESE" CASSEROLE

$3\frac{1}{2}$ cups brown rice penne pasta

$3\frac{1}{2}$ cups water

$\frac{3}{4}$ cup canola oil

$\frac{1}{2}$ cup whole wheat pastry flour

1 onion, chopped

2 cloves fresh garlic, peeled and crushed

$1\frac{1}{2}$ teaspoons salt

2 tablespoons soy sauce

Pinch of turmeric

Black pepper to taste

1 cup nutritional yeast flakes

Preheat the oven to 350 degrees Fahrenheit. Oil a 9 x 13-inch baking dish. Cook the pasta according to the directions on the package; rinse, drain, and set aside. Bring the water to a boil in a covered pot, reduce the heat, and keep simmering. Heat $\frac{1}{2}$ cup of the canola oil in a large saucepan over medium heat. Gradually stir the whole wheat pastry flour into the heated oil and whisk over medium heat until the "roux" is smooth and bubbling. Whisk in the heated water, then stir in the onion, garlic, salt, soy sauce, turmeric, and black pepper. Continue to cook, stirring, for 5 minutes, as the mixture thickens and boils. Whisk in the nutritional yeast and remaining $\frac{1}{4}$ cup canola oil. Mix $\frac{3}{4}$ of the sauce with the cooked pasta and spread into the baking dish. Pour the remainder of the sauce on top. Bake for 15 minutes, uncovered. Broil the top until light brown, 1 to 3 minutes.

SERVES 6

and it's time it became far more widely known and used. It has a distinctive flavor that many people enjoy. The flavor has been described as nutty or cheesy.

Nutritional yeast is available both in the form of yellow flakes and as a yellow powder similar in appearance and texture to a fine cornmeal. It can be found in the bulk aisle of most natural food stores. Stored in a cool, dry place, it keeps very well. In food preparation it is extremely versatile, with a wide variety of uses, as a flavoring and/or thickening agent in soups, sauces, salad dressings, cheesy spreads, casseroles, and more.

Sweet Potatoes: Nutritional All-Stars

Many of us know sweet potatoes as part of our holiday fare, but these naturally sweet tubers can easily be part of meals throughout the year. Their nutritive profile makes them part of any nutritional all-star team.

In 1992, the Center for Science in the Public Interest compared the nutritional value of a wide assortment of vegetables. Taking into account fiber content, complex carbohydrates, protein, vitamins A and C, iron, and calcium, the sweet potato ranked highest in nutritional value. According to these criteria, sweet potatoes earned 184 points, 100 points ahead of the common potato.

In addition, sweet potatoes contain unique root storage proteins that have been shown to have remarkable antioxidant properties. In one study, these proteins demonstrated one-third the antioxidant activity of glutathione. Glutathione is considered to be the most potent endogenous antioxidant in the human body.

Sweet potatoes are superb sources of vitamin A, very good sources of vitamin C and manganese, and good sources of dietary fiber, vitamin B6, potassium, iron, and copper. Their vitamin A levels are particularly outstanding. If you are or have been a smoker, or if you are frequently exposed to secondhand smoke, then regularly eating vitamin A–rich foods such as sweet potatoes can literally save your life. The bioavailability of the beta-carotene (provitamin A) in orange-fleshed sweet potatoes is higher even than that found in dark green leafy vegetables.

Purple-fleshed sweet potatoes have another set of nutritional attributes. They are good sources of anthocyanins, which are stunningly effective antioxidants. In one major study, purple sweet potatoes were found to have greater antioxidant properties than any other food tested.

Another advantage of sweet potatoes is that they grow well under a wide variety of farming conditions and have few natural enemies. Thus, pesticides are rarely used.

Baked sweet potatoes make wonderful "heat and serve" leftovers and are a great food to pack in to-go lunches. Don't forget to poke holes in the skin or they may explode.

SPICY SWEET POTATO BAKES

4 long, thin sweet potatoes

2 tablespoons olive oil

3 tablespoons paprika

$\frac{1}{2}$ teaspoon black pepper

$\frac{1}{2}$ teaspoon onion powder

$\frac{1}{2}$ teaspoon dried thyme

$\frac{1}{2}$ teaspoon dried rosemary

$\frac{1}{2}$ teaspoon garlic powder

$\frac{1}{4}$ teaspoon cayenne pepper

$\frac{1}{2}$ teaspoon salt

Preheat oven to 375 degrees Fahrenheit. Lightly oil a baking sheet or shallow pan. Cut the sweet potatoes in quarters lengthwise, then in half across the middle. Place the olive oil in a small bowl. Mix the spices and salt in another small bowl, then lay the mix out on a plate. Brush or rub each sweet potato piece lightly with olive oil from the small bowl. Roll each oiled piece on the spice plate, using your fingers to remove excess. Lay the pieces on the baking sheet or pan. Bake for 20 minutes on one side. Flip the pieces over and bake for another 20 minutes. Serve hot.

SERVES 4

Split Peas: Small but Mighty

Even if you are already a lover of split pea soup, you may not realize the many nutrients that inexpensive split peas provide. A small but nutritionally powerful member of the legume family, split peas are an excellent source of protein.

Split peas are also excellent sources of several important minerals and B vitamins, all with virtually no fat. They provide a type of insoluble fiber that increases stool bulk, prevents constipation, and helps prevent digestive disorders such as irritable bowel syndrome and diverticulosis. A single cup of cooked split peas provides 65 percent of the recommended daily allowance for fiber.

SPLIT PEA CABBAGE SOUP

Unlike traditional split pea soup, where the vegetables are cooked for a long time along with the split peas, the vegetables in this recipe are cooked separately to preserve their nutrients, then simmered with the peas before serving.

6 cups water
2 cups dry split peas, rinsed and drained
1 or 2 cloves fresh garlic, minced
1 onion, chopped
1 medium potato, chopped
2 medium carrots, chopped
3 stalks celery, chopped fine
8 ounces frozen corn, thawed
3 cups cabbage, shredded or chopped fine
6 mushrooms, sliced
2 teaspoons dried sage
$3/4$ teaspoon black pepper
$1/4$ cup soy sauce
1 (14-ounce) can diced tomatoes

In a large saucepan or soup pot combine the water, split peas, and garlic. Cover and bring to a boil. Reduce the heat and simmer for 1 hour and 15 minutes. Check the heat periodically to ensure the water is bubbling gently. (If it's too high, the peas will boil over.) Place the onion, potato, carrots, and celery in another large saucepan or soup pot with about an inch of water. Cover and cook on medium-high heat until the pot is full of steam. Reduce the heat and simmer for 8 minutes. Add the corn, cabbage, mushrooms, sage, pepper, and soy sauce. Turn up the heat until the pot is again full of steam. Reduce the heat and simmer for 8 minutes. Set aside until the peas are cooked. Add the tomatoes and cooked peas to the vegetables and heat altogether while stirring. Serve hot.

SERVES 8

Split peas have been shown to be of benefit in managing blood sugar levels. They contain large amounts of a particular type of fiber that prevents blood sugar levels from rising rapidly after a meal.

In a major study that examined food intake patterns and risk of death from coronary heart disease, researchers followed more than sixteen thousand men from many different countries. They found that legumes, including split peas, were associated with an 82 percent reduction in risk.

Some people are sensitive to sulfites, a type of preservative used in wine making, found in dried fruits, and commonly added to delicatessen salads and salad bars. People who are sensitive to sulfites may experience rapid heartbeat, headache, or confusion if they consume these foods. If you have ever reacted to sulfites, it could be because your molybdenum levels are low. Molybdenum, a trace mineral, is a crucial component of the enzyme sulfite oxidase, which the body uses to break down sulfites. Split peas are an outstanding source of molybdenum. A cup of split peas provides nearly 200 percent of the recommended daily allowance.

Split peas will keep for several months in an airtight container in a cool, dry, dark place. For longer storage, keep them refrigerated.

Lentils: Packed with Protein

Lentils have been part of the human diet since Neolithic times and may have been the first crop ever domesticated by humans. Traditionally, lentils have been venerated and included in the religious ceremonies of many cultures. Today, we know that with 26 percent protein, lentils have the third highest level of protein from any plant-based food, exceeded only by soybeans and hemp. And they are particularly good sources of two essential amino acids, isoleucine and lysine.

But as high as lentils are in protein, they are equally excellent sources of a number of other key nutrients. They are one of the best plant-based sources of iron and provide substantial quantities of dietary fiber, folate, B vitamins, and many other minerals. In 2006, *Health* magazine selected lentils as one of the world's five healthiest foods.

Lentils cook quickly. This is true for all lentils, but especially for small varieties with the husks removed, such as the common red lentil. They do well in slow cookers, but pressure cookers are not recommended, since the small lentils may clog the pressure relief valve.

TANGY LENTIL-BARLEY STEW

$\frac{1}{4}$ cup olive oil

$\frac{3}{4}$ cup chopped celery

$\frac{3}{4}$ cup chopped onion

1 cup chopped carrot

2 cloves fresh garlic, minced

6 cups water

$\frac{3}{4}$ cup lentils

$\frac{3}{4}$ cup barley

$\frac{1}{2}$ teaspoon dried rosemary

$\frac{1}{2}$ teaspoon dried oregano

$\frac{1}{2}$ teaspoon black pepper

1 (28-ounce) can diced tomatoes

2 tablespoons vegetable broth powder

In a large soup pot, heat the olive oil over medium-high heat. Add the celery, onion, carrot, and garlic, and cook, stirring, for about 5 minutes. Add the water, lentils, barley, rosemary, oregano, and pepper. Cover and bring to a boil, then the reduce heat and simmer for 45 minutes. Add the tomatoes and vegetable broth powder, and simmer for 15 minutes, stirring occasionally. Serve hot.

SERVES 6

The ancient Greeks told of a philosopher eating bread and lentils for dinner. He was approached by another man, who lived sumptuously by flattering the king. Said the flatterer, "If you would learn to be subservient to the king, you would not have to live on lentils." The philosopher replied, "If you would learn to live on lentils, you would not have to give up your independence in order to be docile and acquiescent to the king."

Sunflower Seeds: Far More Than a Snack

Sunflower seeds were once a staple food for many Native American tribes. They are one of the plant kingdom's most abundant sources of vi-

> ### OVEN-ROASTED SUNFLOWER SEEDS
>
> Preheat the oven to 375 degrees Fahrenheit. Spread the raw shelled seeds in a single layer on a cookie sheet, and place the cookie sheet on a middle rack in the oven. Roast for 6 to 8 minutes, until the seeds are golden brown. (They will continue to darken after you remove them, so remove them when they are a bit lighter than you want them.) Salt and season to taste.

tamin E, the human body's primary fat-soluble antioxidant. They are also good sources of vitamin B1, magnesium, manganese, copper, selenium, vitamin B5, and folate.

When vitamin E is absorbed by the human body from sunflower seeds, it neutralizes free radicals, thus protecting brain cells and cell membranes. Vitamin E from sunflower seeds also has significant anti-inflammatory effects that can reduce the symptoms of asthma, rheumatoid arthritis, and other conditions in which free radicals and inflammation play a major role. Sunflower seeds are so packed with vitamin E that a mere two ounces contain nearly 100 percent of the recommended daily allowance.

Though sunflower seeds are most commonly eaten as a healthy snack, they can be included in almost any meal and can be used as garnishes or as ingredients in almost any recipe. The seeds can also be sprouted and eaten in salads. You can enjoy them blended into a creamy base for soups or ground into sunflower butter, or you can munch them raw or lightly roasted. In our household, we roast them and then sprinkle them on hot breakfast cereals, in casseroles, and on salads, and we also just eat them by the handful.

Oats: Hearty, Satisfying, and Delicious

Most of us think of oats as food for horses and cattle, but that's a shame because oats are a wonderful food for people. Higher in protein than any other cereal grain except quinoa, oats also contain essential vitamins (particularly B1, B5, folic acid, and biotin) and minerals (including magnesium, calcium, selenium, manganese, iron, and copper).

NUTTY MORNING OATMEAL

The walnuts and cinnamon aren't added only for flavor. Oats are a comparatively low-glycemic index grain to begin with, but the addition of walnuts and cinnamon creates a nourishing breakfast with a very low glycemic index. This is a tasty and hearty breakfast that will provide you with consistent healthy blood sugar levels and give you plenty of energy all morning.

1 cup rolled oats (not the "quick cooking" or "instant" kind)
2½ cups water
½ teaspoon salt
½ teaspoon cinnamon
⅓ cup raisins
⅓ cup walnuts

Place the oats, water, salt, cinnamon, and raisins in a covered saucepan and bring to a boil. Turn down the heat and simmer for 10 minutes, stirring occasionally. Remove from the heat, stir in the walnuts, and serve hot.

SERVES 3

Oats have more soluble fiber than any other grain and are particularly high in beta-D-glucans, a soluble fiber that has been proven to lower LDL (bad) cholesterol and to reduce the risk of heart disease. In the 1980s, a series of studies found oats to be so heart healthy that there ensued what can only be called an oat bran craze. Oat bran was added to all kinds of foods, including potato chips, which were then claimed to be health foods. Sadly, much of the oats people consume today is in sugary ready-to-eat cereals such as Cap'n Crunch, Froot Loops, and Lucky Charms.

Of course, merely adding oats or oat bran to an unhealthy diet isn't enough. But regular consumption of the soluble fiber in oats, along with a diet low in saturated fat and cholesterol, has been shown to be an effective way to reduce the risk of heart disease.

Oats are also significant sources of phytoestrogens, which have been linked to decreased risk of hormone-related diseases such as breast cancer.

Cabbage: Common but Grandly Nurturing

We sometimes call people "cabbage heads" as a term of disparagement. The French, on the other hand, have terms of endearment for males and for females—*mon petit chou* and *ma petite chou*—that literally translate as "my little cabbage" but which are used to mean "darling" or "sweetheart."

It may be a measure of our elitism that we have come to look down on cabbage as a commonplace food, when, in fact, cabbage, like the other vegetables in the cruciferous family, is extraordinarily rich in phytonutrients that have remarkable health-promoting benefits. Sturdy, abundant, and inexpensive, cabbage is a longstanding dietary staple throughout the world.

Cabbage is an exceptional source of vitamin C. It also contains appreciable levels of the amino acid glutamine, which is an excellent anti-inflammatory.

Many studies have found that people who eat the most cabbage and other cruciferous vegetables have lower risks of cancer—even when compared to people who regularly eat other vegetables. For example, a study of more than one thousand men conducted at the Fred Hutchinson Cancer Research Center in Seattle, Washington, found that men who ate twenty-eight servings of vegetables a week (four per day) had a 35 percent lower risk of developing prostate cancer. But those consuming just three or more servings of cabbage or other cruciferous vegetables a week had a 44 percent lower risk.

A great number of studies have found the consumption of cruciferous vegetables to be associated with a lower incidence of a variety of cancers, including lung, colon, breast, ovarian, and bladder. One study of smokers in Singapore found that regular consumption of cabbage or other cruciferous vegetables reduced lung cancer risk by an amazing 69 percent.

How much cabbage and other cruciferous vegetables do you need to eat in order to lower your risk of cancer? Less than a cup a day.

SUNNY CASHEW COLESLAW

3 carrots, grated

1 medium head cabbage, grated

2 tablespoons raisins

Pinch of paprika

2 tablespoons chopped fresh parsley

1 tablespoon Oven-Roasted Sunflower Seeds (page 179)

½ cup raw cashews

½ cup roasted sunflower seeds

1 tablespoon raw tahini

2 tablespoons canola oil

3 tablespoons apple cider vinegar

5 tablespoons lemon juice

¼ teaspoon black pepper

¼ teaspoon mustard powder

½ teaspoon salt

2 teaspoons onion powder

2 teaspoons organic sugar

2 tablespoons nutritional yeast

¾ cup water

Place the carrots, cabbage, and raisins in a large bowl and set aside. Save the paprika, parsley, and tablespoon of sunflower seeds to use as a garnish. Blend all of the other ingredients in a blender or food processor until creamy. Stir the blended mixture into the carrots, cabbage, and raisins until thoroughly mixed. Garnish with the paprika, parsley, and a tablespoon of sunflower seeds. Place in the refrigerator for at least 1 hour before serving to allow the cabbage and carrots to soften and the flavors to mingle.

SERVES 6

Carrots: Orange Gift from the Earth

Carrots are well known and loved everywhere. Because they are so widely available and so inexpensive, though, we may not realize how nutritious they are.

CREAMY CARROT CURRY SOUP

2 cups chopped carrots

1½ cups chopped onions

3 cups water

½ cup roasted cashews (preferably dry roasted, unsalted, or low salt)

2 tablespoons soy sauce

2 teaspoons curry powder (more if you like it "hot")

¼ cup chopped fresh parsley

In a saucepan, combine the carrots, onions, and water. Cover and bring to a boil, then turn down the heat and simmer for 10 minutes. Place the cooked vegetables, cooking liquid, cashews, soy sauce, and curry powder into the blender and blend until creamy. Serve hot and garnish with parsley to taste.

SERVES 4

Carrots, perhaps not surprisingly given their name, are one of the food kingdom's richest sources of carotenoids. Regular carotenoid intake from carrots and other vegetables has been linked with an up to 50 percent decrease in cancers of the lung, bladder, cervix, prostate, colon, larynx, and esophagus.

There were several famous studies conducted in the 1990s in which long-term smokers were given synthetic beta-carotene, and it not only didn't prevent them from developing lung cancer, it might have made things worse. How does that reconcile with the many studies that have found carrot consumption to be beneficial in the prevention of cancer, and lung cancer in particular? Scientists now believe that carrots' protective effects are the result of the synergistic interaction of several different carotenoids that are abundant in carrots, including alpha-carotene. In the study, subjects were not given the spectrum of carotenoids, nor were they given any alpha-carotene. They were given only isolated beta-carotene. When you eat carrots, on the other hand, you get the full spectrum of carotenoids.

Your grandmother may have told you that carrots were good for your eyes. If she did, she was right. When you eat carrots, the carotenoids in them are converted to vitamin A in the liver, and then travel to the retina where they are transformed into rhodopsin, a purple pigment that is necessary for night vision. This is one of the reasons carrots have been shown to protect against macular degeneration and the development of senile cataracts, the leading causes of blindness in the elderly.

A study of 1,300 elderly people in Massachusetts found that those who ate at least one serving a day of carrots and/or squash had a 60 percent reduction in their risk of heart attacks, compared to those who ate less than one serving a day.

Tofu: Happily Becoming Mainstream

Tofu is made from soy milk much the way cheese is made from cow's milk, but nutritionally, tofu is superior to cheese in many respects. Unlike cheese, for example, tofu is low in calories, contains beneficial amounts of iron, and has no saturated fat or cholesterol. Tofu is also higher in protein than cheese. And while cheese and other dairy products are considered good sources of calcium, tofu, depending on the coagulant used in manufacturing, may also be high in calcium and magnesium.

Further, while cheese consumption is associated with higher rates of heart disease, consumption of soy protein is associated with lower rates of heart disease.

As a food, tofu is extremely versatile. About the only thing you wouldn't want to do with it is just eat it out of the tub. Like whole wheat flour, which also wouldn't be good to simply eat, tofu is best thought of as an ingredient. With it, you can make many wonderful meals. Although a few years ago tofu could be found only in health food and other specialty stores, tofu has become widely available today. It's available in several consistencies—soft to firm—and you can use it in traditional Asian dishes or as a cholesterol-free alternative to high-fat dairy foods, meat, or poultry.

Almost all the soybeans that aren't organically grown in the United States today are genetically modified. If you want to avoid eating transgenic foods, get organic tofu.

TOFU CHIVE DIP AND SPREAD

You can use this as a hearty topping on potatoes, a delicious spread on bagels or toast, a dip for cracker or chips, or a tasty garnish for soups and vegetables.

2 (12.3-ounce) packages Mori Nu Silken Firm Tofu
4½ tablespoons rice vinegar
1½ teaspoons salt
1½ teaspoons onion powder
⅜ cup olive oil
¾ cup finely chopped chives or green onions

Place the tofu, rice vinegar, salt, and onion powder into a food processor and process until well mixed, about 30 seconds. Continue processing while slowly adding the olive oil, and process until smooth, about 30 seconds. Place the mixture into a bowl and stir in the chives or green onions. Serve chilled.

MAKES 2½ CUPS

SEVEN

Kids: The Biggest Financial Decision of Your Life

Mother Nature, in her infinite wisdom, has instilled within each of us a powerful biological instinct to reproduce. This is her way of assuring that the human race, come what may, will never have any disposable income.

— DAVE BARRY

For many of us, our children, grandchildren, and families are sources of immense happiness. Even the challenges of family life are valuable because they can be sources of spiritual growth. Relationships are at the core of the new good life, for they help us to learn that connecting, rather than possessing, is the key to celebrating family, friends, love, and life.

Over the course of our lives, we all make many choices. Some we make through logical analysis, others via intuition, and yet others from emotion. Some choices are so consequential that we live them not only once but a thousand times over, remembering them and experiencing their implications for the rest of our lives.

Whether to have children, and if so how many, is indisputably among the most momentous choices an individual or a couple can or will ever make. It is more than possible that no other single decision you make means as much to the quality of your life and to the life of the planet. It is a decision with enormous spiritual, emotional, and practical dimensions. It is so profound, on so many levels of the human experience, that it may seem trivializing to mention its financial implications.

Still, they exist.

Housing, food, and transportation represent the three biggest expenses in most household budgets. But of all your life choices, the one that may have the greatest impact on your long-term financial security is not about the home you live in, the car you do or don't drive, or the food you eat.

It is the decision about how many children, if any, you have.

Children, of course, are precious beyond description, and the joy and love they bring into the world is literally priceless. I consider the nurturing of wise and healthy children to be a spiritual act, and parenting to be a sacred responsibility. But it takes more than unconditional love to raise even the easiest child, and I think the capacity to look soberly at the expenses that are involved is part of the maturity that parenthood requires.

Whether you are currently in your childbearing years or not, it can be eye-opening to reflect on how much it actually costs to raise a child in the United States today. How would we go about determining those costs? Fortunately, we have good data, because this topic is analyzed and systematically updated each year by the U.S. Department of Agriculture. The federal agency takes into account the average costs nationwide of housing, food, transportation, health care, child care, and education, and issues an annual report titled *Expenditures on Children by Families*.

This analysis calculates the cost of raising a child from birth to age seventeen. It does not include the costs of prenatal care and birthing, nor does it include educational expenses past the age of seventeen. These costs, obviously, can be considerable, but even without them the expenses of raising children are far larger than most people realize.

What a family spends on raising a child depends significantly on their level of income and on the cost of living in their particular region. To illustrate, here are three hypothetical children who come from different economic and geographical circumstances, with dollar amounts derived from official 2008 government figures.

- Monica is born in Selma, Alabama, and raised by a single mother. Monica's mother is limited in her income and isn't getting significant support from Monica's father, and so she doesn't have a lot to spend on her daughter's upbringing. Still, by the time Monica is seventeen, her mother will have incurred costs of $149,000 in raising her, including the costs of housing, food, clothes, toys, day care, medical bills, transportation, and so forth. Her birth wasn't cheap, either. It cost $7,600 in hospital fees and prenatal care, and since Monica's mom didn't have health insurance, she had to pick up that tab. The cost of most colleges or universities are prohibitive for Monica, but she studies hard and wants to go to the local community college. The cost to attend is $121 per credit hour, which comes to $3,000 per school year, or $6,000 in tuition fees for two years. Since she's a full-time student, she lives at home, and her mom assumes the costs of providing for her for those two additional years ($8,000 a year).

  By the time Monica finishes her two years of higher education and is ready to begin supporting herself, her mom will have spent $178,600 raising her. If that amount of money had over the years instead been deposited in equal increments each year in a retirement account at a rate of 5 percent, her mom would by then have had more than $300,000 in the account.

- Willie is born to a middle-class family in St. Louis, Missouri. Between them, his parents make $55,000 a year. Raising Willie from birth to the age of seventeen costs them $204,000 in food, clothing, housing, and other direct expenses. The cost of his birth added another $8,000 in hospital and prenatal care fees. If he attends a local four-year college and lives on campus, his four-year college experience will cost his parents an additional $85,000.

  By the time Willie gets his bachelor's degree at the age of twenty-one, his parents will have spent a total of $297,000 to raise him. If instead they had invested that money over the years in a retirement account paying 5 percent, the account would by now be worth more than $530,000.

- Julie is born to parents who are fairly well off. They live in Baltimore, Maryland, and their combined income is $90,000 a year, which gives them a little more to spend on pampering their young lady as she grows up. Her parents had health insurance that covered the costs of Julie's birth, but still, by the time she's seventeen, they will have spent $298,000 on her meals, clothing, and other expenses.

Julie is serious about her studies and decides to attend a local university that has a fine reputation—George Washington University in Washington, D.C. The cost of attending this school, including living expenses, is currently $53,600 a year. By the time Julie graduates from this four-year university, her parents will have paid $512,400 to raise her. If they had over the years invested that money in a retirement account with a 5 percent rate of interest, and the money had been deposited in equal increments each year, they would now have $915,128 in their account.

THE MOMMY TAX

There is yet another financial cost to having children, beyond what I've described thus far, that's quite considerable. So far I've talked about direct expenses—money out of pocket. But in Ann Crittenden's remarkable book *The Price of Motherhood,* she concludes that women in the United States pay a "mommy tax," losing a staggering amount of income as a result of having children.

Most companies, she notes, believe that the ideal worker is "unencumbered." Indeed, the American workplace can be downright inhospitable to people "burdened" by family responsibilities. Some employers see any sign of life outside the office as inadequate commitment to the job. Crittenden cites numerous studies indicating that even short career interruptions in the corporate world are seriously penalized.

How large is the mommy tax? According to the calculations of economist Shirley Burggraf, a childless husband and wife who each earn $55,750 annually will over the course of time lose $1.35 million in reduced income if they have a child. Burggraf arrives at this figure by computing how much less the parent who shoulders the dominant share of the parenting (usually but not necessarily the mother) will earn over forty-five years (the average number of years in a working lifetime), compared to how much they would have earned if they had remained childless.

The primary breadwinner will presumably continue to earn $55,750 annually. The other parent would have likewise earned that amount if she (or he) were "unencumbered." But the data show that as a result of raising a child, she (or he) instead will earn an average of $25,750 annually over the same forty-five years. Burggraf multiplies $30,000 (the difference between what the two parents earn annually) by 45 to reach the figure of $1.35 million in lowered income. That is the amount of wages forgone by the other parent, who can, at most, work part-time for many years, and whose salary if she (or he) eventually returns to full-time employment will be far less than it would have been if she (or he) hadn't left the workforce to raise a family.

In a middle-income family, the numbers aren't as staggering but are still huge. With one parent earning $30,000 per year as a full-time sales representative, and the other averaging $15,000 as a part-time computer consultant, the mommy tax of lost income over the course of a working lifetime still amounts to more than $600,000.

The mommy tax is highest for well-educated, high-income people, and lowest for less-educated people who have less potential income to lose. But it can take a dreadful toll on lower income families, where the mommy tax can push a family over the brink into desperation and poverty. And in the case of single mothers, it can create virtually impossible challenges.

The phrase "equal pay for equal work" has long been a rallying cry for the women's movement. Despite federal legislation making it illegal to pay men and women different wage rates for equal work, the gap has persisted. Why? Most of the reason is the mommy tax.

Women who aren't mothers do, in fact, earn almost as much as their male counterparts for comparable work—90 percent as much. Women who are mothers, however, do much worse—they earn only 73 percent as much. And single mothers do even worse, earning on average only 61 percent as much as men. Remarkably, the wage gap between women who are mothers and women who aren't is significantly greater than the gap between women who aren't mothers and men.

That's the situation currently in the United States. But Crittenden points out that in countries such as Sweden and France, different family policies have created different outcomes. In France, for example, every mother, rich or poor, married or single, receives not only free health care but a cash allowance for each child. She can spend this allowance any way she wants, including hiring the help of a nanny. Single mothers receive additional benefits, including housing subsidies worth about

$6,000 a year for the first three years of a child's life. After that the benefits are sharply reduced, but excellent public nursery schools are available to every three-year-old child, free of charge. These programs, along with year-long paid maternity leave, allow French mothers to take care of their babies and survive economically.

I don't mean to imply that everything about French policy is ideal, but they have found a way to greatly reduce the mommy tax. This is one of the reasons that the child poverty rate in France is only 7.5 percent. (It's only 4.2 percent in Sweden and 2.4 percent in Denmark.) Painfully, the child poverty rate in the United States is the highest of the world's twenty-four fully industrialized nations, at 21.9 percent.

The phrase "family values" has different meanings to different people. To me, family values are expressed by loving, supporting, and taking care of one another. That's why I would have a hard time explaining family values to the more than twenty-five million U.S. kids living in poverty (including more than one-third of all African-American kids).

I find it heartening, though, that there are many good people of every religious persuasion and of every political orientation who are seeking to relieve this suffering. Since 2006, for example, the organization Moms-Rising (MomsRising.org) has been working to bring together the millions of people who share a common concern about the need to build a more family-friendly America. The group—which now has more than one million members—has the goal of improving family economic security by working together to build a nation where children, parents, and businesses thrive.

In their book *The Motherhood Manifesto,* MomsRising founders Joan Blades and Kristin Rowe-Finkbeiner write, "National policies and programs with proven success in other countries—like family leave, flexible work options, subsidized childcare and preschool, as well as healthcare coverage for all kids—are largely lacking in America. . . . Without paid family leave parents often have to put their infants in extremely expensive or substandard childcare facilities; families with a sick child, inadequate health coverage, and no flexible work options often end up in bankruptcy."

A strong advocate for paid maternity leave, MomsRising points out that the United States today is one of only four countries in the world that doesn't offer paid leave to new mothers. Paid family leave has been shown to reduce infant mortality by as much as 20 percent. The lack of it in the United States is one of the reasons we rank a dismally low thirty-seventh among nations in infant mortality rates.

This is one of the profound problems with the old good life. A way of life that has been failing so many of our children, in truth has been failing all of us.

SMALLER FAMILIES?

I am a father myself, and I believe that being a parent can be one of the most valuable experiences in a human life. It certainly has been that for me. As someone once said, when we have children, we try to teach them about life, but it is they who teach us what life is about.

There are many good reasons that people have children. Just because it is expensive doesn't mean it isn't the right choice for you or your loved ones. But it's a good idea to know what you're getting into. And besides, just as the new good life means smaller houses, smaller cars, smaller waistlines—and, I hope, smaller egos—than we've come to think of as normal, I think it's worth considering whether in some cases it might also mean smaller families.

There was a day when families used to have loads of kids because life expectancies were low, childhood deaths were frequent, and farming families needed farmhands, but in the industrialized world none of these are commonplace anymore. There was also a day when if a child didn't have siblings, he or she might not have other kids to play with and to learn from. In times past, people essentially interacted only with those who lived near them. But when you factor in the increasing role of extended families in our lives today, the increasing mobility of young people, the increasing concentration of people in the world, and, of course, the Internet and the tremendous growth of social networking technologies, those sentiments can seem outdated.

I have known and loved people from large families and from small ones, and I think that each kind of family has its advantages, its own particular gifts, and its blessings. But questions keep nagging at me: Can the earth afford for our population to continue growing? What would human life on this planet be like if ever larger numbers of people tried to live the way we have been living?

In 2009, statisticians from Oregon State University published an article titled "Reproduction and the Carbon Legacies of Individuals" in the scientific journal *Global Environmental Change*. Their central finding? The more children you have, the more your carbon footprint soars. Consider, for example, an American woman who owns a Prius, drives as little as possible, recycles, installs the most efficient lighting, and replaces her refrigerator and windows with energy-saving models. Those steps, obviously and thankfully, lower her carbon footprint. The researchers found, however, that if she has two children who grow up to be typical Americans, her carbon legacy will eventually rise by nearly forty times the amount she has saved by those actions.

The fact is that we Americans, representing 5 percent of the world's population, consume 30 percent of the world's resources and are responsible for an even higher percentage of the world's toxic waste. We actually spend more for trash bags than 90 of the world's 210 countries spend for everything combined. When we have children, there are serious ecological consequences. Our way of life is endangering the lives of all our descendants.

For this and many other reasons, I think it would be a good idea if people thought much more thoroughly about the implications of having children before conceiving. But I do not in any way support coercive population control practices such as those that have been enacted in China. There, totalitarian restrictions mandate that most married urban couples can have only one child. Such draconian measures are not only a violation of human rights, but lead inevitably to forced sterilizations, forced abortions, and infanticides.

I am utterly opposed to any efforts to mandate the number of children that families can have.

At the same time, I think the decision to have a child or children is one of the most profound and significant ones a woman or a couple ever makes. The consequences of reproduction are extremely important, and I think they deserve the highest degree of reflection and responsibility.

My friend and colleague Mathis Wackernagel is the creator of the concept of the "ecological footprint." He is also the founder and director of the Global Footprint Network, an organization whose latest data show that, at the current rate of growth in humanity's population and resource consumption, by the early 2030s we would require the ecological services of two planets to keep up with our demand. Globally, we have already exceeded the carrying capacity of our one and only planet.

At this moment, there are about one trillion pounds of human flesh on the planet. That's quite a footprint.

There is a mathematical equation involved in all this that one way or another has to come into balance. Somehow, some way, our numbers multiplied by our impact must eventually come into equilibrium with the capacities of the planet. Right now, we are far from that balance. Given our current numbers, we are consuming and polluting at a rate the earth cannot possibly sustain for much longer. If we don't find a sane, ethical, and humane way to reduce our consumption, our pollution, and our numbers, then nature may find a way to do that job for us, and it might not be pretty. It could, in fact, take the form of catastrophe, disaster, and suffering so widespread as to be unparalleled in human history.

It's a sad fact of life today that when people think about having children, their future is shadowed by so many financial and environmental concerns. On the positive side, though, I know many young couples who had considered having children to be prohibitively expensive in today's consumer society, and so had chosen to remain childless. As they've discovered the many financial and time-saving advantages that come with shifting to a simpler low-cost lifestyle, they've reopened their minds to the possibility of being parents, whether through procreation or adoption.

WHY WE STOPPED AT ONE

My wife and I had only one child, a beautiful son we named Ocean. Our reasons for stopping at one were many, including that we didn't want to dilute our resources. And by that I don't just mean money, although that certainly played a role, as during our childbearing years we had very little of it.

But beyond money, we wanted to conserve our time and our emotional and physical energy. We wanted to give our child, each other, our friends, and our work a quality of attention and focus that we suspected would not be possible if we were to add additional little ones to the mix. Every parent tries to give their second, third, fourth, or even fifth child as much undivided attention as they can, but as the numbers get larger it does get more difficult. There are only so many hours in the day. We felt, instinctively, that in our case we could have a greater impact on the world and bring more love into it by having just one.

Having only one child meant I could be home and spend more time with my son, because I did not have to work as many hours as would have been needed if we had more children. This was precious to me, as I know it is to many others. Having more time to enjoy your relationships, children included, is one of the great rewards of the new good life. For many, the choice to work less and live simply so they can spend more time at home and with their loved ones is deeply rewarding. Plus, your children get more of you, which is what they really want and need.

There are, of course, downsides to having only one child. With all their expectations, hopes, and fears focused on just one child, parents have to guard against the tendency to become overprotective and excessively attentive, because this could make an only child afraid of the world beyond his or her parents, and hinder the child's relationships with peers. Recognizing this danger, we made it a priority to help Ocean find his own confidence and inner wisdom. We also tried to make sure our expectations of him were realistic. At times I failed miserably at this, but thankfully, in this effort, he was most helpful. One day, when he was twelve, I asked Ocean how I was doing as a dad. "Pretty well," he said, "but please lower your expectations of me." In the discussion that ensued, he made it clear that he wasn't asking me to lower my opinion of him, just what I expected from him. I respected the wisdom of what he was telling me and tried diligently thereafter to honor his request.

We also made it a point to let Ocean get to know other trusted adults, to include him in group activities with other families, and to give him as many opportunities to play with other kids as we could manage.

Ocean is now thirty-five, and I respect and admire him greatly. His marriage to Michele is now fifteen years along and seems to be thriving and filled with love and understanding, which is quite an achievement given the challenges they face in raising two special-needs children. As a father in this situation, Ocean is extraordinarily patient, reassuring, and inspiring. Plus, he is doing remarkable work in the world as the director of a nonprofit organization.

WHAT REALLY SPOILS CHILDREN?

I did have a fear that having only one child might lead to our son being spoiled. No parent wants to raise a spoiled brat—a kid who is selfish, demanding, and insensitive to others. And many of us suspect that children who have no siblings can end up spoiled rotten.

But what is it that spoils children? I don't think it's an abundance of love and thoughtful attention. I think it more likely happens when we substitute material things for genuine love, when we try to give them everything they want, when we try to appease their every desire, when we indulge them with loads of toys and feel like failures if they aren't always happy. I think spoiling happens when we give our kids junk food that provides short-term pleasure, instead of providing them with real nourishment.

The truth is that we live in a culture where, as environmentalist Bill McKibben puts it, "almost everyone is a little spoiled, where spoiling children underwrites a significant part of the economy."

If a child's needs become so paramount to the parents that they sacrifice everything, the child feels insecure, with little chance to learn how to live a self-reliant life. If parents can't tolerate any discomfort from their child, if they can never say no to him or her, the child grows fearful. If parents have no sources of joy other than their children, the children may believe they are the center of the universe.

What spoils kids is when they are taught to fill up their emptiness from the outside by purchasing things and activities, rather than learning how to fill themselves up from the inside through making good choices, caring, and creativity. It's not love that spoils our kids. They become spoiled when we ply them with too many toys, too much stimulation, and too much of the wrong kind of attention. They become spoiled when they learn, often from our example, to identify their self-worth with other's approval, with how they look, with how much stuff they have, with how expensive their clothes are, or with how large their homes are. We spoil our kids when we teach them to meet their deepest spiritual and emotional needs with material things. We spoil them when we don't help them to learn to deal with disappointment or to learn about the joys of helping others.

It's not smaller families that spoil children; it's smaller hearts and smaller thoughts. Spoiling happens when kids aren't helped to know their own inner beauty, when they feel they will be valued only for their looks, possessions, or performance. Spoiling happens when children aren't celebrated for who they are, when they are forced to pretend, to put on a mask, to ignore their own deepest promptings and truth. Spoiling happens when kids aren't valued for their inner qualities, their kindness, their laughter, their inspirations, their passion for life.

It took about 165,000 years of human history on planet Earth for the human population to reach one billion, which it did around 1800.

One hundred thirty years later, in 1930, there were two billion people on the planet.

Thirty years later, in 1960, there were three billion of us.

Fourteen years later, in 1974, there were four billion.

Thirteen years later, in 1987, there were five billion.

Twelve years later, in 1999, there were six billion.

Eleven years later, in 2010, there were seven billion.

WE HAVE BEEN FRUITFUL AND MULTIPLIED

On the first page of the first book of the Bible, in the beginning of Genesis, we are enjoined "to be fruitful, and multiply, and fill the earth." It appears that we've done that quite successfully.

More people have been born since 1950 than were born during the history of the planet prior to that date. I find that truly profound. More people have been born during my lifetime than in the previous four million years since our ancestors first stood upright. Maybe we should consider our going forth to multiply and fill the earth to have been accomplished. What would it mean if we were to check this one off our to-do list?

Bill McKibben writes,

When you check something off a list, you don't just throw the list away. You look farther down the list, [to] see what comes next. And the list, of course, is long. The Gospels, the Torah, the Koran, and a thousand other texts sacred and profane give us plenty of other goals toward which to divert some of the energy we've traditionally used in raising large families, goals on which we've barely begun. Feed the hungry, clothe the naked, comfort the oppressed; love your neighbor as yourself; heal the earth. We live on a planet where three billion people don't have clean water, where species die by the score each day, where kids grow up without fathers, where violence overwhelms us, where people judge each other by the color of their skin, where a hypersexualized culture poisons the adolescence of girls, where old people and young people need each other's support. And the energy freed by having smaller families may be some of the energy needed to take on these next challenges, to really take them on, not just to announce that they're important, or to send a check, or to read an article, but to make them central to our lives.

It's been an article of faith in the old good life that bigger is better, and many are the men and women who've enlarged their egos by producing many children. But don't you think, when you come right down to it, that it's as silly to measure the quality of a family by the number of its children as it is to gauge the value of people's lives merely by the numbers in their bank accounts?

RAISING STRONG, HAPPY AND CREATIVE CHILDREN IN THE MIDST OF A CONSUMER CULTURE (WITHOUT SPENDING AN ARM AND A LEG)

And what if you have children? How do you raise them without going bankrupt in the process? How do you raise them so they won't fall prey to the mindless consumerism that is doing so much harm to the planet? How do you help them to understand that "toys aren't us"?

In a day when Barbie and Bratz dolls are marketed to three-year-olds, and the worst junk food is not only sold but advertised in public schools, how do you protect your children? How do you defend them from both the obvious and the subtle ways that a commercial culture deliberately turns kids into consumers?

Growing up is never easy, even in the best of environments. Perhaps every generation of adults asks the perennial question, "What's the matter with kids today?" But today's youth are being targeted by sophisticated and predatory marketing that teaches them to value so many of the wrong things.

As Barbara Ehrenreich writes, "We worry about so many dangers to our children—drugs, perverts, bullies—but seldom notice the biggest menace of all: the multibillion-dollar marketing effort aimed at turning the kids into oversexed, status-obsessed, attention-deficient little consumers."

Thanks to the success of this effort, contemporary youth in the

United States have become perhaps the most brand-oriented, consumer-involved, and materialistic generation in history. A survey of youth from seventy cities in more than fifteen countries found that a higher percentage of kids in the United States want to become rich and famous than in any other country in the world. And a higher percentage of children in the United States than anywhere else in the world believe that the clothes they wear and the brands they buy identify who they are and define their social status.

As a parent, what can you do? Every family is unique, with its own struggles and its own opportunities. Here are a few ideas that might help:

Communication: The Key to Connection

Probably the single most important key to living joyfully with your children is communication. Whether they were born into a family already living simply or are part of a family's transition to a more sustainable lifestyle, kids want to be included in the discussions and choices that impact their lives. To include them, you need to be clear with yourself about what you value, how and why you are choosing to live the way you are, and how you want to speak about it.

Of course, the conversations you have with your kids will vary greatly, depending on the age and maturity of the child. But from an early age, your children will greatly appreciate being told why you do things the way you do.

Even very young kids can understand that excess packaging uses up the earth's resources and crowds our landfills. They can understand that you might want to buy products made by workers who are treated well and paid fairly. They can enjoy choosing foods that make their bodies strong and healthy. And they can appreciate that you are choosing to spend less money on things so that you can have more time to work and play together.

Older children benefit greatly when they are included in family deliberations about how to spend time and money. They often have a lot to contribute when families discuss and clarify their values and priorities. In the process, they develop healthy habits and ways of thinking that will serve them throughout their lives.

Children may have to deal with issues around peer pressure, fitting in, and social inclusion. Their peers may have taken on the belief that their self-worth and happiness depend on purchasing the latest products. You may want to offer guidance, but it's also helpful to listen to your children's concerns and reservations about living a different lifestyle than many of their friends and classmates.

You can talk with your children about the insidious powers of media and advertising, so that you can help them to know what they truly want and value. Is it the latest fad items? Or is it friendship, love, and a sense of belonging? Are there alternatives to buying and spending money that can help them find satisfaction and joy? These kinds of conversations are a lot easier when they are begun early in life. But it's never too late to begin questioning the assumptions and values of an excessively materialistic culture.

Some parents allow teens to decide how (within certain limitations) they wish to spend the money they earn themselves. Others give an allowance with a similar understanding.

Some families work together to create a family mission statement. The value of doing so is not just in the final document. It's also in the communication, focus, clarity about priorities, and learning about values. Stephen Covey, author of the bestseller *The 7 Habits of Highly Effective Families,* says the creation of a family mission statement has been the most transforming event in his own family's history.

Contribution: Everyone Needs to Make a Difference

Most children have a natural desire to help others. You can support and encourage this feeling by providing them with opportunities to make a difference to their families, friends, and the wider community. One family I know created, as part of their mission statement, the principle that each family member would do something for somebody every day for which they did not get paid.

Children who know they are making a positive contribution to others have a sense of their worth that doesn't depend on consumption. If you make it a point always to thank and appreciate your kids for the things they do for you and for others, they will grow up deriving pleasure and self-esteem from helping out.

You can volunteer as a family at local soup kitchens, food banks, or river or beach cleanups. Or your kids can get involved with other groups of youth doing service work in your community. Roots & Shoots (rootsandshoots.org) is an international volunteer organization for children founded by Jane Goodall. It has branches in many locations with ongoing projects and opportunities to make a difference.

Instead of buying birthday and other holiday gifts, you can invite your children to have donations made in their names to a cause of their choice. Learning about the work being done by various nonprofit organizations will give them a valuable window into the world of service. And forgoing a present in order that an organization doing good can receive a donation can strengthen your kids' self-esteem and generosity. YouthGive.org is an organization that makes it easy for kids to get involved in giving to good causes.

Of course, if children have grown accustomed to receiving many gifts on their birthdays and other holidays, they may not be eager to be so munificent. Asking them to take a step that is too large can lead them to associate generosity with deprivation and resentment. The art is to take small, gradual steps to wean, educate, and inspire them.

Working Together: How to Share Values and Have Fun While Getting Something Done

If you do chores together, the experience will feel less like a burden or obligation and more like a time for your kids to learn and practice real life skills. What's required is that you take a little extra time and make having fun as important as getting the job done. It may take longer, but there will be opportunities for learning and for meaningful conversations.

There are a wide variety of tasks in which children of different ages can participate. These include sorting and delivering recyclables to the recycling center (small children are fascinated by the enormous bins and big trucks there), cleaning house and sorting laundry (good for developing motor skills), caring for pets, gardening, and, of course, cooking. Younger kids enjoy learning to pour, measure, and stir. Older children can help with planning, budgeting, shopping, and preparing healthy family meals or snacks.

With a little creativity and attention, most tasks can become enriching and pleasurable opportunities to learn, to grow, and to enjoy being together.

If you're going to the store or to a farmers market, there are countless opportunities for kids to learn new things and express themselves. Younger children might enjoy running around the produce department looking for vegetables that begin with a certain letter or that are orange or purple. When they are a bit older, they can practice reading the signs, filling up bags, weighing the veggies and reading the scales, comparing prices, and learning to count out the money at the cash register.

You can have discussions about why you buy the food you do. You might talk about why you don't buy strawberries in December that are shipped from far away, and what foods are most nourishing. If you buy organic food, you can talk about what pesticides do to foods and to the people who grow them.

It's natural to want to protect your children from the pain in the world, but when they reach the appropriate level of maturity you can discuss world hunger with them. You can explain that not everyone can afford to buy the food they need, and talk about ways to help. We had that discussion with our son when he was eight, and he decided that he would henceforth give his allowance to groups that were providing food to the hungry. This turned out to be a long-term arrangement. He saved what we gave him and periodically would send it in to groups he had researched and believed to be doing the most good with the dollars they had.

Turn Off the TV—and Turn On Life

Perhaps the single best protection you can offer your children is to eliminate or reduce television watching. Today, the vast majority of children in the United States have televisions in their bedrooms. This has consequences.

- **TV turns kids (and adults) into consumers.** A study published in the *Journal of Developmental and Behavioral Pediatrics* in 2001 came to the not-all-that-surprising conclusion that the more TV kids watch, the more they bug their parents to buy them toys. Another survey found that people spend an extra $208 annually for each hour of television they watch weekly.

- **TV turns off children's brains.** The more television kids watch, the more addicted they become to the passive and trancelike state it produces. Perhaps this is why studies have shown that children who watch more TV are more likely to become drug addicts.
- **TV promotes violence.** By the time the average child in the United States is eighteen, he or she has seen two hundred thousand dramatized acts of violence, including forty thousand dramatized murders. The consequences to children are now well known. These include increased aggressive behavior and emotional desensitization to violence in real life.
- **TV teaches the wrong values.** Even nonviolent shows are often filled with commercials that reinforce attitudes of entitlement and selfishness. The message they convey to kids is that being cool is of utmost importance, and the way to be cool is to buy the products that are advertised.
- **TV makes kids fat.** The more television children watch, the more likely they are to become obese. They also end up eating more of the types of foods that are advertised: fast foods, convenience foods, candy, and soda.

On the other hand, living TV-free vastly reduces your kids' exposure to commercial propaganda and violence. Children who watch less television get more exercise and are healthier. Living TV-free gives them more time for real-life experiences and opportunities to develop their creativity, intelligence, and social skills.

The less TV is watched in your home, the fewer the number of junk food ads your kids (and you) will be exposed to. You don't have to allow corporations without a conscience to have unlimited access to your children. You don't have to turn your kids' minds over to those who would prey on them.

If you're going to have a TV in the house, here are some ideas to keep the beast under control:

- Some parents choose to limit television watching, rather than eliminate it completely. If you can bring your children into the conversation about why you are setting limits and what those limits will be, they will feel less like victims and more like participants in an adventure of self-discovery.

- If you do have a TV, it can be helpful to keep it tucked away in a closet or cupboard, or covered with something beautiful. Keeping it out of sight reduces the temptation to turn it on habitually.
- Eliminating TV watching during meals is a good place to start cutting back. This provides an opportunity to eat more consciously, appreciate the food that has been prepared, and enjoy being together.
- Some families decide to make certain shows or days of the week off-limits. You may limit the number of hours per week or create a system where kids earn TV-watching time in exchange for doing chores or other character-building activities.
- Turning off the sound during commercials not only protects your household from being deluged by toxic messages, it can also foster an awareness of just how many commercials we are exposed to for every program we watch.
- Some families own a TV but use it only for watching carefully selected videos and DVDs. Family movie nights can be a fun way to relax together. You can set up comfortable spaces for watching, with lots of pillows for cuddling. After the movie is over, you can invite younger children to talk about their favorite parts of the movie or when they felt scared, excited, sad, and so forth. You can take a turn, too. Children may like to play out some of the characters and reenact their favorite scenes. This is a good way to become present and connected after watching a film.
- With older children you may want to introduce documentaries and movies with educational, inspiring, or uplifting messages. Take some time afterward to talk about your responses to the films, especially if they have a lot of emotional intensity or new information.

Help Your Kids to Become Media Literate

You can talk to your children about the ads you see in magazines, on packaging and billboards, and through other media. A good starting point is to explain how these commercials are designed to convince people to buy certain products, and you can question together the underlying messages they send.

You can ask, "What does this commercial want you to do? How does it make you feel?" When children become aware of how manipulative ads can be, they develop their capacity to resist the ads' underlying assumptions.

You can help children to notice how the tone, sounds, colors, music, and entertainment qualities of the ads are designed to draw them in and to make the products appear inviting. You can discuss the beliefs and assumptions about life and relationships that appear in television programs and films. (Make sure younger kids understand that the people they see who are endorsing and promoting products are paid to do so.)

Developing a critical eye will help your children navigate the minefield of today's corporate advertising and media. As they wean themselves from the trance of the consumer culture, their own values will be strengthened. They will gain more power to create meaningful lives filled with caring, cooperation, and creativity.

Connecting with Nature: A Key to Fun and Health

In times past, children spent much of their free time outdoors. But kids today often live in urban and suburban environments where automobile traffic keeps them from playing in the streets. In some neighborhoods, there are other problems that restrict kids to the indoors. Drug dealing, robberies, accidental violence from gunshots, and other criminal activities can combine to make outdoor space dangerous for children. This is a tragedy. As a society, we owe our children a world in which it is safe to step outside and play.

Children pay a heavy price when they are confined indoors. Their levels of activity and exercise are diminished. Their autonomy is reduced, and their ability to connect socially with others is greatly limited. As a result, children who spend most or all of their time indoors are more susceptible to commercialization.

Studies show that children who play outside do better in school, have less problems paying attention, are healthier, have less stress and anxiety, and are generally happier and more productive than their cooped-up peers.

Experiencing nature can nurture a child's sense of well-being and belonging, and stimulate their sense of adventure. Hiking, biking, canoeing, skateboarding, sledding, bird watching, lake and ocean swimming, sports, and other inexpensive outdoor exercise can be fun for the whole family and foster a sense of physical vitality and confidence in young people.

Develop Healthy Family Rituals

Dinnertime offers a perfect opportunity for families to connect and bond with one another. Everyone needs to take time to eat, so why not make it a positive experience of coming together to be nourished on every level? You might want to take turns offering a prayer or blessing before the meal, or sing a song together. Or you can go around the table and have each person say what they feel thankful for.

During the meal, it can be fun for each person to share a happy moment from their day. Or each person can share a highlight and a low point from their day. It's nice to have some kind of a go-round, so that even the family members who are shy will have a chance to talk and receive everyone's attention.

Reading to children can be of tremendous importance. So can making music, playing games, or doing art projects as a family. The point is to create a family culture that is safe, fun, nurturing, and stimulating for both children and adults. This will give your children the best chance to grow up into self-reliant, caring, creative, and successful people.

And always kiss your children goodnight, even if they've already fallen asleep.

Priceless Family Fun

Juliet B. Schor is a widely recognized expert in economics and family studies. Discussing ways that families have been successful in keeping the corporate culture at bay, she writes:

> One woman started a mother-daughter book club, with discussion of the book and an activity. One household had family movie nights, with row seating, ushers, and popcorn. Another specialized in elaborate but low-budget theme parties—Greek mythology, insects, Peter Pan, and Eskimos (complete with a full-scale igloo). Other popular activities were wood-working, playing board games after

school, and unorganized sports. These activities . . . typically involved parents and kids together. One family makes a yearly pilgrimage to a mine to collect rocks, another took the kids out of school for nearly a year of travel, a third are avid canoeists and campers.

One of our family's favorite games to play with children, particularly when we have guests, is called "Two Truths and a Lie." Each person has a turn to make three statements about themselves. Two must be true, and one must be false. The listeners then have an opportunity to ask questions and then to guess which of the three statements is the lie. The person making the statements attempts to trick the listeners into guessing incorrectly by choosing truths that seem unlikely, and by inventing a lie that seems like it might really have happened. It's a great way to learn new and interesting things about one another, and even young children seem to get the concept with a little coaching.

Breaking Free from Commercial Exploitation

In recent years, marketers have devoted an enormous amount of money and ingenuity to exploiting young people's desire to belong, convincing them that in order to be accepted and popular, they need to constantly buy the latest and newest thing. Gene Del Vecchio, a former advertising executive and the author of *Creating Ever-Cool: A Marketer's Guide to a Kid's Heart,* describes the effort to make young people chronically feel they must buy new things. "Part of cool," he says candidly, "is having something that others do not. That makes a kid feel special. It is also the spark that drives kids to find the next cool item."

Every time you acquire books, toys, games, clothes, and other items for your kids, you have an opportunity to reinforce this mindset or to step beyond it. While being a good parent in the old good life might have meant constantly buying new sets of clothes and toys, only to see them outgrown physically and/or developmentally every year or two, families now are relearning the value of hand-me-downs. As with other forms of sharing, this provides a way to save money and resources. It also help kids to grow up valuing relationships more than shopping and thus to have a better sense of where their true wealth lies.

Right now, there are millions of kids "upstream" from yours, likely with abundant hand-me-downs to share. There are many ways you can take advantage of this flow and then, when the time comes, pass on what your kids no longer need to another lucky family. These include:

- **Get downstream.** If you know someone with a child a little older than yours and with reasonably similar lifestyle interests, you can ask if they would like to share what their kid outgrows with your family. You can offer to pick up items from their house to save them the trouble of getting rid of things they no longer need.
- **Get to know the kids' used stores.** Most cities have one or more secondhand stores for kids. Typically, they buy quality used items for 25 percent of the estimated (new) retail value, and then sell them for 50 percent of the estimated retail value. My son and his wife are downstream from several families, and if ever their twins need something that hasn't been handed down, they sell some old things the twins have outgrown at the used store and use the money to get whatever they need. Their net clothing and toys budget for the twins averages about fifty dollars a year, and some years it is nothing at all—and there is never a shortage of clothes or toys in the home (or strewn around the living room either, for that matter).
- **Check out Freecycle.org, a network made up of 4,812 groups with 6,552,000 members around the globe.** It's a grassroots and entirely nonprofit movement of people who are giving (and getting) stuff for free in their own towns. It's all about reuse and keeping good stuff out of landfills. Each local group is moderated by a local volunteer, and membership is free. Lots of kids stuff is given away on the Freecycle Network.
- **Share books.** In many communities, libraries are a wonderful and remarkably useful free resource for kids. There are also a host of online book-sharing co-ops such as PaperBackSwap.com, where people who offer to share a book have the opportunity to receive a book.

Your Kids Are Watching

You may sometimes feel that your children aren't listening to you, but I can assure you they are always watching you. They may not seem to be heeding your words, but they are paying a great deal of attention to your example. They are great imitators, so be careful what you give them to imitate.

One child, when grown up, wrote a poem of gratitude to her mother. Mary Rita Schilke Korzan didn't thank her mom, Blanche Schilke, for the money she spent on her, for the presents she bought her, or for the advice she gave her. She didn't thank her mother for sending her to the best schools or for making sure she had designer clothes. But it's a poem that I think any parent would be grateful and happy to some-day receive from a grown child, and it is a poignant reminder that the example we set for our children by the way we live is our real message to them:

> *When you thought I wasn't looking,*
>> *You hung my first painting on the refrigerator,*
>>> *And I wanted to paint another one.*

> *When you thought I wasn't looking,*
>> *You fed a stray cat,*
>>> *And I thought it was good to be kind to animals.*

> *When you thought I wasn't looking,*
>> *You baked a birthday cake just for me,*
>>> *And I knew that little things were special things.*

> *When you thought I wasn't looking,*
>> *You said a prayer,*
>>> *And I believed there was a God that I could always talk to.*

> *When you thought I wasn't looking,*
>> *You kissed me goodnight,*
>>> *And I felt loved.*

> *When you thought I wasn't looking,*
>> *I saw tears come from your eyes,*
>>> *And I learned that sometimes things hurt*
>>>> *But that it's alright to cry.*

When you thought I wasn't looking,
    You smiled
        And it made me want to look that pretty, too.

When you thought I wasn't looking,
    You cared,
        And I wanted to be everything that I could be.

When you thought I wasn't looking,
    I looked,
        And wanted to say thanks
            For all those things you did
When you thought I wasn't looking.

EIGHT

Safe, Clean, and Natural

There are approximately three million things I'd rather do on a sunny day than clean the house. Does that make me sound like a typical man, whose idea of helping with the vacuuming is to lift his legs and whose idea of housework is to sweep the room with a glance?

I do not, I fully acknowledge, wake up in the morning bursting with eagerness to wax the linoleum. At the same time, it is only fair that I do my share, so I have developed a dedicated interest in finding the easiest, cheapest, and most nontoxic ways to accomplish the purpose.

And what, while we're on the subject, is the actual purpose of house-cleaning?

It isn't to rid the world of all bacteria. That's impossible in the first place, and it would be fatal to the human race if it were to be accomplished. And the purpose, at least for most of us, isn't to have a spotless, picture-perfect home. That's nearly impossible and would take most of our precious waking hours.

The point, as far as I am concerned, is to create a healthy and comfortable environment. I like to say that our house is clean enough to be healthy and dirty enough to be happy.

In a triumph of modern marketing, though, most of us have been convinced that in order to keep our homes clean and make our lives worthwhile we need the help of an arsenal of modern cleaning products. There are three problems with this. First, it's not true. We can clean just as well and in many cases better without them. Second, these products are expensive. Americans spend more than $20 billion a year on cleaning products. And third, they are full of chemicals, many of which are known or suspected to be serious health and environmental hazards.

In 2005, American Red Cross workers collected blood from human subjects and sent the blood to two independent laboratories to be analyzed for chemicals. The results found that each person's body was contaminated with an average of two hundred industrial chemicals and pollutants, including pesticides, stain repellents, flame retardants, plasticizers, and a host of chemicals found in modern cleaning and beauty products. These kinds of studies had been done before, but what made this study newsworthy—what, in fact, made it mind-boggling—was that this was the first study that had ever tested the blood of newborns. The blood had been taken from the umbilical cords of randomly selected babies, immediately after the cords had been detached from the infants.

All of us—even newborns—live, today, in an environment that is suffused with chemicals that did not exist fifty years ago. If we want to reduce the burden of toxic chemicals in our bodies, we need to reduce the amounts of toxic chemicals in our environments, and that includes the products we use to clean and beautify our homes and bodies.

What happens if we clean for image and a spotless look rather than for a healthy home environment? Ellen Sandbeck, author of *Green Housekeeping,* reminds us, "If we clean just for appearances, rather than health, we may end up rubbing our burning eyes, scratching our rough, reddened skin, and suffering asthma attacks while wearing soft, fragrant, toxic clothing in gleaming homes that make us dizzy with the aerosolized essence of mountain meadows. Then we can look out the windows and watch the robins fainting on our perfect lawns."

It is a strange irony that so many of the most widely used products currently sold as cleaning and beauty aids actually pollute our environments and our bodies. This is the toxic paradox. Instead of supporting health, many of these products undermine it.

Fortunately, there are in almost every case alternatives made from safe, natural ingredients that work at least as well and are far less toxic, less expensive, and more pleasant to use.

THINGS YOU SHOULD NEVER (OR ALMOST NEVER) BUY

Bleach- and Ammonia-Based Household Cleaners

For decades, manufacturers of cleaning products have used the most powerful weapons in their chemical arsenals, with virtually no attention to how these agents affect the environment or human health. As a result, many people use bleach- and ammonia-based products to clean their toilets and bathrooms. Though these products are extremely effective at killing bacteria and mold, they are also extremely hazardous. Even when used correctly, they can cause eye, nose, and throat irritation. When used to clean closed-in areas such as shower stalls, they produce vapor concentrations that can cause serious lung damage and can burn the skin and eyes.

Drain uncloggers, toilet bowl cleaners, in-the-tank toilet cleaners, oven cleaners, and disinfecting sprays are particularly likely to include these chemicals. Chlorine and ammonia have valid industrial uses, and chlorine certainly has an important role in water purification. But for household uses, they are serious overkill.

Everyone recognizes the distinct "swimming pool" odor of chlorine bleach (more precisely, sodium hypochlorite). You'd think that this strong, irritating odor would keep children from playing with it, but products containing bleach are among the leading causes of poisoning in children. The American Association of Poison Control Centers reports that more than 120,000 children under the age of five are harmed in incidents involving household cleaners each year.

Most commercial laundry bleaches contain chlorine. Not only are these products dangerous to human health and the environment, they also damage fabrics and make them wear out rapidly. Is having "whiter than white" clothes and towels worth using one of the most dangerous and reactive elements on the planet?

If products containing ammonia and those containing chlorine bleach are mixed together, the result is both poisonous and highly explosive. When combined or mixed, they form chlorine gas and chloramines, which can cause severe and irreversible damage to the lungs. Chlorine gas has been used as an agent of chemical warfare. It is deadly.

Although products containing chlorine bleach or ammonia are effective at killing most pathogens, they are so toxic that they are almost never worth the risk, particularly when there are other products that are far less dangerous and are equally effective for most cleanup jobs. To clean dishes, for example, a small amount of liquid castile soap and hot water are generally quite sufficient to prevent cold or flu viruses from spreading in a household. Bon Ami is a safe alternative to Comet and Ajax. See pages 226–232 for specific cleaning and disinfecting formulas that are nontoxic and inexpensive.

Carpet Cleaners and Spot Removers Containing PERC or TCE

Most carpet cleaners and spot removers rely on powerful chemical solvents that dissolve dirt and grease, often including perchloroethylene (PERC) or trichloroethylene (TCE). These chemicals are toxic to the nervous system, and they are carcinogens. PERC is the agent used in most dry-cleaning. Short-term exposure to high doses can cause dizziness, decreased motor skills, and vision trouble.

A far less toxic form of carpet cleaning and the method that nearly all carpet manufacturers and carpet fiber producers recommend is called "hot water extraction," or "steam cleaning." The term "steam cleaning" is a little misleading, because there is actually little or no steam involved. This cleaning process involves spraying a fine stream of hot water and detergents into the carpet at high pressure. The dirt, soil, and grime thus loosened up is then sucked up by a powerful vacuum into a holding tank. This can be done from a truck-mounted unit outside your home, with only the hose and floor tool brought inside, or by a portable system brought into the home or office. See page 232 for inexpensive and nontoxic alternatives to using commercial carpet cleaning solutions.

Antimicrobial Soaps and Dish Liquids

Chemicals found in antibacterial soaps and other "germ-fighting" household products pose significant risks to human health and to the environment. Are they worth the risk?

The Soap and Detergent Association defends their use, citing a Food and Drug Administration (FDA) advisory panel of experts who said in 2005 that these chemicals are effective in reducing infection. That same committee, however, voted 11 to 1 that outside a hospital or other health care setting, these products are no more effective than regular soap and water in fighting infections. The vast majority of experts not on the payroll of industry agree. Rolf Halden, cofounder of the Johns Hopkins University Center for Water and Health, says that frequent hand washing with plain soap is just as effective for maintaining public health.

Similarly, the American Medical Association (AMA) advises: "There is little evidence to support the use of antimicrobials in consumer products." In fact, overuse of antimicrobial products is contributing to antibiotic resistance by encouraging the emergence of so-called supergerms. For this reason, the AMA released a report in 2000 stating "the use of common antimicrobials . . . in consumer products should be discontinued."

The two most common chemicals found in antimicrobial soaps, detergents, and other personal care products are triclocarban (TCC) and triclosan (TCS). Both of these chemicals are known to cause allergies, reproductive problems, skin irritations, and thyroid hormone disruption. TCC degrades into two substances, both of which are carcinogens. TCS, meanwhile, is a precursor to environmentally persistent dioxins, which are among the most poisonous compounds on the planet.

Antibacterial and chlorinated products also damage septic systems by killing the bacteria on which the systems depend.

Don't waste your money on dish liquids, hand soaps, toothpastes, and hand lotions that are "antibacterial." They aren't necessary, they are expensive, and they present a health risk.

Watch out for sponges that "resist odors" or "kill odors." This means they have been treated with a chemical disinfectant. Stick with pure cellulose sponges and be sure to squeeze them out thoroughly after each use. If they start to smell, boil them in hot water for five minutes. Some people put sponges through their dishwashers, but the water in dishwashers isn't typically hot enough to guarantee that the sponges will emerge germ-free.

Oven Cleaners

Most oven cleaners contain sodium hydroxide, an extremely corrosive substance that can react violently if mixed with other chemicals. Oven cleaners are designed and formulated to dissolve almost any organic material they contact. Unfortunately, this includes your skin and eyes. It doesn't take much exposure for the mist from aerosol oven cleaners to cause lung damage and chemical burns. The fumes are seriously toxic.

If you put a sheet of aluminum foil on the floor of your electric oven, making sure it doesn't touch the heating elements or cover the vents, and replace it when it gets dirty, you will save yourself a lot of oven-cleaning time. Aluminum foil is inadvisable on the bottom of some gas ovens, in which case you can place a cookie sheet on the bottom oven rack to catch any drippings from above. Many ovens have a self-cleaning feature, but if yours doesn't, a nontoxic and inexpensive way to clean your oven is to use the formula on page 228.

Drain Cleaners

All chemical drain cleaners are extremely hazardous. If even a single drop splatters into a human eye, severe damage (including blindness) can result. A single drop will also burn human skin.

Most drain cleaners contain strong acids, such as sulfuric acid and hydrochloric acid. In the chemical industry, sulfuric acid is known as oil of vitriol. It is so notoriously corrosive—a mere drop can cause permanent disfigurement—that in times past it was used as an agent of warfare. It is the origin of the word "vitriolic," which the dictionary defines as "filled with or expressing violent and bitter hatred toward somebody or something."

Drain cleaners wreak havoc on septic systems and sewage treatment plants. They are expensive and do nothing to prevent the problem from recurring. And if children accidentally play with them, the results can be horrible. Even if you don't have children, they are a liability to have in your home.

The best drain cleaner? Prevention. Don't pour grease down the kitchen sink. Don't flush dental floss, tampons, sanitary napkins, condoms, or paper towels down the toilet. People sometimes put ridiculous stuff in their toilets—diapers, cat litter, coffee grounds, cigarette butts, plastic bags, small toys, and a stunning array of other items. None of that ever belongs in a toilet. Don't flush down anything other than what your body produces and toilet paper.

See page 230 for how to clean out a clogged drain inexpensively, without using toxic chemicals.

Fabric Softeners or Dryer Sheets

Fabric softeners and dryer sheets are a great way to add to your body burden of toxic chemicals. How, you might wonder, could products with sweet names like Soft Ocean Mist, Clean Breeze, and Spring Awakening be anything but beneficent? The active chemical ingredients in products such as these have strong and pungent odors, so the manufacturers use heavy fragrances to cover up these smells. These fragrances include among their ingredients hormone-disrupting phthalates and neurotoxic chemicals such as toluene and styrene. Even fabric softeners and dryer sheets that are marketed as nontoxic often include chemicals such as alpha-terpineol, benzyl acetate, camphor, benzyl alcohol, limonene, ethyl acetate, pentane, and chloroform. According to the manufacturer's material safety data sheets, with sufficient exposure these chemicals:

- cause headaches, central nervous system disorders, and loss of muscular coordination
- irritate mucous membranes and impair respiratory function
- cause nausea, vomiting, dizziness, or drowsiness
- cause liver or kidney damage
- cause skin disorders and allergic reactions
- cause cancer

You become exposed to the chemicals in fabric softeners and dryer sheets when you breathe the aromatic molecules in the air near the clothes and when you touch the clothes or other fabrics with any part of your skin. Commercial fabric softeners and dryer sheets are actually designed to leave a chemical residue on the clothes in order to reduce static cling.

When animals are exposed to air containing fumes from fabric softener sheets, they develop irritation of the eyes, nose, throat, and lungs. Some have severe asthma attacks.

See page 231 for an effective fabric softener formula that uses only inexpensive and completely nontoxic ingredients, that leaves no film on fabrics, and that has the added benefit of aiding in eliminating any residual soap or detergent that might otherwise have remained in the fabrics.

Air Fresheners

Air fresheners are used in three-quarters of American households today, and are nearly a $2 billion a year industry. But the scented sprays, gels, and plug-ins don't actually "freshen" the air. They merely mask odors by filling the air with chemicals that overwhelm and desensitize the olfactory cells in our noses that allow us to detect scents. It would be more accurate to call them air polluters.

Air fresheners have been linked to breathing difficulties, developmental problems in babies, and cancer in lab animals. The chemicals in air fresheners are particularly dangerous to people with asthma or other respiratory problems. When the Natural Resources Defense Council analyzed fourteen common air fresheners, it found that twelve products, including some advertised as "all natural," contained the hormone-disrupting chemicals known as phthalates. Studies have shown that phthalates disrupt testosterone production, cause malformation of sex organs, and produce adverse changes in the genitals of baby boys.

Looking for an inexpensive and nontoxic way to deodorize your house? Put baking soda on your carpets, douse cotton balls in your favorite essential oil and place them around the house, or just bake fresh bread or cookies. Or put a few drops of essential oil into a spray bottle filled with water. Spray into the air, not onto furniture or faces.

Another alternative is to grow houseplants. The only true air fresheners, houseplants raise oxygen levels in indoor air while removing toxins and particulate matter. When NASA scientists researched how to create clean air for space missions and planned moon bases, they discovered that particular houseplants are extraordinarily effective at removing common pollutants including ammonia, formaldehyde, and benzene. At the very top of their list is the areca palm (also known as the yellow palm or butterfly palm). Quite tolerant of a range of indoor conditions, it releases voluminous amounts of moisture into the air, removes chemical toxins efficiently, and is beautiful to look at, making it a perfect low-maintenance houseplant.

And, of course, if you want indoor air that doesn't poison you and others, don't smoke indoors or allow others to do so.

Air Purifiers and Electronic Air Cleaners That Produce Ozone

Ozone in the upper atmosphere is critical to life on our planet. High above the earth, it acts as a protective shield, absorbing ultraviolet radiation that would otherwise be lethal to most terrestrial life. But you don't want excess ozone in the air you breathe.

Manufacturers and vendors of ozone devices describe ozone as "energized oxygen," "pure air," "saturated oxygen," "activated oxygen," or "super oxygen"—all terms implying that ozone is a healthy kind of oxygen. It is not. Ozone is a toxic gas with vastly different chemical and toxicological properties from oxygen. According to the EPA, "When inhaled, ozone can damage the lungs. Relatively low amounts can cause chest pain, coughing, shortness of breath, and throat irritation. Ozone may also worsen chronic respiratory diseases such as asthma and compromise the ability of the body to fight respiratory infections."

The companies that sell ozone generators say their products reduce mold, mildew, odors, and bacteria. It's true that ozone can be a powerful disinfectant, and ozone can play an important role in water purification. But it makes no sense to purposefully introduce it into the air you breathe. Don't waste your money on these products. See pages 226–232 for nontoxic and inexpensive ways to reduce mold, mildew, odors, and bacteria.

Too Much Stuff

Clutter, as well as being unsightly, consumes more of your precious time than you may realize. To mop a completely bare floor takes maybe ten minutes. But if the floor is cluttered and you have to move a lot of stuff out of your way as you go and then put it back afterward, the whole process may take an hour. And it's not just floors. Whenever items are stored on countertops, on tables, on dressers, or on any other horizontal surface (including sofas and beds), they will slow down your housecleaning. Cleaning professionals say that getting rid of clutter would eliminate 40 percent of the housework in the average American home.

Clutter devours time in other ways, too. According to the American Demographics Society, every day Americans collectively waste nine million hours searching for misplaced items. If you can't find it, what exactly is the point of owning it? Have you ever had the experience of purchasing something you needed, only to discover later that you already owned it but had been unable to find it?

Clutter costs you time and money. In the never-ending battle between order and chaos, clutter sides with chaos every time. The irony is that you have paid good money, which represents significant amounts of your life energy, for the things that added together create the clutter in your home and in your life. Anything that you possess that does not add to your life or your happiness eventually becomes a burden.

I don't like clutter, but I still tend to accumulate more things than I need. So every year or two, I go through my attic and closets, giving away or recycling everything that I possibly can. If something isn't demonstrably useful or beautiful, if it isn't clearly adding to my life, it goes. The point is to reduce clutter, produce simplicity, and support an emotional and mental spaciousness. My deeper goal in cleaning out my attic and closets is a life uncluttered by scattered thinking and unnecessary obligations.

INEXPENSIVE, NONTOXIC, EFFECTIVE, AND SAFE HOUSEHOLD CLEANING PRODUCTS

Once viewed as part of a fringe lifestyle, natural and nontoxic products are now going mainstream. With each passing year, they are occupying an ever larger place in world trade. Using nontoxic household cleaners may not seem like a life-changing act, but increasing numbers of people are finding this to be a significant step toward weaning themselves away from dependence on chemicals that damage human health and the environment.

And it can save a lot of money. The average U.S. household spends more than $200 a year on cleaning products. You can easily save $100 or more annually, and do just as good a job with far less toxicity, if you base your cleaning around simple natural products—particularly liquid castile soap, distilled white vinegar, and baking soda.

Castile Soap

Traditionally, soaps have been made by combining rendered animal fat with lye. From a cleaning perspective, though, there has always been a problem with such soaps. They react with the minerals in hard water to form a stubborn scum that doesn't dissolve in water. This is why synthetic cleaners and detergents were invented. Made from petroleum and containing an assortment of chemicals, they don't combine with water-soluble minerals and so don't leave a residual scum.

As a result of this advantage, detergents have almost totally replaced traditional soaps. Nearly all bath soaps on the market today, both solid and liquid, are actually detergents. The problem is, they contain toxic ingredients.

There is, however, an excellent alternative. Castile soap is soap made from vegetable oils. Available as both a liquid and in bar form, it is gentler than traditional soap, dissolves more completely, and no matter how hard the water, doesn't form a scum.

There are many brands of castile soap. One of the most widely available and highest quality is Dr. Bronner's. Made from olive and coconut oil, Dr. Bronner's liquid castile soaps are a little more expensive than some other castile soaps, but they are ultraconcentrated, which actually makes them a bargain. If you use Dr. Bronner's full strength in a squirt or spray bottle, it may clog the opening. This won't happen if you dilute it sufficiently.

As well, Dr. Bronner's products are made entirely from food-grade ingredients, are certified organic and fair trade, and the company gives 40–70 percent of its profits to social causes, including orphanages throughout the world. Despite many buyout offers, the company remains family owned. And uniquely among companies of its size, the highest paid employee at Dr. Bronner's makes no more than five times the salary of the lowest paid employee.

In addition to Dr. Bronner's, there are a few other brands of castile soaps that are all-natural blends of organic ingredients and contain no dangerous chemicals. Like Dr. Bronner's, these products don't form hard scums and so minimize the need to use abrasive cleaners on sinks and other surfaces.

Unfortunately, in the United States there is no legal definition of what constitutes "castile soap," so some manufacturers have begun jumping on the bandwagon, selling cheaper products that are actually chemical soups, listing only a few of the ingredients, and calling them castile soaps.

Distilled White Vinegar

Today, we are surrounded by so many sophisticated medical miracles and complex chemical products that we often fail to notice agents that have been used safely and effectively for hundreds of years. Distilled white vinegar is a prime example.

Although called "white" vinegar, this form of vinegar is not actually white. It's clear. It's also the cheapest of all forms of vinegar. Economical, nontoxic, and friendly to the environment, it is an extraordinarily versatile and effective cleaning agent. An excellent solvent for many cleaning jobs, its acidity makes it effective for killing most mold, bacteria, and germs. It can be used as a rinse aid in dishwashers and a fabric softener in laundering (see page 231), and it beautifully shines and polishes chrome faucets. As it dries, the vinegar smell disappears completely.

You can use it to mop a floor or to wipe down tabletops, appliances, and toilet seats. One caveat, though: Vinegar can harm marble and other stone surfaces, so it's best not to use it there.

In addition to its admirable household-cleaning properties, vinegar has many healing body care uses. You can soothe a sore throat by gargling with a mixture of vinegar, water, and honey. You can soak your feet in distilled white vinegar to thwart the fungus that causes athlete's foot. And you can rub it into your scalp, then rinse and shampoo, to get rid of dandruff.

If you have a problem with a cat scratching your furniture, spray it (the furniture, not the cat) with distilled white vinegar and the cat will probably stop.

Distilled white vinegar is self-preserving and doesn't need refrigeration. Its shelf life is almost indefinite. If you buy it by the gallon, you'll save money over small bottles.

Baking Soda

Sodium bicarbonate, known as baking soda, is an inexpensive and completely nontoxic product with an extraordinary number of household uses, including cleaning, deodorizing, and fire extinguishing.

Most baking soda today comes from trona, an ore found in great quantities in a particular part of Wyoming. Fifty million years ago, the land surrounding Green River, Wyoming, was covered by a six-hundred-square-mile lake. As the lake evaporated, it left a two-hundred-billion-ton deposit of trona sandwiched between layers of sandstone and shale. The trona deposit at the Green River Basin is so large that it can meet the entire world's needs for sodium bicarbonate for thousands of years to come. Baking soda is thus one of the few resources that we are in no danger of exhausting.

There is one other place where baking soda is manufactured today—the human body. Humans produce sodium bicarbonate for many critical purposes, including to maintain the correct acidity level of the bloodstream, to neutralize the plaque acids in the mouth and thus protect the teeth, and to neutralize stomach acids and thus prevent ulcers. Endogenous sodium bicarbonate also helps people to breathe, by carrying carbon dioxide from bodily tissues into the lungs, from which it is exhaled.

Many people are familiar with baking soda's leavening abilities, but fewer are aware of its outstanding cleaning capabilities. Most forms of dirt and grease are composed of fatty acids that can be neutralized by baking soda just as well as they can by soaps or detergents. Once neutralized, these acids dissolve in water and can be easily wiped away. Baking soda is an excellent alternative to harsh, toxic chemical cleaners.

Most unpleasant odors, too, are acid-based. This includes human body odor, pet urine odor, and most forms of bad breath (halitosis). Commercial "deodorizers" rely on added fragrances that mask odors. The National Academy of Sciences has identified the ingredients in fragrances as neurotoxins (chemicals toxic to the human brain and nervous system). Baking soda, in contrast, has no toxicity, and rather than mask odors, it effectively neutralizes them.

It's not a good idea to dissolve baking soda in water to use as a cleaner on surfaces and objects that will be hard to rinse afterward. On the other hand, baking soda makes a great scrubber for sinks, tubs, and toilets, where it can easily be rinsed. It is gentle, won't scratch, and is safe to use on porcelain. Some people keep it in a shaker bottle for ease of use. You can employ a sugar shaker for this purpose or make your own shaker by using a hammer and nail to punch holes in the lid of a jar.

Buying baking soda in bulk will save you a lot. It can be purchased quite inexpensively by the pound or more at many hardware stores. Some pool-supply companies sell it for noncooking purposes under the name sodium bicarbonate. You can also buy it in quantity at restaurant supply stores and at megastores. If you store it in an airtight and waterproof container, it will keep for a very long time. It does not need to be refrigerated.

Hydrogen Peroxide

Hydrogen peroxide is very effective for household cleaning, thanks to its antibacterial, antifungal, antimold, and antimildew properties. It not only cleans and disinfects the surfaces and objects you clean with it, it also keeps your sponges, mops, and scrubbing pads cleaner as well. It's nontoxic for people, plants, animals, and the earth. And it's inexpensive.

At its full strength, hydrogen peroxide has many industrial uses, but for household purposes the ideal product to use is much weaker—3 percent hydrogen peroxide and 97 percent water. It is also available in a 35 percent strength, but you have to be careful with that level of concentration. All the suggested uses in this book are based on a 3 percent solution.

When exposed to light, hydrogen peroxide breaks down rapidly, so it must be stored in a bottle that doesn't allow for the transmission of light. A plastic spray bottle nozzle can be screwed onto a hydrogen peroxide bottle, creating a sprayer with the necessary light-blocking characteristics.

You can use 3 percent hydrogen peroxide either straight or diluted in an equal amount of water as a mouthwash if you have trench mouth, canker sores, or other mouth infections. This will also help to whiten your teeth.

Hydrogen peroxide can also be used to wash or soak fruits and vegetables to kill bacteria. Research published by the *Journal of Food and Science* in 2003 found that hydrogen peroxide was effective at decontaminating apples and melons that were infected with strains of E. coli.

To kill germs and leave a fresh smell, put a little on your dishrag or sponge when you wipe down your kitchen and bathroom counters and tabletops. Similarly, to kill bacteria such as salmonella that might be growing on a wooden cutting board, pour hydrogen peroxide on it after rinsing with water.

To whiten clothes and fabrics in your laundry, you can add a cup of hydrogen peroxide to the rinse cycle as a safe alternative to chlorine bleach. If there is blood on clothing, apply hydrogen peroxide directly to the soiled spot, let sit a minute, then rinse with cold water. Repeat if necessary. Be careful not to overdo it, though, if you don't want to bleach out color from the fabric. Test for colorfastness in an inconspicuous area first.

Washing Soda

Extremely inexpensive, washing soda could be considered baking soda on steroids. It's highly alkaline, can be used to remove stubborn stains from laundry, and has a variety of other uses around the house, including to descale coffee machines, bathroom tiles, and other objects that may have accumulated mineral deposits as a result of hard water. It has no toxic fumes, but it is more caustic than baking soda, so wear gloves when using it.

Washing soda is useful in making laundry soap, cleaning deep grease (it's much safer than commercial solvents), removing stains, and unclogging drains. It's not a good idea to use it on fiberglass or aluminum, as it could scratch. Keep it out of the reach of children and pets.

Washing soda is available at some supermarkets and hardware stores. If you have trouble finding it, you can locate a retailer in your area that carries it by calling Church & Dwight Consumer Relations at (800) 524–1328 with your zip code.

Borax

Humans have used borax for more than four thousand years. Since the 1800s, it has been mined near Death Valley, California. Dirt cheap, borax has many industrial uses, but in the home it is used as a natural laundry-cleaning booster, multipurpose cleaner, fungicide, insecticide, herbicide, and disinfectant. An off-white color, odorless, and alkaline, borax crystals can be mixed with other cleaning agents for added power.

Although you certainly wouldn't want to eat it, borax is relatively safe and is quite effective without being toxic. It is useful in a lot of the ways that baking soda is, but it's stronger and disinfects more, so it's good for mold, mildew, and deeper dirt. In general, use baking soda first and use borax only in situations where something stronger is needed. It will enable you to get even stubborn stains clean without resorting to toxic chemicals.

Borax should not be used where it might get into food, and it should be safely stored out of the reach of children and pets. By far the leading brand in the United States is 20 Mule Team Borax.

Cream of Tartar

Found in the spice/baking section of most markets, cream of tartar is comparatively expensive (around three dollars an ounce). However, you need only a tiny amount (¼ teaspoon or less) to remove most stubborn stains on tubs and sinks, and it stores indefinitely. It is an effective non-toxic product and can eliminate the need for strong and toxic bleaches. A by-product of the wine industry, cream of tartar works magically on tubs and sinks.

Flexible Plastic Drain-Cleaning Sticks

Costing only two or three dollars, these are great tools to clean hair and other gunk out of drains. Over time they will save you a lot of aggravation, a lot of time, and hundreds of dollars in plumbing costs. You can find these simple-to-use devices in many hardware stores in the plumbing department. They are far less expensive, and for their intended purpose far more useful, than aluminum or other metal "snakes."

NONTOXIC, INEXPENSIVE, AND EFFECTIVE CLEANING FORMULAS

There are many "natural cleaners" on the market today. Some are made by good companies, including the widely available Dr. Bronner's, Shaklee (sold person-to-person and via the Internet), and Seventh Generation, based in Burlington, Vermont.

The problem with natural cleaning products in general is that they are almost always more expensive than their typical commercial counterparts, and sometimes much more. Plus, there is a great deal of hype and greenwashing in the industry. There are no regulations that govern the use of words such as "natural" or "organic" in cleaning products and no requirements that products list all their ingredients.

Today, the "natural cleaner" market in the United States is dominated by Green Works, which accounts for nearly half of the nation's sales. Green Works is owned by Clorox, the chemical giant whose name derives from its bestselling product—chlorine bleach. Another leading brand of "natural cleaner," Simple Green, is made from the solvent 2-butoxyethanol, a known environmental hazard that causes a whole range of health problems. The major cleansing ingredient in Jason "pure, natural and organic" liquid soaps, body washes, and shampoos is sodium myreth sulfate, a proven skin and eye irritant that is made with the carcinogenic petrochemical ethylene oxide.

Fortunately, there are excellent alternatives. The formulas that follow are effective and use only nontoxic and inexpensive ingredients. They can save you a stack of cash while sparing your body and your home environment from exposure to toxic chemicals. These formulas were developed by my wife, Deo, who for years helped support our family by cleaning homes. Her "Shiny Bright Housecleaning Service" specialized in the use of nontoxic and truly natural ingredients.

You might want to get a few plastic spray bottles for liquids, a few squeeze bottles, some airtight containers for powders and scrubs, and some shakers (sugar shakers work well) for scouring powders. Be sure to label your containers clearly.

For Dish Soap

You can use liquid castile soap for hand-washing dishes. Dilute in a squeeze bottle, using 1 part castile soap to 3 parts water. If you are using Dr. Bronner's liquid castile soap, dilute even more, as it is very concentrated.

For General Cleaning of Kitchen and Bathroom Surfaces: Counters, Appliances, Glass Stovetops, Cupboards, and Tiles

For a good spray cleaner that cuts grease and neutralizes odors, dilute 1 cup of white vinegar with 1 cup of water in a spray bottle. Add ¼ teaspoon of liquid castile soap. Shake thoroughly. Spray and wipe with a clean, dry cloth. The vinegar odor will dissipate quickly. (Do not use this on stone or marble.) For tougher jobs, use 100 percent vinegar.

For marble or stone surfaces, make a solution of ¼ teaspoon of castile soap in 2 cups of water. Spray and wipe with a clean, dry cloth.

For tougher jobs, spray with a solution of ½ teaspoon of baking soda, 2 teaspoons of borax, and ½ teaspoon of liquid castile soap in 2 cups of hot water. Shake well to dissolve, and shake periodically before spraying. Wipe with a clean, dry rag.

For Kitchen and Bathroom Sinks

Sprinkle baking soda on a damp sponge for a light scour, then rinse. For a heavier duty scour, mix 1 part baking soda, 1 part borax, and 1 part salt.

For a quick and whitening scour, sprinkle your sink with baking soda, then pour a little 3 percent hydrogen peroxide on your cloth or scrubber, and wipe. Rinse well.

To remove stains in porcelain enamel sinks and tubs, wet the stain, sprinkle with cream of tartar, and scrub with a moist cloth or scrubber. If you need more power, make a paste of cream of tartar and hydrogen peroxide to scrub the stain.

For Cleaning Ovens

For a good, inexpensive, and nontoxic oven cleaner: Mix 2 tablespoons of liquid castile soap and 2 tablespoons of borax with 2 cups of hot water in a spray bottle. Shake thoroughly. Spray the oven with this mixture, coating the sides, top, and bottom of the oven. Wait 20 minutes, then scrub, rinse, and wipe dry. This also works on oven racks. You can place them outside on newspaper to spray and scrub.

If you need a stronger cleaner, add 1 tablespoon of washing soda to the solution. Make sure the water is warm to dissolve the washing soda. For extremely stubborn spots you can scour with some straight washing soda on your scrubber (wear gloves).

For Burned Food in Pots and Baking Dishes

Stir 2 tablespoons of baking soda per quart of water into your pot or baking dish. For pots, bring to a boil, then let cool. For baking dishes, place in the oven at 350 degrees Fahrenheit and then allow to cool. After cooling, the burned-on food will scrape off easily. Alternatively, you can put baking soda into your pot or dish and add boiling water, let cool, and then clean.

Cast-iron pans will need a little re-oiling after this treatment. Place the pan on a hot burner for a minute or two to dry it thoroughly. Then, while it is still hot, lightly oil the pan and leave it on the hot burner a few minutes longer. Remove the pan from the burner and wipe the excess oil off the surface.

For nonstick cookware, use a plastic or other soft scrubber to avoid scratching the surface, and use a medium (not high) setting to heat the baking soda solution.

For Toilet Bowls

For routine cleaning, sprinkle the toilet bowl with baking soda and brush clean. If you prefer a spray, you can spritz a little white vinegar onto the rim and bowl and brush clean.

When you need a more powerful cleaning, combine ½ cup of vinegar and ½ cup of baking soda in the toilet. Let sit a few minutes, then scrub.

If a toilet bowl has a high degree of built-up minerals: Use a toilet plunger in the bowl until the water empties out. Fill the bowl with white vinegar and let it sit overnight. In the morning, scrub with your toilet brush and other cleaning tools. The vinegar will have loosened the minerals enough that you can now remove them.

For Showers and Tubs

For a simple dry scrub, sprinkle with baking soda, scour with a cloth or nonscratch scrubber, and rinse. For heavier cleaning and to remove built-up soap scum, wet the surface, then sprinkle with borax. Scrub, then rinse. If you need a strong disinfecting cleaner, spray with a solution of 1 teaspoon of borax, ½ teaspoon of liquid castile soap, ½ cup of hot vinegar, and ½ cup of hot water. Scrub, then rinse well.

For Grout Stains

To remove grout stains, apply 3 percent hydrogen peroxide and let sit 20 minutes. Scrub with a toothbrush and rinse thoroughly.

For Disinfecting

Spray toilet rims, cutting boards, counters, and other surfaces you wish to disinfect with hydrogen peroxide, followed by vinegar spray. Let sit

20 minutes or so before rinsing. Never mix vinegar and hydrogen per-oxide in the same bottle.

To Remove Mold (and Help Prevent Recurrence)

Spray moldy areas on walls, tiles, or tile grout with 100 percent white vin-egar. Wait a few minutes, then rub with a cloth or scrubber and wipe clean. Do not rinse. Repeat if needed. The vinegar smell will dissipate quickly.

If you need a stronger treatment, use 3 percent hydrogen peroxide in place of vinegar. Test walls for colorfastness before applying, as hydro-gen peroxide may change the color.

If you have a chronic mold problem, spray with hydrogen peroxide and allow to sit for several hours. Spray again, then proceed as above.

For Faucets and Chrome

Spray with 100 percent white vinegar and polish with a dry cloth. To re-move hardened minerals, soak overnight in a rag drenched in vinegar, then use a toothbrush and baking soda to scrub clean. Rinse, spray with vinegar, and polish.

For Sluggish or Clogged Drains

First remove trapped debris by using a flexible plastic drain-cleaning stick, available at many hardware stores. These sticks are thin enough to slide between the small gaps in your drain fitting. Then pour ½ cup of baking soda into the drain, followed by 1 cup of heated white vinegar. It will sizzle for a while, and you can use your drain stick to help loosen things up. Follow this with a couple quarts of boiling water. (Do not at-tempt to use this remedy directly after using a commercial drain cleaner, as it may cause a reaction.)

If the drain is completely backed up and you need a more powerful approach, pour 1 cup of washing soda around the drain and let it sit. The washing soda will slowly seep into the clogged drain and, in most cases, it will begin to open. Follow this with boiling (or hot) water. When water is beginning to move down the drain again, you can open it fur-ther by pouring ½ cup of baking soda followed by 1 cup of heated white vinegar into the drain. Flush with boiling water.

If your drain is severely blocked, you may need to use an auger (snake) available at hardware stores. Use a toilet auger for toilets to avoid scratching the porcelain, and a crank auger for sinks and tubs.

As a preventive measure, to keep drains clear, use your drain stick to remove hair on a regular basis. Every month or so, pour 1 cup of baking soda into the drain and wash it down with boiling (or hot) water.

For Mirrors and Windows

A solution of 1 part white vinegar to 3 parts water works well to clean windows and mirrors. If you buy vinegar by the gallon, this mixture costs less than one cent per ounce. Biokleen glass cleaner at my local store costs sixteen cents per ounce.

If windows or mirrors are very dirty, use equal parts vinegar and water. If commercial window cleaners with wax have been used in the past on your windows, they may smear when you attempt to clean them with vinegar. In this case, make a solution of 2 cups of water, ½ cup of vinegar, and ½ teaspoon of liquid castile soap in a spray bottle. Spray, wait 30 seconds, then wipe clean. From then on you can clean with vinegar and water.

For Cleaning Floors

Combine 1 cup of vinegar and ½ teaspoon of liquid castile soap in a bucket of warm water. For marble and stone floors, omit the vinegar. There is no need to rinse afterward.

For Laundry Detergent

For the toughest cleaning jobs, there is a way to greatly enhance the cleaning power of any natural laundry detergent. Add ½ cup each of borax and washing soda and use hot water. This will clean better than even the most toxic and most heavy-duty laundry detergents on the market.

For Fabric Softener

To soften fabrics and remove excess soap or detergent, use ½ cup of vinegar diluted with ½ cup of water in your rinse cycle. The vinegar smell will be completely gone when the clothes are dry.

If your washing machine has a built-in rinse or fabric softener dispenser, simply pour the diluted vinegar into the dispenser. If your washing machine doesn't have a dispenser, you can either add the diluted vinegar at the beginning of the rinse cycle or use the Downy Ball.

The Downy Ball costs about three dollars, is available on eBay and elsewhere online, and doesn't require you to watch for when the rinse cycle begins. It's designed to dispense liquid fabric softener (or vinegar) in top-loading clothes-washing machines at the right time in the washing cycle. It's made by Downy, the manufacturer of chemical fabric softeners, but it works even better with vinegar.

Using vinegar as a fabric softener has many advantages. It decreases your exposure to toxic chemicals, and it reduces static and wrinkles in your clothing and makes them feel better. Even towels that are line dried will feel fluffy and soft. If you ever want to remove detergent buildup in your washing machine, run the machine through a wash cycle without any clothes, using hot water and a cup of vinegar.

If some types of synthetic fabrics still emerge from the dryer with a degree of static cling, try line drying them or only partially drying them in the dryer. And a reminder: Never use bleach and vinegar at the same time. Mixing them together in a washing machine (or anywhere else) may create toxic fumes.

For Carpet Cleaning

To freshen and deodorize carpets, sprinkle them with baking soda, work it in with a brush or stiff broom, and let it sit several hours. Sweep to remove some of the baking soda before vacuuming thoroughly.

An effective way to deeply clean wall-to-wall or large carpets is with a steam extraction machine, which you can rent from hardware stores, supermarkets, and equipment rental stores. Before steam cleaning, vacuum thoroughly.

Commercial carpet-cleaning solutions, which are often used with steam extraction machines, may contain toxic chemicals and perfumes. You can replace these with a mixture of castile soap and white vinegar. This will dissolve stains and neutralize odors. Mix the vinegar (instead of commercial cleaning solution) with water in the proportion recommended on the machine. Add a teaspoon of castile soap per gallon of water. The vinegar odor will dissipate once the carpet dries.

THE TRUTH ABOUT COSMETICS SAFETY

You probably expect a shampoo or other body care product that is labeled "pure, natural and organic," to be what it says it is. But unlike the food industry, where products must meet certain standards to be labeled "organic," there are today no legal standards for organic or natural personal care products sold in the United States. Words such as "organic," "pure," "natural," and "gentle" can be used as marketing claims on any personal care product without any guidelines or regulations. The top-selling shampoo in the country, for example, is Clairol Herbal Essences shampoo, which has for years claimed to offer users "the organic experience." It's been an extraordinarily effective marketing theme, but the product itself may have no ingredients whatsoever that are actually organic in any meaningful sense of the term.

The commercial cosmetic industry defines "organic" as "any compound containing carbon" and defines "natural" as "any ingredient derived from a natural substance." By those definitions, all plastics and petroleum-derived pesticides are organic, and literally everything on Earth is natural.

In 2008, Dr. Bronner's sued a collection of companies that market "organic" personal care products over the validity of their organic labels. The lawsuit alleged that it's false advertising and unfair to the public to label as "organic" products whose primary ingredients are chemicals derived from petroleum. Dr. Bronner's lawsuit was backed by the Organic Consumers Association, which represents nearly one million members, subscribers, and volunteers, including several thousand businesses in the natural foods and organic marketplace.

It's well known that products we apply to our bodies can be absorbed through the skin, so you would think that products that are applied to the skin would be subject to some kind of regulation and scrutiny for their health effects. In reality, though, the FDA has no power to perform even the most rudimentary functions needed to ensure the safety of the $35 billion worth of cosmetics and other personal care products sold each year in the United States. Today, the FDA:

- Does not review or approve cosmetic products or ingredients before they are sold to the public.

- Does not require manufacturers to file data on ingredients or report cosmetic-related injuries.
- Does not require companies to test cosmetic products for safety before marketing.
- Does not have the authority to recall defective or harmful cosmetics.

In 2004, European Union countries took heed of the data coming from literally thousands of research studies and banned more than 1,100 ingredients then in widespread use in cosmetic, body care, and cleaning products. The ingredients were banned because they were known or suspected of causing cancer, birth defects, or fertility problems. By contrast, the U.S. FDA has in its history banned a grand total of nine.

Today in the United States, there are virtually no restrictions on the ingredients that companies making cosmetics and other personal care products are allowed to use. The result is that toxic chemicals can be found in everything from sunscreen to nail polish, from mascara to baby shampoo, from deodorants to shaving creams, from lipstick to colognes. According to a 2005 analysis of cosmetic ingredients by the Environmental Working Group (a nonprofit organization dedicated to using the power of science to protect public health and the environment), more than half of cosmetics products for sale in the United States contain chemicals that can act like estrogen or disrupt hormones in the body.

How, then, can you know what products are safe? Fortunately, the Environmental Working Group has developed an extraordinarily thorough website, cosmeticsdatabase.com, that provides a guide to the safety of a vast array of cosmetics and personal care products.

An example of the Environmental Working Group's findings: In 2009, the organization reported that out of 1,691 sunscreens and other sun-blocking products currently on the market, 60 percent either didn't protect skin from sun damage or contained hazardous chemicals, or both. Not satisfied merely to point out the problem, the organization's website provides a guide to enable you to find safe sunscreen products that work.

BEYOND HELPLESSNESS

One Sunday in the summer of 2009, the front page of *The New York Times* reported two painful news stories. One spoke of the many suicides among Iraqi vets. The other announced that another 1.5 million unemployed Americans were facing the imminent loss of their unemployment benefits.

A couple pages further along, on a very different note, there appeared two lavish ads for perfumes. One full-page ad, for a new fragrance marketed by John Varvatos, spoke of "an intricate yet bold blend of rose absolute and a coffee bean accord." The other ad, also taking up an entire page, was for a fragrance by Marc Jacobs and proclaimed a startling new fragrance endowed with "an intoxicating swirl of rich layers, wrapping the skin in sensuous florals, blooming with the signature note of fuchsia peony."

Some might say that this grating juxtaposition reflects the human capacity to find something beautiful even in dark times, and perhaps it does. But I could not help but think of two other things.

I found myself remembering another full-page ad in *The New York Times,* this one from a few years previous. Sponsored by three nonprofits—the Environmental Working Group, Coming Clean, and Health Care Without Harm—the ad showed a full-page photo of a beautiful young pregnant woman sniffing a bottle of perfume. "Sexy for her," said the heading over the photo. "For baby, it could really be poison."

"Toxic chemicals linked to birth defects," the ad stated accurately, "are being found at alarming rates in women of childbearing age. And according to new laboratory tests, these same chemicals are being added to popular cosmetics and beauty aids." The tests had found phthalates—industrial chemicals that have been shown to damage the liver, kidneys, and lungs, and which have been strongly linked to birth defects—in 72 percent of the cosmetic products on the market in the United States, and in every single fragrance tested.

Since that time, the evidence has continued to mount. One study found that men who used cologne or aftershave within twenty-four hours of urine collection had more than twice the levels of a particularly dangerous type of phthalate (diethyl phthalate) in their bodies as men who did not use the products.

What's the point of using products to make you look or smell beautiful on the outside, if they are potentially making you sick on the inside? That was one of my thoughts as I saw this somewhat jarring juxtaposition in the paper between so much human suffering, on the one hand, and these expensive and potentially toxic perfumes, on the other.

The other thought that came to me then was about our human capacity for denial, about how often we want to turn away from suffering because we don't know how to bear it, because we don't know how strong and able we are. So often we feel helpless in the face of life's pressures and pain, and we retreat into distractions and indulgences. But what if we knew we weren't really helpless? What if we knew that there really are ways we can live that are healthy for our bodies, our communities, and our world? What if we knew that we could choose ways of life that are thriving and sustainable, that don't depend on pollution or harm?

The perfumes that were advertised so lavishly in *The New York Times* that day come in exquisite bottles. They are expensive and sensually intoxicating, and like almost all commercial perfumes today they contain ingredients that can be harmful. Products like that can have a certain appeal when we feel unable to do anything about the larger problems on the planet. But what if our daily lives were full of choices we made in favor of what is simple, inexpensive, and nontoxic? Would we be more rooted in what is enduring? Would we be more confident in our ability to make a positive difference? Might we see more opportunities to bring healing and beauty into the world? Might we feel less alone, less afraid, and less inclined to divert our attention and seek escape? Would we feel more trust in our ability to be resourceful and thrive even in times of economic downturn?

I love beautiful scents and fragrances as much as anyone, and I take great pleasure in essential oils and other natural scents. The smell of cinnamon, of freshly brewed coffee, of vanilla and jasmine, of roses and freshly cut grass, delight and inspire me. But how much harm has been done when we buy unhealthy products to push away our feelings, to mask over what is real and alive and happening in us and in our world?

The new good life isn't about covering up our inner lives with an outer mask, with façades or pretense. It's about living from our inner beauty, from our capacity to make good choices, and our ability to alleviate suffering. It's not about poisoning ourselves and our future. It's about being lit from within by our capacity to respond to what life brings us with as much love as we can, and with as much love as it takes.

BEAUTY THAT IS SOUL DEEP

I have a dear friend and colleague, Victoria Moran, who in her fifties is one of the most beautiful, vibrant, and energetic women you could ever meet. Yet in her early life she experienced herself as fat and dumpy. Somewhere along the line Victoria started thanking God at night for the good in her day, stopped asking to be thin and gorgeous, and began asking if she could be strong and helpful. In her book *Lit from Within,* Victoria has written eloquently about how someone truly becomes beautiful:

> Your physical self is by no means the totality of who you are. It does, however, reflect who you are: a unique spiritual being of extraordinary beauty and importance. When you understand this and see yourself in this way, you will treat your body as if it housed a soul, and you will live your life as though it were part of a grand design. You will be rewarded with an unmistakable radiance that comes from deep within and shows on the outside, too. . . .
>
> You don't have to look like the women [and men] in the magazines. They usually represent one idea of beauty, an idea dependent on youth and abetted by cosmetics, lighting, and the art of the touch-up. What you'll have instead is a glow that can be neither bought nor bottled.
>
> Until quite recently, contemporary culture didn't put much stock in having a lovely soul. This was probably because nobody could figure out how to make a profit from it. Whatever the reason, that message to devalue the beauty that arises from deep within crept into the collective consciousness. In reality, though, inner beauty is the only kind that truly matters because it's the only kind that goes the distance.
>
> You can count on it to persist, even if you don't feel well or you've been up all night with a sick child or when you're ten—or thirty—years older than you are now. And since this beauty is soul-deep, you may even be able to take it with you when you go.
>
> You can think of its outward expression as charisma or grace, as class or poise. When you have it, your eyes really are windows to the soul. Your smile can put anyone at ease. An irresistible attraction

emanates from your personality so that, regardless of your age or body type, you are beautiful. . . . This is the radiance that can light up a room, light up your life, and give you the kind of beauty that passing years will never diminish.

This is the kind of beauty that is truly worth celebrating, and it can't be purchased in the cosmetics section at Bloomingdale's. Fortunately, we don't have to acquire it from outside ourselves. We have only to discover it and set it free.

NINE

The Economics of Happiness

When you have dismissed the serpents of vanity and greed, conquered the lizards of self-importance, and lulled the monkey mind to sleep, your steps will be lighter.

When you have given up everything to make a friend a cup of tea and tend her broken heart, stood up against the violation of innocent children and their fathers and mothers, made conscious choices to live simply and honor the earth, your steps will be lighter.

When you have grown still on purpose while everything around you is asking for your chaos, you will find the doors between every room of this interior castle thrown open, the path home to your true love unobstructed at all.

—SAINT TERESA OF AVILA

When I left Baskin-Robbins and the fortune my father had made selling ice cream, I did so because I didn't want to live a life of affluence based on a product that could harm people's health. I also recoiled at the idea of inheriting a life of privilege while so many others had to struggle for their basic livelihood. I once heard it said of George

W. Bush that he was born on third base and thought he had hit a triple. I'm not sure what base I was born on, but I walked off the field to play an entirely different game.

I didn't take the steps I did because I thought money is bad. On the contrary, I believe money is good and important. Without it, it's impossible to thrive in the modern world and difficult even to survive. But money isn't a god. It's something to use, not something to crave or to worship, and certainly not something that should rule our lives.

It seems that something has gone terribly wrong in our relationships with money. Somehow we have come to make money into an end in itself, more important than human life, more important than the natural world, more important than our spiritual well-being.

The mainstream media called me a "rebel without a cone," but my rebellion was about a lot more than ice cream. My rebellion was against profit seeking without conscience, against economic activity unbounded by morals, concern for the vulnerable, future generations, or the limits of nature.

My problem was not with comfort or monetary wealth. My problem was with a way of life in which those who have more than they need are envied or extolled, while those who are materially poor are scorned or forgotten.

I felt acutely that I had only so many days on this earth, and while I held this brief candle I wanted to walk a different path. Far deeper in me than the desire to inherit money was the need to truly inherit my life, the need to find, befriend, and become true to myself. The trust fund I wanted to enrich my life was the trust in my heart. The treasure I wanted to inherit was my own soul, for that is a treasure you can never lose.

In the more than forty years since I made the decision to walk away from Baskin-Robbins and the wealth that would have been mine, I have never once, not for a single moment, regretted it.

At the time, I had never heard the phrase "follow your bliss." That phrase did not become widely known until twenty years later, when Joseph Campbell, a lifelong student and teacher of mythology, was interviewed by Bill Moyers, in what was to become one of the most popular series ever presented by PBS, *The Power of Myth*.

In one of the interviews, Moyers asked Campbell, "Do you ever have the sense of . . . being helped by hidden hands?"

Campbell replied,

All the time. It is miraculous. I even have a superstition that has grown on me as a result of invisible hands coming all the time—namely, that if you do follow your bliss you put yourself on a kind of track that has been there all the while, waiting for you, and the life that you ought to be living is the one you are living. When you can see that, you begin to meet people who are in your field of bliss, and they open doors to you. I say, follow your bliss and don't be afraid, and doors will open where you didn't know they were going to be.

By "following your bliss," Campbell obviously didn't mean doing whatever you please. He meant something far deeper, vastly more difficult, and infinitely more life giving than any kind of self-indulgence. He meant identifying whatever burning needs have been instilled in your soul, finding whatever it is that you are truly passionate about, and attempting to give yourself over to your essential purpose as fully as possible. In so doing, and in surmounting the obstacles life is certain to provide, he believed you will achieve your fullest potential and serve your community to the greatest possible extent.

Campbell's idea that your deepest happiness is found in being true to your greatest purpose is not exactly what the Macy's department store chain had in mind when, a few Christmas seasons ago, they provided consumers with shopping bags that carried the message, printed in bold letters right at the top: "Who says you can't buy happiness?" Apparently Macy's didn't mind contradicting a message inherent in every major world religion in order to make money off the birth of Christ.

Of course, Macy's isn't alone. Coca-Cola has spent enormous sums on a massive global marketing campaign presenting Coke vending machines as "happiness factories." And Nestlé has based much of its advertising on slogans such as "Happiness is as easy as Nesquik."

In reality, though, products such as Coke and Nesquik contribute less to happiness than they do to obesity, a physical condition associated more with feelings of depression and anxiety than with joy.

I wonder, sometimes, if it's possible for us to comprehend the price we've paid in the pursuit of the old good life. Have we been deluding ourselves? Have we as a society bought into assumptions about money and happiness that not only aren't true, but are tearing the heart out of our lives and our world?

The Value of Money

There seem to be two schools of thought about the relationship between money and happiness: On the one hand, there are those who say money isn't that important. "You can only become truly accomplished at something you love," writes Maya Angelou. "Don't make money your goal. Instead, pursue the things you love doing, and then do them so well that people can't take their eyes off you."

In her camp is the environmental advocate John Muir, who once said that he was better off than the billionaire E. H. Harriman. "I have all the money I want," Muir explained, "and he hasn't."

On the other hand, there are those who say that money is essential, and that there is something spiritually pretentious and elitist about pretending otherwise. It's not the love of money that is the root of all evil, they would say, but the lack of money. Maybe money can't directly buy happiness, but it certainly can buy lots of things that contribute tremendously to happiness. While it is possible to be happy with less, it is far easier to be happy with more. They would argue that those who believe money is not important have probably never watched their children go hungry.

I believe there is truth in both camps. Up to a certain point, money is vital to happiness for almost everyone. It can buy food, clothing, and housing and provide for other basic needs. Once a person's basic needs are met, though, money takes on a different meaning.

For a family barely scraping by, $500 could be the difference between paying the rent or being evicted—between having a place to sleep and being homeless. To someone more affluent, $500 might simply mean a few hours spent shopping for clothes, or that much more financial security and increased savings.

Flying on an airplane recently, I had a vivid reminder of how differently people in different economic classes experience money. In the seat pocket in front of me, I found the ubiquitous Sky Mall "shopping magazine." This "magazine" is actually a catalog that offers thousands of items for sale, not a single one of which appears to me to be something anyone actually needs.

Some seven hundred million bored airline passengers, many of them presumably among the more affluent members of modern society, peruse the catalog each year, making $150 million in purchases. One of the catalog's perennial bestsellers is a lawn ornament called the "Zombie of Montclaire Moors," a ghoulish piece of plastic resin that you can buy for around $100. Promising to "bring the flesh-hungry undead to your daffodil bed," what this macabre lawn decoration actually does, I think, is give passersby the impression that your house is occupied by a raving lunatic.

Leafing through the catalog, I also find that I can spend $329.99, plus shipping and handling, for a "putting game . . . a piece of equipment . . . [that] has no physical cup. Instead the device's software creates a 'virtual' cup that can be set to any distance on a 'virtual' green . . . allowing you to simulate any length putt up to 32 feet."

The executives behind the Sky Mall catalog say they are providing amusement and relaxation to airline passengers. And I confess that on some long flights, feeling restless and uncomfortable, I've perused the pages hoping to find something of interest. But the items offered have always seemed relentlessly frivolous, and they remind me of a painful irony. The cost of the putting game, for instance, could provide food and housing for a year for an impoverished family in Africa. The cost of the ghoulish lawn ornament could pay for several cataract surgeries in many parts of the world, restoring sight to the blind.

Money can and does make an enormous difference to those in need, and this is every bit as true in wealthier nations as it is in poorer ones. Every human being needs food, shelter, rest, clothing, and a sense of control over their lives. Those who are unemployed and unable to pay their bills, those who don't have enough to meet their basic needs, are far more prone to feelings of helplessness and despair, and far more likely to be victims of violence. Plus, it can be expensive to be poor. In the United States today, inner-city residents who don't have cars to get to supermarkets often buy their groceries from corner stores where the food selection isn't healthy and everything costs more.

In much of the country, it's almost becoming a crime to be poor. A 2009 report from the National Law Center on Homelessness and

Poverty found that the number of laws against the publicly poor— ordinances that make it illegal to sleep, eat, or sit in public spaces—has been rising in cities across the nation. "If you're lying on a sidewalk, whether you're homeless or a millionaire, you're in violation of the ordinance," said a city attorney in St. Petersburg, Florida, trying to make the case that antiloitering legislation doesn't discriminate against the destitute. It's a line of reasoning that has deep historical roots. "The law, in its majestic equality," wrote the French novelist Anatole France, "forbids the rich as well as the poor to sleep under bridges, to beg in the streets and to steal bread."

MONEY AND HAPPINESS

What does science tell us about the relationship between money and happiness? A vast amount of research about the question has been conducted globally in the last few decades. As more and more scientists have become involved, the studies, experiments, and forms of research have become increasingly sophisticated. No longer must scientists simply rely on what people tell them. What people say can be verified. Well-being can be assessed by various empirical measures with high consistency, reliability, and validity.

In his book *Happiness: Lessons from a New Science,* economist Richard Layard explains: "We now know that what people say about how they feel corresponds closely to the actual levels of activity in different parts of the brain, which can be measured in standard scientific ways." People who say they are happy "have relatively high levels of electrical activity in the left prefrontal region of the brain," and "are also more likely to be rated as happy by friends," "more likely to respond to requests for help," "less likely to be involved in disputes at work," and also "less likely to die prematurely."

Does the data support the idea that money brings happiness? Surprisingly, only insofar as it lifts people out of poverty. Once that point is clearly passed, the link between monetary wealth and happiness is actually very small.

For example, the people of Denmark and Sweden have consistently been found to be among the happiest in the world. These prosperous societies score at or near the top of most measures of quality of life, happiness, and social well-being. What makes things interesting, though, is that the people of Costa Rica, according to these same studies, are actually happier, even though the per capita gross domestic product (GDP) of Costa Rica is only one-fourth that of Denmark and Sweden.

Similarly, the Guatemalans are happier than people in the United States, despite income levels only a tenth as high. And the people of Honduras are as happy as those of the United Kingdom, even with a per capita GDP that is only 12 percent as great.

The list goes on and on. The El Salvadorians are happier than the Japanese or the French, despite having only one-sixth the income. In fact, the more you look at the data comparing people's monetary wealth with their levels of happiness, once you get past the poverty line the harder it is to see any correlation at all. Surveys of the richest Americans, for example, show happiness scores identical to those of the Amish, a people who intentionally live almost entirely without cars or telephones. The happiness scores of the richest Americans, in fact, are only slightly higher than those of Masai tribesmen, a semi-nomadic African people who live without electricity or running water.

Of course, the lowest life-satisfaction scores come from the world's most destitute people. The happiness numbers for homeless people in Calcutta, India, for example, are among the lowest ever recorded. But when these people have enough money to move off the street and into a slum, their levels of happiness and satisfaction rise and become nearly equivalent to those of a sample of college students from forty-seven nations.

Daniel Kahneman won the 2002 Nobel Prize in economics. He subsequently paired up with Princeton University economist Alan Krueger to study whether increased income produces additional happiness. Their conclusion? "The belief that high income is associated with good mood (happiness) is greatly exaggerated and mostly an illusion."

Although a few studies have suggested otherwise, the vast preponderance of research indicates that past a certain point, the ability of money to bring happiness seems to dwindle to almost nothing. Psychologist David Lykken, summarizing his extensive studies on the subject, says that "people who go to work in their overalls and on the bus are just as happy, on the average, as those in suits who drive to work in their own Mercedes." How about the ultrarich? According to a study by psycholo-

	LIFE SATSIFACTION SCORE (as per World Database Happiness)	PER CAPITA GDP (in U.S. dollars)
Costa Rica	8.5	$9,606
Denmark	8.2	$37,400
Sweden	7.7	$36,500
Guatemala	7.6	$4,700
Canada	7.6	$38,400
United States	7.4	$45,800
El Salvador	7.2	$5,800
Honduras	7.1	$4,100
United Kingdom	7.1	$35,100
Kuwait	7.0	$39,300
Brazil	6.8	$9,700
France	6.5	$33,200
China	6.3	$5,300
Japan	6.2	$33,600
Taiwan	6.2	$30,100
Zimbabwe	3.3	$200
Tanzania	3.2	$1,300

gist Ed Diener and his colleagues, the *Forbes* 100 wealthiest Americans are barely happier than the average person.

These findings go so strongly against the grain of conventional thinking that even the researchers conducting these studies have at times been resistant to accepting the conclusions. The prevailing economic theory is that more income gives people more opportunities to make choices that bring higher levels of satisfaction. But the data is robust, consistent, and compelling. "I was raised in an economic classroom to believe that money buys . . . happiness," writes Andrew Oswald, a British economist who has been a pioneer in the study of the economics of happiness. "I have had to revise that opinion."

The science is now so strong that it's being reported even in publications that are the foremost proponents of wealth accumulation. In 2004, *Forbes,* a magazine that proudly calls itself "the capitalist tool," published an article by senior editor Matthew Herper that announced: "It's official: Money can't buy happiness. . . . Increases in income just don't seem to make people happier."

Similarly, a 2004 article in *The Wall Street Journal*—another publication not generally considered to be on the leading edge of the movement for voluntary simplicity—declared: "To be sure, income is an accurate predictor of well-being when it raises someone from, say, homelessness to a janitorial job, because the jump up the economic ladder brings basic needs like food and shelter. With increasing wealth, however, extra money doesn't buy much extra happiness." The article quoted researchers Ed Diener of the University of Illinois and Martin Seligman of the University of Pennsylvania. After analyzing more than 150 studies on wealth and happiness, they wrote: "Although economic output has risen steeply over the past decades, there has been no rise in life satisfaction . . . and there has been a substantial increase in depression and distrust."

Money, it seems, is a little like beer. Most people like it, but more is not necessarily better. A beer might improve your mood, but drinking ten beers not only won't increase your happiness tenfold, it might not increase it at all.

Meanwhile, our single-minded focus on expanding our capacity for consumption has generated a bevy of unhappy consequences. It's driven species to extinction, polluted our air and water, and destabilized the atmospheric gases that we depend on for the viability of our climate. It's produced people who are isolated, anxious, and greedy, led to a level of wealth inequality that is staggering, and brought us unprecedented and utterly unsustainable levels of debt.

We keep thinking that having more of the things money can buy will make us happier. Despite our current economic problems, we still have bigger homes, more cars, more appliances, and more possessions than any people have ever had at any time in history. We have accumulated so much stuff that a new industry has arisen and increasingly flourished—self-storage lockers, buildings, and warehouses.

But has acquiring all this stuff been worth the costs? While we've been on this multidecade shopping binge, our rates of depression, obesity, heart attacks, divorces, and suicides have skyrocketed. Antidepressants are now the most commonly prescribed drugs in the United States. As a nation, we consume two-thirds of the global market for drugs prescribed to combat chronic sadness and hopelessness. One study found that today, the average American child experiences higher levels of anxiety than did the average child *under psychiatric care* in the 1950s. And yet, when Americans were asked in a survey what single factor they believed would most improve the quality of their lives, the most common answer was "more money."

Maybe we're caught in ancient fears of not having enough to make it, primal fears of not having what we need to survive. Maybe we're stuck believing that nothing is ever enough, that true satisfaction is impossible because danger lurks around every corner. Maybe we've been bombarded from an early and vulnerable age with the message that money and the things it can buy are our only ticket to happiness. And maybe we've been hampered, as a people, by the fact that the primary index we have created to measure our economic well-being is absolutely guaranteed to get everything wrong.

POINTING US IN THE WRONG DIRECTION

How do we measure a nation's economic performance? How do we determine whether an economy is flourishing or not? The answer, for more than seventy-five years, has been the gross national product (GNP) and its nearly identical twin, the gross domestic product (GDP).

No numbers have mattered more to the thinking and decisions of our policy makers. Other important economic statistics are calculated as percentages of the GDP. So central and so basic to our economic thinking has the GDP become that virtually every nation on Earth uses its GDP as its fundamental measure of economic progress. The reason the United States is considered the world's most prosperous nation is because it has the largest GDP. Economists, politicians, and other leaders take for granted that the higher a nation's GDP, the better off are its people.

Unfortunately, using the GDP or the GNP to measure well-being and genuine progress makes about as much sense as using a fork to eat soup. It's the wrong tool for the job. Two months before he was assassinated, Robert F. Kennedy explained why:

> Our gross national product counts air pollution and cigarette advertising, and ambulances to clear our highways of carnage. It counts special locks for our doors, and the jails for the people who break them. It counts the destruction of the redwoods, and the loss of our natural wonder in chaotic sprawl. It counts napalm, nuclear warheads, and armored cars for the police to fight the riots in our cities. Yet the gross national product does not allow for the health of our children, the quality of their education, or the joy of their play. It does not include the beauty of our poetry or the strength of our marriages, the intelligence of our public debate or the integrity of our public officials. It measures neither our wit nor our courage, neither our wisdom nor our learning, neither our compassion nor our devotion to our country. It measures everything, in short, except that which makes life worthwhile.

How can we develop a healthy relationship to wealth and to genuine economic progress when our most fundamental gauge to assess societal well-being is so askew? The GDP, like the GNP, simply adds together all monetary expenditures. The GDP does not care one whit what it is we're consuming, about how equitably distributed a country's wealth might be, nor whether the money we spend is ours or is borrowed from future generations. It doesn't care about infant mortality rates or the amount of violence in a society. It doesn't take into any account how many in a nation are homeless, unemployed, or hungry. It is entirely possible for the nation with the world's highest GDP to also have the world's highest poverty rate and the world's highest level of national debt.

The GDP rises whenever money changes hands. When families break down and children require foster care, the GDP grows, but not so when parents successfully care for their children. People who max out their credit cards buying things they don't need make the GDP look good. People who save their money and live sensibly don't. Seen through such a lens, the most economically productive people are cancer patients in the midst of getting a divorce. Healthy people in happy marriages, in contrast, are economically invisible, and all the more so if they cook at home, walk to work, grow food in a home garden, and don't smoke.

The more people drive, the higher the GDP rises, due to the greater production of gasoline and cars. No account is taken of the number of hours wasted in traffic jams or the pollution unleashed into the atmosphere. In recent years, the GDP has gotten substantial boosts from toxic waste spills such as the *Exxon Valdez* disaster and the boom in prison construction. The whole thing is reminiscent of Edward Abbey's reflection that "growth for the sake of growth is the philosophy of the cancer cell."

Meanwhile, anything that doesn't involve monetary exchange simply does not register to the GDP. Unpaid service such as housework and child care might as well not exist. Natural resources such as rivers and oceans, topsoil and forests, the ozone layer and the atmosphere, are seen as essentially valueless, unless, of course, they are exploited and converted into revenue. But even then, the GDP measures the resulting economic activity in a manner that is fundamentally misleading. As economist Mark Anielski points out, by counting the depletion of natural resources as current income rather than as the liquidation of assets, the GDP "violates both basic accounting principles and common sense."

ALTERNATIVES TO THE GDP

At this writing, we are experiencing the worst financial crisis in the last seventy-five years. One of the reasons the crisis took so many economic experts by surprise is that the systems we use to measure our economic well-being failed us. They did not register that the euphoric growth performance of the world economy prior to the 2008 downturn was, in fact, utterly unsustainable. It is clear now that much of the then-heralded economic growth was a statistical mirage, based on real estate and stock prices that had been grossly inflated by bubbles. If we had had a better measurement system, would we have seen the problems earlier? Would governments have been able to take precautionary measures to avoid or at least minimize the present turmoil?

As long as we continue to rely on the GDP, our leaders will lack a timely and reliable set of wealth accounts—the "balance sheets" of the economy. Fortunately, many efforts are under way to develop economic indexes that are far more reliable measures of genuine wealth and progress than the GDP. Amartya Sen is a Nobel laureate in economics from Harvard who has received more than eighty honorary doctorates for his work in understanding the underlying mechanisms of poverty, famine, and gender inequality. He is also one of many leading economists who recognize that, as he put it in 2008, "the gross domestic product is very misleading and something must be done to get better measures of well-being." Professor Sen and another Nobel laureate in economics, Joseph Stiglitz, are cochairmen of the Commission on the Measurement of Economic Performance and Social Progress, established in 2008 by Nicolas Sarkozy, the president of France, to develop an alternative to the GDP.

The government of China, similarly, is increasingly recognizing that the nation's torrid economic growth has come at a growing ecological and social cost. Mark Anielski, author of a groundbreaking book on alternatives to the GDP titled *The Economics of Happiness: Building Genuine Wealth,* is working with the Chinese government on how to adopt "green GDP accounting." The goal is to take quality of life and the environment into account when measuring the country's economic health.

There are many other alternatives under development, including one being created by the Organisation for Economic Co-operation and Development, an international consortium of thirty countries that are committed to democracy and the market economy.

I'm heartened to see the many efforts under way to develop alternatives to the GDP that take into account the health of our lives, the strength of our communities, and the sustainability of the environment. And yet it is no simple task to develop a monetized system that can measure the real determinants of well-being and do justice to the vast complexities of modern economic life. It may be that no single alternative index will emerge to entirely replace the GDP, and we will come to rely on a variety of indexes, each with its own perspectives, to provide us with as complete a picture as possible of the real state of our economic affairs and our societal well-being. And then perhaps we will be able to develop policies that lead to our ultimate goal—a sustainable prosperity shared by all.

POTENTIAL ALTERNATIVES TO
THE GROSS DOMESTIC PRODUCT

The Index of Sustainable Economic Welfare is based on the ideas of economists William Nordhaus and James Tobin in their Measure of Economic Welfare.

The United Nations Human Development Index is published annually in the Human Development Report by the United Nations Development Program; it includes factors such as life expectancy, health, education, and literacy.

The Living Planet Index was developed by the World Wide Fund for Nature and the United Nations Environmental Program; it focuses on the status of global biological diversity.

The Quality-of-Life Index compares the economies of 183 countries by looking at 200 factors as diverse as contraception use, children's well-being, homicides, housing prices, traffic congestion, alcohol and drug addiction, and life expectancy; it is published annually in *The Economist.*

National Accounts of Well-Being measure and report on the well-being of populations in order to provide a more meaningful measure of national success and help governments make decisions to improve the lives of their citizens. They were developed from European Social Survey and World Values Survey data by the New Economics Foundation.

The Genuine Progress Indicator was created by Redefining Progress in the belief that if policy makers measure what truly matters to people—health care, safety, a clean environment, and other indicators of well-being—economic policy will naturally shift toward sustainability.

The Happy Planet Index shows the relative efficiency with which nations convert the planet's natural resources into long and happy lives for their citizens; it was developed and is published annually by the New Economics Foundation.

The Genuine Wealth Assessment is a values-based well-being analysis and management tool developed by economist Mark Anielski. It can be used by individuals, communities, nations, and business enterprises to better measure and manage their most important assets: the things that make life worthwhile. It seeks to integrate people (human capital), relationships (social capital), the environment (natural capital), physical infrastructure (built capital), and money (financial capital).

GROSS NATIONAL HAPPINESS

Only one nation on the planet has officially switched away from the GDP as its primary index for evaluating its economic life. The small Asian country of Bhutan, which a few decades ago had among the lowest life expectancies on Earth, has formally made "gross national happiness" its primary measure of progress. The shift was launched by King Jigme Singye Wangchuck, who acceded to the throne in 1972 and over the course of his reign voluntarily reduced the scope of his powers and instituted the country's first democratic elections. What, you may wonder, has happened to the well-being of this nation as a result?

Though household incomes remain very low, the people of Bhutan have made extraordinary progress in many of the things that truly matter. Forty years ago, Bhutan had no public education system, but now there are free schools at all levels throughout the country. The literacy rate, which was less than 10 percent as recently as the early nineties, now tops 50 percent and continues to increase rapidly.

Forty years ago, there was not a single sanitary hospital in the country. Now, all Bhutanese citizens have access to free health care. Government policies ensure that people have a great deal of free time with their families, including paid maternity leave. The elderly are provided for both by their extended families and by pension programs offered by the government.

Perhaps the most remarkable part of Bhutan's commitment to gross national happiness is a stunning dedication to preserving the country's natural resources. While the forests of all its neighboring countries have been decimated in recent years, Bhutan retains the highest original forest cover of any nation on earth. The hunting of animals is prohibited, and livestock grazing, logging, and mining are strictly controlled and limited. Plastic bags are banned, and there are stringent fuel-quality laws. The nation has an annual holiday to honor the king, but instead of pomp and parades, the people spend the day planting trees. Consistent with the Buddhist doctrine of respect for all life, the new constitution gives inalienable rights to wildlife and trees as well as to people.

How has all this affected the health of the people? In a stunningly short time, the nation of Bhutan has experienced one of the most dramatic increases in life expectancy in world history. In 1984, life expectancy in Bhutan was forty-seven years. Today, it is sixty-six years.

As the Bhutanese experience demonstrates, gross national happiness is more than a utopian fantasy. It can actually be an effective development strategy, at least for a small undeveloped nation with a relatively homogeneous culture. But could such a scenario be applicable to the economies of vastly larger, more highly differentiated, and culturally diverse societies? Quantifying happiness is a complex and difficult task under the best of circumstances, and constructing a "well-being" index that could replace the GDP is an enormously challenging undertaking, particularly given how deeply materialistic assumptions have become ingrained in our thinking.

The Bhutanese experience is based on an understanding that has fallen out of fashion in modern consumer culture, namely that happiness is not limited to the enjoyment of temporary material comforts and pleasures. Perhaps it's time for us to enter a fundamental conversation with ourselves and with one another. What is it that we truly value? What is the source of our deepest and most abiding happiness?

FINDING OUR LOST SOULS

Just as the GDP has been a misleading indicator at a national level, guiding us to falsely equate the making and spending of money with societal well-being, so, too, have we been led at a personal and family level to measure our success almost entirely in material terms. There are aspects of modern culture that have made us want to be rich more than to be satisfied, content, and healthy. They have fostered greed and envy and led us to feel entertained rather than repulsed by ads like the one for Twix candy bars that glorifies selfishness as it triumphantly declares "Two for me. None for you!"

We have paid dearly for this mistake, because it has divided us from one another and brought distance between us and our souls. If we want to obtain genuine wealth and enduring well-being, I believe there are few things more important for us to do today than to awaken from this cultural trance and to bring our economic lives into congruence with our true values.

In this task, my dear friend Lynne Twist, author of *The Soul of Money,* has been a mentor and an inspiration to me, as she has been to tens of thousands of others. She believes that our greatest joy and sense of purpose can be discovered if our use of money becomes a spiritual practice—if we are able to make it an instrument of our intention and our integrity.

Lynne and her husband, Bill, have given an extraordinary amount of money and time over the years to building a world in which all people can experience thriving, just, and sustainable ways of life. She recalls when she first made a major contribution to an organization dedicated to ending world hunger: "It realigned my priorities. My financial life started to be more in alignment with my deep sense of self and soul. I began to have an experience of prosperity that was unrelated to any quantity of money or acquisitions."

We've all seen money used to create accumulation and self-importance, but Lynne came to see that it could also be used to express her love for people and her affirmation of life. "Lining money up with our soul, with our deepest dreams and highest aspirations," she says, "is the source of our prosperity. . . . Money used this way connects us to the whole of life."

Lynne believes that using money as a direct expression of one's deepest sense of self is immensely powerful. She also knows that it isn't easy. "I'm still working on it," she writes. "I waste money. I buy products that are part of the problem rather than part of the solution. I get excited about money, and disappointed about money, and frustrated and conflicted over money issues. But I am also on a path, in a practice . . . that I believe are useful and important in our time."

When we let go of making the accumulation of more money the central goal of our lives, we have the capacity for a greater life, a life beyond just getting and having. What's needed, as Lynne Twist puts it, is that you let the way you are with money "stand for who you are, your love, your heart, your word, and your humanity."

DOES MONEY CORRUPT?

One of the most subtle and insidious beliefs that for many people generates a disconnection between their values and their money choices is the idea that money is dirty or corrupt. It's remarkable how deeply buried in people's unconscious such convictions can be. But the fact that such beliefs are unconscious does not make them less powerful; in fact, it may give them even greater influence.

I have a friend who is prejudiced against the wealthy. I've heard him frequently say that rich people are greedy. In order to obtain their wealth, he believes, they must have taken advantage of others. Or, if they happen to have inherited their money, then they must be lazy. If you want to know what God thinks of money, he says, just look at the people He's given it to.

There is a kernel of truth in my friend's beliefs, because there certainly are people with wealth who are selfish and mean, who have acquired their fortunes through exploiting others, and even through violence and brutality. And I have no doubt that there are some inheritors who are more to be pitied than envied, for they have become indolent and disconnected from any sense of purpose. But I believe my friend's disdain for the wealthy is a serious error, because such people are not found only, or even disproportionately, among the wealthy. Self-centered, manipulative, and lazy people exist at every rung of the economic ladder, in every social and economic class. This is true now, it has been true in the past, and presumably it will always be the case. There simply is no consistent correlation, positive or negative, between character and wealth.

I must say with some sadness that my friend, like others who believe that wealthy people are less compassionate than others, has a hard time relating to those with money, because his judgments get in the way. He has never been able to develop financial security in his own life, and I wonder if his prejudice against the wealthy is playing a part in his continuing financial malaise.

There is a truth that my friend is unable to see. If wealthy people are able to bring their relationship with money into accord with their deepest values and heart's purpose, they are then in an absolutely wonderful position to make a positive difference.

We need to take the shame out of having money just as much as we need to take the shame out of not having it. For then we can more fully grasp that our handling of money, our thinking about money, our making and spending and giving of money, can be a spiritual practice with profound ramifications for our own healing and for the healing of our greater community.

Consider, for example, the extraordinary case of Zell Kravinsky. Zell grew up in a tiny house in Philadelphia and now lives in a modest home not far from there, in Jenkintown, Pennsylvania. His father was a workingman and his mother was a teacher. He spent years teaching emotionally troubled inner-city kids and has also taught at the University of Pennsylvania. One year he was voted by student evaluations as the most highly appreciated faculty member at the university.

Over the years, Zell has made a series of compounding real estate investments that made him a great deal of money. What has he done with his fortune? Not what my friend, the one who believes all rich people are selfish, would expect. In fact, not what many of us would expect.

After amassing a fortune of more than $45 million, Zell Kravinsky donated virtually all of his money to charities working on what he cares about most: the improvement of public health. He set aside about $80,000 for his children's education, but other than that, he gave it *all* away.

Zell made the largest contribution ever to the foundation supporting the Centers for Disease Control and Prevention, and he made major donations to the Johns Hopkins Bloomberg School of Public Health and the Ohio State University School of Public Health. Though he could have afforded to live as lavishly as he might have wanted, he lives relatively simply today, with his wife and children in a home that he bought some years ago for under $150,000.

Zell believes that regardless of how much money you do or don't have, if you have a charitable impulse then you should find a way to act on it. "So many people could be cared for with small sums of money," he says, "especially in global public health. About 500,000 children a year become blind in poor countries for lack of vitamin A. Many children die from infections that vitamin A would have prevented." One of the programs he set up through Johns Hopkins focuses on supplying vitamin A where it will do the most good.

After giving his fortune away, Zell decided to reward himself. Some people might reward themselves with a rich dessert or a luxury vacation. Not Zell Kravinsky. He decided to treat himself by making a kidney donation. He says this was something he had always wanted to do. "If you can save another person's life without losing your own, why wouldn't you do it?" he asks, as if dumbfounded that anyone should think his actions to be unusual. After Kravinsky learned that many African Americans in need of a kidney die because they have difficulty obtaining one, he sought out a hospital in Philadelphia that would allow him to fulfill his wishes. He didn't have a particular recipient in mind, but he did ask that his kidney go to a lower-income black person.

Such purely altruistic donations are extremely rare. About six thousand kidneys are taken from living donors in the United States each year, with nearly all of them going to family members or close friends of the donor. Less than thirty a year are donated to complete strangers.

Some people think Zell is a saint, but he's actually quite human. He struggles with his decisions, just like the rest of us. Like many of us he's doing the best he can. The difference is that he has found a way to use his money to express his soul. "I truly believe all of us are brothers and all of us are sisters," he says. "If we could all embrace each other, there'd be no more war, no more ethnic jealousy."

I treasure Zell's example because I believe he is someone who has deepened his relationship with his sense of purpose and brought it to bear, profoundly, on his relationship with money. And that's something we can all seek to do, regardless of how much money we do or don't have.

"There are many ways to give," Zell says. "A bus driver who always has smiles for his passengers is a philanthropist. Taking care of a sick relative is philanthropy. You don't have to give money or an organ. What you don't need could be critical for others."

I'm certainly not saying that you have to give everything you have to others who are less fortunate. What's important is that you do whatever you need to do so you can speak of money and the human spirit in the same breath, so your decisions around money are made not from fear, but from choice. What's important is that, whatever the numbers in your bank account, you are able to find laughter, joy, and beauty in who you are.

THE NEW GOOD LIFE

After a long and difficult life that had brought him much hard-earned wisdom, the Nobel Peace Prize winner Albert Schweitzer said, "One thing I know: The only ones among you who will be really happy are those who will have sought and found how to serve."

For none of us, though, is this particularly easy. It takes work and discipline, listening and surrender, to discover your true calling. It takes tenacity and dedication to develop your innermost gifts. It takes all of your strength and all of your weakness to become the person you are meant to be.

I've been rich and I've been poor, and frankly, being rich is easier. But I also have seen the poverty of a rich society, and I have learned that you don't need to have gobs of money to do great things and to help others. You can be rich in caring and compassion, you can be generous with your devotion and your concern. And I have also come to see that the gifts that come from a calm mind and a steady heart are more valuable than those that come from a self that is lost in delusion, no matter the size of the wallet.

The old good life taught that wealth depends on the multiplication of wants and material possessions. But I believe your genuine wealth depends, rather, on fully expressing and celebrating the gifts you have to give to the world—and receiving the gifts that others have to give to you, as well.

So go forth and be fruitful, go forth and be creative, passionate, and fully alive. Go forth and bring the wisdom of your soul to bear on every choice, every experience, every breath, and every moment.

The new good life is yours whenever you appreciate life, whenever you live with a sense of meaning and purpose that goes beyond the material veil, whenever your heart is filled with wonders, large and small. It is yours when you see life anew, when your faith is restored, when you find the sacred in the midst of the mundane and the beauty of your spirit in the way that you live.

May your time on this earth fill your heart to overflowing. May love be your blanket, peace your pillow, and joy your constant companion.

Acknowledgments

I am deeply grateful to all of the people who in so many ways supported me and made it possible for me to write *The New Good Life*.

My thanks to Ocean Robbins. His keen eye, huge heart, superb communication skills, and thoughtful connection to the issues of our day helped me to visualize, articulate, and hone this book every step of the way.

My thanks, also, to Doug Abrams. It was Doug who first conceived the idea for this book, helped me to develop its structure, and who, as the book's agent, connected me with Marnie Cochran at Random House. Marnie was the book's editor, and I am grateful to her for the quality of attention she brought to the book, her perceptive support, and for the many times she helped me to see my blind spots.

My thanks to Deo Robbins, who, after forty-three years of marriage, still amazes and delights me by loving me even with all my flaws. Her patience, kindness, and unconditional love are lights to my heart and bring joy to my world.

My thanks to Judith Morgan, my dear friend and muse extraordinaire, who stood by me time and again. And to Michele Robbins. I can't imagine a more wonderful daughter-in-love.

My thanks, also, to Craig Schindler, Charlie Bloom, and Vicki Robin, fabulous friends who each gave valuable insights and feedback along the way. And to Jim Glackin and Ellen LaConte for their reflections and support.

My appreciation to all the members of the Turning Tide Coalition, including Tracy Apple-Howard, Van Jones, Joe Kresse, Laura Loescher, Catherine Parrish, Neal Rogin, Aqeela Sherrills, Lynne and Bill Twist, and Mathis Wackernagel, for so many kinds of partnership over the past ten years.

This book could not have been written without the help and support I received from many generous, kind, and loving people. Individually and collectively, they reached out to me and to my family in our time of need. Space does not permit me to name everyone who was there to help, but I could never have made it without the extraordinary munificence of Glenn and Amy Bacheller, Marna Broida and Ian Weiss, Patti Breitman and Stan Rosenfeld, Joe Keon, Grant Abert, Val and Ted Fitch, Tom Scholz, Ariel and Rebecca Nessel, Cate Coslor, Angeles Arrien, Chiu-Nan Lai, Kathy Stevens, Karl and Jeanne Anthony, Katchie Shakti Egger, Larry and Ann Wheat, Jules Oaklander, Diane Greenberg, Preet Marwaha, Tatiana Wrenfeather and John Oettinger, Kathleen Gildred, Marianne Williamson, Dean Ornish, T. Colin and Karen Campbell, Tom Campbell, Joshua and Marcy Jones, Rory Freedman, Carol and Francis Janes, Laura Tan, Jill Nunamaker, Morty Cohen, Li Shin Chiu, and Gene Baur.

My heartfelt thanks also to the others whose generosity and thoughtfulness made an enormous difference. This includes Guy Benintendi, Frank and Eileen Burrous, Ravi Chand, Salima Cobb, Sally and Joseph Dorsten, Tom Gegax, Marilee Geyer, Caryn Hartglass, Paul Hawken, Marilyn Hays, Keith Herman, Julia Butterfly Hill, Sheila Hoffman and Spenser Beard, Allen Huang, Yang Shioubih Huang, Elliot Kalman, Jeff and Patty Knutson, Diane Leigh, Steve Landry, Jeremy and Charlotte Levin, Walter and Rhea Linn, David Loye and Riane Eisler, Victoria Lui, Joanna Macy, Dixie Mahy, Victoria Moran, Jeff and Sabrina Nelson, Danila Oder, Teresa Ohmit, John Owen-Totton, Susan Parsons, Gregg and Lauri Roberti, Martin Rowe, Jessica Simkovic and Yaakov Weintraub, Nina Simons, Robert Singer, John Steiner and Margo King, Coumba Toure, Marsha Veit, Stacey Vicari, Zoe Weil, and many others.

I give thanks for the lives of all prophets, teachers, healers, and revolutionaries, living and dead, acclaimed or obscure, who have rebelled, worked, suffered, and lived for the cause of love and joy.

And I give thanks for each and every one of us who has worked to create a life with less fear and more love, less pain and more joy, less illusion and more wisdom.

More from John Robbins

You are invited to visit www.johnrobbins.info for tools, leading edge information, and a comprehensive resource guide to help you live and share the message of this book.

When you visit, you will find:

- Organizations, websites, books, films, and tools to help you live the new good life
- Information about events with John Robbins and how to contact him
- Articles by and videos featuring John Robbins
- Questions and answers on important topics

Please visit www.johnrobbins.info.

Notes

INTRODUCTION

xii   **In many states, unemployment is**   Jennifer Steinhauer, "California Jobless-
ness Reaches 70-Year High," *The New York Times,* September 19, 2009.

xii · **People who have never before**   Jason DeParle and Robert Gebeloff, "Across
U.S., Food Stamp Use Soars and Stigma Fades," *The New York Times,* No-
vember 28, 2009. See also Julie Bosman, "Newly Poor Swell Lines at Food
Banks," *The New York Times,* February 20, 2009.

xii   **a ship to travel from the Atlantic to the Pacific**   Christopher Flavin and
Robert Engelman, "The Perfect Storm" in *State of the World 2009: Into a
Warming World: A Worldwatch Institute Report on Progress Toward a Sustain-
able Society,* ed. Linda Starke (W. W. Norton and Company, 2009), 5.

CHAPTER 1: RAGS AND RICHES

6   **gargantuan in its excesses and grotesque in its inequalities**   This was later
borne out and described in the 1996 United Nations Development Program's
Human Development Report.

14   **Americans now spend nearly seven**   John De Graaf, David Wann, and
Thomas Naylor, *Affluenza: The All-Consuming Epidemic* (San Francisco:
Berrett-Koehler, 2001), 41.

14   **Thirty-four percent of Americans polled**   Ibid., 184.

23   **He stole more money**   Erin Arvedlund, *Too Good to Be True: The Rise and Fall of Bernie Madoff* (New York: Portfolio, 2009). For an interview with Richard Glantz regarding my loss in the Madoff fraud, see Jerry Oppenheimer, *Madoff with the Money* (Hoboken, N.J.: Wiley, 2009), 224–28. For an interview with me published shortly after the Madoff fraud was discovered, see David Ian Miller, "What's Left When the Money's Gone?" *San Francisco Chronicle,* February 23, 2009, http://www.sfgate.com/cgi-bin/article.cgi?f=/g/a/2009/02/23/findrelig022309.DTL.

CHAPTER 2: GETTING TO KNOW YOUR MONEY TYPE

28   **Recognizing that people have widely**   Brent Kessel, *It's Not About The Money: Unlock Your Money Type to Achieve Spiritual and Financial Abundance* (New York: HarperCollins, 2008); Olivia Mellan, *Money Harmony: Resolving Money Conflicts in Your Life and Relationships* (New York: Walker and Company, 1994); Deborah L. Price, *Money Therapy: Using the Eight Money Types to Create Wealth and Prosperity* (Novato, Calif.: New World Library, 2000); Laura Rowley, *Money and Happiness: A Guide to Living the Good Life* (Hoboken, N.J.: John Wiley and Sons, 2005); David Keirsey, *Please Understand Me II: Temperament, Character, Intelligence* (Del Mar, Calif.: Prometheus Nemesis, 1998); Carol Pearson, *Awakening the Heroes Within: Twelve Archetypes to Help Us Find Ourselves and Transform Our World* (San Francisco: HarperSanFrancisco, 1991); and Helen Palmer, *The Enneagram in Love and Work: Understanding Your Intimate and Business Relationships* (San Francisco: HarperSanFrancisco, 1995).

45   **It wasn't until 2002, when the Kennedy**   Robert Dallek, *An Unfinished Life: John F. Kennedy 1917–1963* (Boston: Little, Brown, and Co., 2003).

49   **"Our enormously productive economy"**   Victor Lebow, "Price Competition in 1955," *Journal of Retailing,* Spring 1955.

CHAPTER 3: FOUR STEPS TO FINANCIAL FREEDOM

67   **Distilled from work**   Joe Dominguez and Vicki Robin, *Your Money or Your Life: Transforming Your Relationship with Money and Achieving Financial Independence* (New York: Viking, 1992).

89   **It's a sickness that some call "affluenza"**   De Graaf, Wann, and Naylor, *Affluenza.*

CHAPTER 4: WHEREVER YOU LIVE IS YOUR TEMPLE—IF YOU TREAT IT LIKE ONE

94   **"rascals who like to sell people houses"**   Wainwright Evans, "Your Dream Home Brought Down to Earth," *Better Homes and Gardens,* May 1929.

95   **article that described Rush Limbaugh's**   Zev Chafets, "Late-Period Limbaugh," *The New York Times Magazine,* July 6, 2008.

95   **After Aaron Spelling's death in 2006**   Issie Lapowsky, "Candy Spelling: Tori Spelling's Actions Killed Her Father, Aaron Spelling," *New York Daily News,* May 29, 2009.

95   **"I always wanted a house big enough"**   Margot Adler, "Behind the Ever-Expanding American Dream Home," *All Things Considered,* National Public Radio, July 1, 2009.

96   **Percent of U.S. homes with 2.5 bathrooms**   Nathan Fox, "This New House," *Mother Jones Magazine,* March/April 2005.

96   **"We were as poor as church mice"**   Charlie and Linda Bloom, *Secrets of Great Marriages: Real Truth from Real Couples About Lasting Love* (Novato, Calif.: New World Library, 2010).

97   **"the delicate dance of need and greed"**   Shay Salomon, *Little House on a Small Planet: Simple Homes, Cozy Retreats, and Energy Efficient Possibilities* (Guilford, Conn.: Lyons Press, 2006), 201.

100   **"Habitat for Humanity builds more than"**   Cynthia Kersey, *Unstoppable: 45 Powerful Stories of Perseverance and Triumph from People Just Like You* (Naperville, Ill.: Sourcebooks, 1998), 24.

104   **"I thought I needed the new car"**   Mark Anielski, *The Economics of Happiness: Building Genuine Wealth* (Gabriola Island, B.C.: New Society Publishers, 2007), 100–104.

116   **"Katrina-like disasters could become commonplace"**   Mike Tidwell, *The Ravaging Tide: Strange Weather, Future Katrinas, and the Coming Death of America's Coastal Cities* (New York: Free Press, 2006), 3–6.

118   **Studies have shown that when**   Richard Douthwaite, *The Growth Illu$ion: How Economic Growth Has Enriched the Few, Impoverished the Many, and Endangered the Planet* (Gabriola Island, B.C.: New Society Publishers, 1999), 125.

118   **In 1998, when Enrique Peñalosa became**   Lester Brown, *Plan B 2.0: Rescuing a Planet Under Stress and a Civilization in Trouble* (New York: W. W. Norton and Company, 2006), 204–5.

118   **"High quality public pedestrian space"**   Enrique Peñalosa, "Parks for Livable Cities: Lessons from a Radical Mayor," keynote address at the Urban Parks Institute's Great Parks/Great Cities Conference, Chicago, Illinois, July 30, 2001. Cited in Lester Brown, *Plan B 4.0: Mobilizing to Save Civilization* (New York: W. W. Norton and Co., 2009), 144–45.

119   **median price for a home sold in Detroit**   Tim Jones, "Detroit's Outlook Falls Along with Home Prices," *Chicago Tribune,* January 29, 2009.

120   **I love San Francisco, but**   Fox, "This New House."

120   **Author Shay Salomon notes a trend**   Salomon, *Little House on a Small Planet,* 62–63.

123   **Research by economists Victor Stango and**   Victor Stango and Jonathan Zinman, "Fuzzy Math, Disclosure Regulation and Credit Market Outcomes" (working paper, Dartmouth College, November 2007), cited in James Surowiecki, "Caveat Mortgagor," *The New Yorker,* July 6, 2009.

123   **Economists Karen Pence and**   Karen M. Pence and Brian Bucks, "Do

Homeowners Know Their House Values and Mortgage Terms?" FEDS working paper no. 2006–03, May 2, 2006.

124 **Trailer residents reported acute** Harry Sawyers, "FEMA's Formaldehyde Woes May Change Particleboard Business," *Popular Mechanics,* August 22, 2008. See also Bill Walsh, "Formaldehyde and Kids," *Healthy Building News,* May 30, 2007.

124 **"A growing body of evidence"** U.S. EPA Office of Radiation and Indoor Air, "The Inside Story: A Guide to Indoor Air Quality" (6609J), http://www.epa.gov/iaq/pubs/insidest.html.

125 **"watery eyes, burning sensations"** U.S. EPA, "An Introduction to Indoor Air Quality," http://www.epa.gov/iaq/formalde.html.

125 **"When children breathe in fumes"** Rebecca Kahlenberg, "The Hidden Toxins in Your Home," *Parents Magazine,* July 2005.

CHAPTER 5: LIFE IS TOO SHORT FOR TRAFFIC

128 **walks less than three hundred yards** Robert Wood Johnson Foundation presentation, Pro-Walk, Pro-Bike Conference, St. Paul, Minnesota, 2002.

128 **eight billion hours a year stuck** Jane Holtz Kay, *Asphalt Nation: How the Automobile Took Over America and How We Can Take It Back* (New York: Crown, 1997), 14.

129 **nearly 20 percent of our income** U.S. Bureau of Labor Statistics 2008 Consumer Expenditure Survey.

130 **"systematic attempt of business to make"** Vance Packard, *The Waste Makers* (New York: D. McKay Co., 1960).

130 **"put Americans on the acquisitive treadmill"** Dan Neil, "When Cars Were America's Idols," *Los Angeles Times,* June 1, 2009.

130 **"The Ladder of Success was"** Ibid.

131 **"The worst auto accidents you'll ever"** Dave Ramsey, *The Total Money Makeover: A Proven Plan for Financial Fitness* (Nashville: Thomas Nelson, 2003).

131 **he calculated the costs of owning** David Leonhardt, "Big Vehicles Stagger Under the Weight of $4 Gas," *The New York Times,* June 4, 2008.

133 **"As long as you can get"** National Public Radio, *Car Talk,* October 6, 2008.

133 **emissions to be toxic** Commonwealth Scientific and Industrial Research Organisation, "New Car Drivers Exposed to Toxic Emissions," media release reference number 2001/290, December 19, 2001.

138 **phenomenon has emerged called "casual carpooling"** Adam Starr, "Carpooling Quietly Booms in San Francisco," *Good,* February 7, 2009.

138 **"While the Bay Area's layout"** Ibid.

142 **Amsterdam became the first major city** Brown, *Plan B 4.0,* 153.

144 **"on the whims of OPEC's despots"** Laura Rosen, "James Woolsey, Hybrid Hawk," *Mother Jones,* May/June 2008.

144 **"Ninety-seven percent of the fuel"** Set America Free Coalition, http://www.setamericafree.org/.

144   **The study found that a shift**   Electric Power Research Institute and the Natural Resources Defense Council, "Environmental Assessment of Plug-In Hybrid Electric Vehicles," July 2007. www.my.epri.com/portal/server.pt ?open=514&objID=223132&mode=2.

145   **"Recharging batteries with off-peak"**   Brown, *Plan B 4.0*, 92.

145   **"undeniably, unbelievably efficient"**   Kim Reynolds, "First Drive: 2008 Tesla Roadster," *Motor Trend*, January 22, 2008.

146   **German automaker Daimler-Benz declared**   "The Car of the Perpetual Future," *The Economist*, September 4, 2008.

146   **General Motors CEO Jack Smith**   Ibid.

146   **Ford's CEO, Jacques Nasser**   Ibid.

147   **"hydrogen fuel-cell technology won't"**   Dan Neil, "Honda FCX Clarity: Beauty for Beauty's Sake," *Los Angeles Times*, February 13, 2009.

147   **U.S. energy secretary Steven Chu announced**   Matthew L. Wald, "U.S. Drops Research into Fuel Cells for Cars," *The New York Times*, May 8, 2009.

147   **The resulting "Consumer Greendex" found**   Sarah van Schagen, "Americans Ranked as World's Least Green Consumers—Again," *Grist*, May 14, 2009.

149   **waiting without shade in the heat**   Kay, *Asphalt Nation*, pg 36.

149   **Rosa Parks might find bus service**   Ibid., 37.

149   **the "Great American Streetcar Scandal"**   Al Mankoff, "Revisiting the American Streetcar Scandal," *Intransition: Transportation Planning, Practice and Progress*, Summer 1999.

150   **Lobbyists from the oil and auto industries**   Eric Schlosser, *Fast Food Nation: The Dark Side of the All-American Meal* (Boston: Houghton Mifflin, 2001), 16.

150   **It has long been considered a basic legal principle**   Edward Humes, *Eco Barons: The Dreamers, Schemers, and Millionaires Who Are Saving Our Planet* (New York: HarperCollins, 2009), 254.

150   **"Consumers and, ultimately, taxpayers have"**   Ibid.

151   **The bus system in Curitiba, Brazil**   Bill McKibben, *Deep Economy: The Wealth of Communities and the Durable Future* (New York: Times Books, 2007), 153.

152   **In Japan, bullet trains**   Brown, *Plan B 4.0*, 93–94. See also Deborah Hastings, "Anyone Aboard for High-Speed Rail?" Associated Press, March 26, 2009.

152   **By 2007, trips into the city**   Brown, *Plan B 4.0*, 148.

CHAPTER 6: EATING BETTER, SPENDING LESS

158   **"A survey of National Merit scholars"**   Barbara Kingsolver, *Animal, Vegetable, Miracle: A Year of Food Life* (New York: HarperCollins, 2007).

161   **When a team of researchers**   Jessie Fan, et al., "Household Food Expenditure Patterns: A Cluster Analysis," *Monthly Labor Review*, April 2007, 38–51.

162   **Environmental Working Group released**   Olga Naidenko, et al., "Bottled Water Contains Disinfection Byproducts, Fertilizer Residue, and Pain Med-

ication," *EWG Research: Bottled Water Quality Investigation: 10 Major Brands, 38 Pollutants,* October 2008, http://www.ewg.org/reports/bottledwater.

164   **seminal report titled *Livestock's Long Shadow,*** Food and Agriculture Organization of the United Nations, *Livestock's Long Shadow: Environmental Issues and Options,* Rome, 2006, http://www.fao.org/docrep/010/a0701e/a0701e00.htm.

164   **"The evidence is strong"** Ezra Klein, "The Meat of the Problem," *The Washington Post,* July 29, 2009. See also Mike Tidwell, "The Low-Carbon Diet," *Audubon Magazine,* January 2009.

165   **"producing beef for the table"** Nathan Fiala, "How Meat Contributes to Global Warming," *Scientific American,* February 4, 2009. See also Christopher L. Weber and H. Scott Matthews, "Food-Miles and the Relative Climate Impacts of Food Choices in the United States," *Environmental Science and Technology,* April 16, 2008; Bryan Walsh, "Meat: Making Global Warming Worse," *Time Magazine,* September 10, 2008; Jim Motavelli, "The Meat of the Matter: Animals Raised for Food Are Warming the Planet Faster Than Cars," *E Magazine,* July/Aug 2008; and Julliette Jowit, "UN Says Eat Less Meat to Curb Global Warming," *The Observer,* September 7, 2008.

165   **University of Chicago study** Gidon Eshel and Pamela Martin, "Diet, Energy and Global Warming," *Earth Interactions* 10 (2006).

165   **Worldwatch Institute published a seminal report** Robert Goodland and Jeff Anhang, "Livestock and Climate Change," *World Watch Magazine,* November/December 2009, 10–19.

166   **"Children born today will find their"** Flavin and Engelman, "Perfect Storm," 5.

168   **"A medium-size buttered popcorn"** William Grimes, "How About Some Popcorn with Your Fat?" *The New York Times,* May 1, 1994.

168   **Has commercial popcorn improved since** Mary MacVean, "Movie Popcorn Still a Nutritional Horror, Study Finds," *Los Angeles Times,* November 19, 2009.

181   **a study of more than one thousand men** J. H. Cohen, et al., "Fruit and Vegetable Intakes and Prostate Cancer Risk," *Journal of the National Cancer Institute,* January 2000.

181   **One study of smokers in Singapore** Bin Zhao, et al., "Dietary Isothiocyanates, Glutathione S-transferase-M1, -T1 Polymorphisms and Lung Cancer Risk Among Chinese Women in Singapore," *Cancer Epidemiology, Biomarkers and Prevention,* October 2001.

183   **There were several famous studies** For example, G. E. Goodman, et al., "The Beta-Carotene and Retinol Efficacy Trial: Incidence of Lung Cancer and Cardiovascular Disease Mortality During 6-Year Follow-up After Stopping Beta-carotene and Retinol Supplements," *Journal of the National Cancer Institute,* December 2004.

184   **A study of 1,300 elderly** J. M. Gaziano, et al., "A Prospective Study of Consumption of Carotenoids in Fruits and Vegetables and Decreased Cardiovascular Mortality in the Elderly," *Annals of Epidemiology,* July 1995.

CHAPTER 7: KIDS: THE BIGGEST FINANCIAL DECISION OF YOUR LIFE

187   **derived from official 2008 government figures**   Mark Lino and Andrea Carlson, *Expenditures on Children by Families, 2008,* USDA Center for Nutrition Policy and Promotion, Publication No. 1528, 2008, 2009.

189   **But in Ann Crittenden's remarkable book**   Ann Crittenden, *The Price of Motherhood: Why the Most Important Job in the World Is Still the Least Valued* (New York: Metropolitan Books, 2001), 87–109.

189   **calculations of economist Shirley Burggraf**   Shirley P. Burggraf, *The Feminine Economy and Economic Man: Reviving the Role of Family in the Postindustrial Age* (New York: Basic Books, 1996), 61.

190   **Women who aren't mothers do**   Jane Waldfogel, "Understanding the 'Family Gap' in Pay for Women with Children," *The Journal of Economic Perspectives,* Winter 1998.

191   **Painfully, the child poverty rate**   UNICEF Innocenti Research Center, "Child Poverty in Perspective: An Overview of Child Well-being in Rich Countries," Innocenti Report Card 7, 2007, Florence, Italy, 7.

191   **"National policies and programs"**   Joan Blades and Kristin Rowe-Finkbeiner, *The Motherhood Manifesto: What America's Moms Want and What to Do About It* (New York: Nation Books, 2006), 15.

192   **"Reproduction and the Carbon Legacies"**   Paul Murtaugh and Michael Schlax, "Reproduction and the Carbon Legacies of Individuals," *Global Environmental Change,* October 30, 2008.

193   **We actually spend more for trash bags**   De Graaf, Wann, and Naylor, *Affluenza,* 85.

196   **"almost everyone is a little spoiled"**   Bill McKibben, *Maybe One: A Personal and Environmental Argument for Single-Child Families* (New York: Simon & Schuster, 1998), 38.

197   **"When you check something"**   Ibid., 198–99.

198   **"We worry about so many dangers"**   Barbara Ehrenreich, front cover quote for Juliet B. Schor, *Born to Buy: The Commericalized Child and the New Consumer Culture* (New York: Scribner, 2004).

199   **A survey of youth from seventy cities**   Schor, *Born to Buy,* 13.

202   **A study published in the *Journal of Developmental***   Thomas Robinson, et al., "Effects of Reducing Television Viewing on Children's Requests for Toys: A Randomized Controlled Trial," *Journal of Developmental and Behavioral Pediatrics,* June 2001.

202   **Another survey found that people**   Juliet B. Schor, *The Overspent American: Why We Want What We Don't Need* (New York: Basic Books, 1998).

205   **Studies show that children**   Romina Barros, Ellen Silver, and Ruth Stein, "School Recess and Group Classroom Behavior," *Pediatrics,* January 26, 2009.

206   **"One woman started a mother-daughter"**   Schor, *Born to Buy,* 208.

207   **"Part of cool"**   Gene Del Vecchio, quoted in Schor, *Born to Buy,* 48.

211   **Mary Rita**   Mary Rita Schilke Korzan, *When You Thought I Wasn't Looking: A Book of Thanks for Mom* (Kansas City, Mo.: Andrews McMeel Publishing, 2004).

CHAPTER 8: SAFE, CLEAN, AND NATURAL

212 **In 2005, American Red Cross** Todd Zwilich, "Study Shows Toxic Chemicals in Newborns," *WebMD Health News,* July 14, 2005. See also Stacy Malkan, *Not Just a Pretty Face: The Ugly Side of the Beauty Industry* (Gabriola, B.C.: New Society Publishers, 2007), 1–2.

212 **"If we clean just for appearances"** Ellen Sandbeck, *Green Housekeeping* (New York: Scribner, 2006), 3.

215 **Rolf Halden** Alana Herro, "Antimicrobial Soaps: Worth the Risk?" Worldwatch Institute, November 1, 2006, http://www.worldwatch.org/node/4698.

215 **"There is little evidence to support"** *Reports of the Council on Scientific Affairs: Use of Antimicrobials in Consumer Products,* 2000 Annual Meeting of the American Medical Association, CSA Rep. 2, A-00.

215 **"the use of common antimicrobials"** Ibid.

217 **When animals are exposed** Rosaline Anderson and Julius Anderson, "Respiratory Toxicity of Fabric Softener Emissions," *The Journal of Toxicology and Environmental Health,* May 2000.

218 **When the Natural Resources Defense Council analyzed** Jane Kay, "Environmental Groups Petition U.S. to Regulate Air Fresheners," *San Francisco Chronicle,* September 20, 2007.

218 **When NASA scientists researched** B. C. Wolverton, *How to Grow Fresh Air: 50 Houseplants That Purify Your Home and Office* (New York: Penguin, 1997).

219 **"When inhaled, ozone can damage"** U.S. EPA, "Ozone Generators That Are Sold as Air Cleaners," April 1, 2009, http://www.epa.gov/iaq/pubs/ozonegen.html.

219 **getting rid of clutter would eliminate** Sandbeck, *Green Housekeeping,* 13.

219 **According to the American Demographics Society** Ibid.

224 **Research published by the *Journal*** G. M. Sapers, et al., "Efficacy of 1% Hydrogen Peroxide Wash in Decontaminating Apples and Cantalope Melons," *Journal of Food Science,* July 20, 2006, 1793–97.

234 **In 2004, European Union countries** Malkan, *Not Just a Pretty Face,* 26.

235 **"Sexy for her"** *The New York Times,* July 10, 2002, cited in Malkan, *Not Just a Pretty Face,* 25.

235 **One study found that men** Susan M. Duty, et al., "Personal Care Product Use Predicts Urinary Concentrations of Some Phthalate Monoesters," *Environmental Health Perspectives,* November 2005, 1530–35.

237 **"Your physical self is"** Victoria Moran, *Lit from Within: Tending Your Soul for Lifelong Beauty* (San Francisco: HarperSanFrancisco, 2001), 1–3.

CHAPTER 9: THE ECONOMICS OF HAPPINESS

240 **one of the most popular series** Joseph Campbell with Bill Moyers, *The Power of Myth* (New York: Doubleday, 1988).

243   **inner-city residents**   DeNeen L. Brown, "Poor? Pay Up" *The Washington Post,* May 18, 2009. See also Barbara Ehrenreich, "Too Poor to Make the News," *The New York Times,* June 14, 2009.

243   **A 2009 report from**   *Homes Not Handcuffs: The Criminalization of Homelessness in U.S. Cities,* National Law Center on Homelessness and Poverty Publications, 2009.

244   **"If you're lying on a sidewalk"**   Alan Gomez, "Cities Clamp Down on Panhandlers," *USA Today,* June 9, 2009.

244   **In his book *Happiness***   Richard Layard, *Happiness: Lessons from a New Science* (New York: Penguin, 2005), 10–11, 202–3.

245   **Surveys of the richest Americans**   Ed Diener and Martin Seligman, "Beyond Money: Toward an Economy of Well-Being," *Psychological Science in the Public Interest* 5, no. 1 (July 2004).

245   **college students from forty-seven nations**   Robert Biswas-Diener and Ed Diener, "Making the Best of a Bad Situation: Satisfaction in the Slums of Calcutta," *Social Indicators Research* 55 (2001): 329–52.

245   **"The belief that high income"**   Anielski, *Economics of Happiness,* 218.

245   **"people who go to work"**   David Lykken, *Happiness: The Surprising Ways We Can Make the Most of What Nature Gives Us* (New York: Golden Books, 1999), 17.

245   **According to a study by psychologist**   Ed Diener with J. Horwitz and Robert Emmons, "Happiness of the Very Wealthy," *Social Indicators* 16 (1985): 263–74.

247   **"I was raised in an economic"**   Anielski, *Economics of Happiness,* 215.

247   **"It's official: Money can't"**   Matthew Herper, "Money Won't Buy You Happiness," *Forbes,* September 21, 2004.

247   **"To be sure, income is"**   Sharon Begley, "Wealth and Happiness Don't Necessarily Go Hand in Hand," *The Wall Street Journal,* August 13, 2004.

247   **Money, it seems, is a little like beer**   McKibben, *Deep Economy,* 42.

248   **As a nation, we consume**   Barbara Ehrenreich, *Bright-Sided: How the Relentless Promotion of Positive Thinking Has Undermined America* (New York: Henry Holt and Company, 2009), 3.

248   **One study found that today**   McKibben, *Deep Economy,* 36.

248   **And yet, when Americans were asked**   Angus Campbell, *The Sense of Well-Being in America: Recent Patterns and Trends* (New York: McGraw-Hill, 1981), 68.

248   **guaranteed to get everything wrong**   Megan McArdle, "Misleading Indicator," *The Atlantic,* November 2009.

249   **"Our gross national product counts"**   Robert F. Kennedy, remarks at the University of Kansas, March 18, 1968.

250   **"violates both basic accounting principles"**   Anielski, *Economics of Happiness,* 31.

251   **Professor Sen and another Nobel**   David Jolly, "G.D.P. Seen as Inadequate Measure of Economic Health," *The New York Times,* September 14, 2009.

253   **free schools at all levels**   Stephen Herrera, "Zen and the Art of Happiness,"

Ode, December 2005. See also Jeff Greenwald, "Happy Land," *Yoga Journal,* July–August 2004.

254 **Today, it is sixty-six years**   Andrew C. Revkin, "A New Measure of Well-Being from a Happy Little Kingdom," *The New York Times,* October 4, 2005.

255 **"It realigned my priorities"**   Lynne Twist with Teresa Barker, *The Soul of Money: Transforming Your Relationship with Money and Life* (New York: W. W. Norton and Company, 2003), 253.

255 **"Lining money up"**   Ibid., 254.

255 **"I'm still working on it"**   Ibid.

255 **"stand for who you are"**   Ibid., 257.

257 **"So many people could be"**   Zell Kravinsky, "Bolder Giving in Extraordinary Times," www.boldergiving.org/inspiring_stories.

Index

ABOUT THE AUTHOR

Widely considered one of the world's leading experts on the dietary link between the environment and health, JOHN ROBBINS is the author of the million-copy bestseller *Diet for a New America*. His work has been the subject of cover stories and feature articles in the *San Francisco Chronicle,* the *Los Angeles Times, The Washington Post, The New York Times,* and *People* magazine. Robbins has been a featured and keynote speaker at hundreds of major conferences, including those sponsored by the Sierra Club and UNICEF, and is the recipient of many awards, including the Rachel Carson Award and the Albert Schweitzer Humanitarian Award. He is the founder of EarthSave International, a nonprofit organization dedicated to healthy food choices, preservation of the environment, and a more compassionate world. Robbins lives with his wife, Deo, their son, Ocean, and daughter-in-law, Michele, and their grandchildren, River and Bodhi, outside of Santa Cruz, California.

ABOUT THE TYPE

This book was set in Granjon, a modern recutting of a typeface produced under the direction of George W. Jones, who based Granjon's design upon the letter forms of Claude Garamond (1480–1561). The name was given to the typeface as a tribute to the typographic designer Robert Granjon.